Communications
in Computer and Information Science 943

Commenced Publication in 2007
Founding and Former Series Editors:
Phoebe Chen, Alfredo Cuzzocrea, Xiaoyong Du, Orhun Kara, Ting Liu,
Dominik Ślęzak, and Xiaokang Yang

Editorial Board

Simone Diniz Junqueira Barbosa
Pontifical Catholic University of Rio de Janeiro (PUC-Rio),
Rio de Janeiro, Brazil
Joaquim Filipe
Polytechnic Institute of Setúbal, Setúbal, Portugal
Ashish Ghosh
Indian Statistical Institute, Kolkata, India
Igor Kotenko
St. Petersburg Institute for Informatics and Automation of the Russian
Academy of Sciences, St. Petersburg, Russia
Krishna M. Sivalingam
Indian Institute of Technology Madras, Chennai, India
Takashi Washio
Osaka University, Osaka, Japan
Junsong Yuan
University at Buffalo, The State University of New York, Buffalo, USA
Lizhu Zhou
Tsinghua University, Beijing, China

More information about this series at http://www.springer.com/series/7899

Polina Eismont · Olga Mitrenina
Asya Pereltsvaig (Eds.)

Language, Music and Computing

Second International Workshop, LMAC 2017
St. Petersburg, Russia, April 17–19, 2017
Revised Selected Papers

 Springer

Editors
Polina Eismont (ID)
Saint Petersburg State University
of Aerospace Instrumentation
Saint Petersburg, Russia

Asya Pereltsvaig (ID)
Santa Clara University
Santa Clara, USA

Olga Mitrenina (ID)
Saint Petersburg State University
St. Petersburg, Russia

ISSN 1865-0929   ISSN 1865-0937 (electronic)
Communications in Computer and Information Science
ISBN 978-3-030-05593-6   ISBN 978-3-030-05594-3   (eBook)
https://doi.org/10.1007/978-3-030-05594-3

Library of Congress Control Number: 2018963719

© Springer Nature Switzerland AG 2019
This work is subject to copyright. All rights are reserved by the Publisher, whether the whole or part of the material is concerned, specifically the rights of translation, reprinting, reuse of illustrations, recitation, broadcasting, reproduction on microfilms or in any other physical way, and transmission or information storage and retrieval, electronic adaptation, computer software, or by similar or dissimilar methodology now known or hereafter developed.
The use of general descriptive names, registered names, trademarks, service marks, etc. in this publication does not imply, even in the absence of a specific statement, that such names are exempt from the relevant protective laws and regulations and therefore free for general use.
The publisher, the authors, and the editors are safe to assume that the advice and information in this book are believed to be true and accurate at the date of publication. Neither the publisher nor the authors or the editors give a warranty, express or implied, with respect to the material contained herein or for any errors or omissions that may have been made. The publisher remains neutral with regard to jurisdictional claims in published maps and institutional affiliations.

This Springer imprint is published by the registered company Springer Nature Switzerland AG
The registered company address is: Gewerbestrasse 11, 6330 Cham, Switzerland

Preface

In his 1871 book *The Descent of Man and Selection in Relation to Sex*, Charles Darwin put forward a so-called Caruso theory: Singing, he surmised, was akin to peacock's tail in that it gave a male an edge in attracting more females. But, as noted by Berwick and Chomsky [1: 3], things did not stop at sexual selection: Darwin thought that singing led to improvement of the vocal apparatus, and better vocal competence led in turn to a general increase in brain size, which subsequently allowed for the development of language, including language used for internal thought. While some aspects of Darwin's thinking on the matter have become outdated, the Caruso theory experienced something of a revival in the past 25 years, especially in the works of Robert C. Berwick and William Tecumseh Fitch (see, for example, [2]). Yet, the issue of the relation between language and music remains highly controversial and provocative.

In order to shed new light on the connection—or disparity—between language and music, we conducted two International Workshops on Language, Music, and Computing. (The latter was added to the mix largely, but not exclusively, because of the role that computers play in the scientific study of both linguistic outputs and music.) The first edition of this workshop was held in 2015 and became a great success [3]. The second workshop took place during April 17–19, 2017, in Saint Petersburg, Russia, and attracted about 100 scholars from around the world including such countries as France, Japan, USA, India, Germany, Russia, Thailand, Croatia, Spain, Georgia, etc. Among the keynote speakers we are proud to name Prof. Sabine Iatridou (Massachusetts Institute of Technologies, USA); Prof. Sergi Jorda (Universitat Pompeu Fabra, Spain); Prof. Meryl Goldberg (California State University San Marcos, USA); and Dr. Elena Riekhakaynen (Saint-Petersburg State University, Russia).

The present volume contains 17 articles based on papers selected from the list of more than 50 presentations presented at the Second Workshop on Language, Music, and Computing. The papers went through a thorough double-blind peer-review process. The volume is divided into five blocks, each of which covers a distinct subtopic: the universal grammar of music, the parallelism between music and singing, language as music, technical aspects of computational study of both language and music, and formalizing the informal. The following is a brief overview of the contributions and their impact on the field.

Part One, "The Universal Grammar of Music," contains three contributions that present opposing views on the use of the concept of universal grammar, developed in a Chomskian approach to linguistics, and applying such linguistic concepts to the study of music. Thus, the articles in this section of the volume represent the lively debate that characterizes the field today: some scholars believe that generative grammar is applicable to music (cf. the paper by Oriol Quintana), while others challenge extending concepts of the generative grammar to the domain of music (cf. the paper by Rafael Barbosa). The third contribution in this section, by Rodmonga Potapova and Vsevolod Potapov, uses a semiotic approach and considers speech and music as two subsystems of the common semiotic interpersonal communication system with regard to semantics, semiotic syntactics, and pragmatics.

The second part of the volume, "The Surface of Music and Singing," focuses on the acoustic and articulatory parallelism between music and the aspect of language that is closest to music, namely, singing. The first contribution, by Karina Evgrafova, Vera Evdokimova, Pavel Skrelin, and Tatjana Chukaeva, investigates synchronization of musical acoustics (pitch, frequencies, durations) and articulatory movements in Russian classical romance. Their research employs the method of electromagnetic articulography (EMA) to study the difference of vowel articulation in singing and in speaking. Chawadon Ketkaew and Yanin Sawanakunanon in their contribution compare rhythmic properties of speech, pop, and folk songs in Thai using the normalized pairwise variability index (nPVI). The study questions whether music with lyrics exhibits the same influences as does instrumental music, and shows that the two types of pop songs pattern differently with respect to the nPVI and ascribe this difference to the influences of Western music and folk melodies, respectively. Gregory Martynenko, the author of the third contribution, analyzes a corpus of five performances of a certain vocal piece by Sergei Rachmaninoff by different vocalists and proposes to extend this research in the future by examining other characteristics besides tempo: height, loudness, and timbre. The closing article in this section, by Ilya Saitanov, examines traditional dance melodies from Macedonia (Greece) and shows that tonality, mode, meter, and tune may vary in different performances of the same melody.

The third part of the volume, "Language as Music," contains four contributions that focus on the study of linguistic phenomena from the perspective of such articulatory and acoustic characteristics that are also useful in the study of music: tempo, speech breaks, etc. Jana Jurčević's article examines sound symbolism of Croatian occasional expressions (*auuuuuch, brm brm brm*, etc.) used in chats in social communication platforms such as Facebook Messenger, WhatsApp, and Hangouts. She adopts the position that sound symbolism plays a much greater role in oral communication than the standard structuralist view of linguistics would allow. Elena Riekhakaynen and Alena Balanovskaia in their paper focus on the processing of Russian spoken words by native speakers and second-language learners. The authors discuss different methods of studying slips of the ear showing how they can contribute to the understanding of speech processing. The next article, by Natalia Bogdanova-Beglarian, studied speech breaks in oral discourse, based on the annotated part of the Russian corpus "One Speaker's Day." Sociolinguistic analysis of the data showed that speech breaks are more frequent in the speech of men (rather than women), seniors (as opposed to children, youth, and middle-aged speakers), and unemployed and retired people (in contrast to the speech of managers, who produce significantly fewer speech breaks than other speakers in other groups). This study also investigates what causes disfluencies and how the speaker gets out of communicative difficulties. The contribution by Tatiana Sherstinova is based on the same speech corpus of everyday Russian containing long-term audio recordings of conversations made in natural circumstances. The focus of her investigation is the audible non-linguistic (paralinguistic) elements in conversation, such as laughter, inhalation noise, cough, various e-like and m-like vocalizations, tongue clicking, hesitations, yawns, etc. The analysis uncovered some specific unexpected results such as laughter is the undeniable leader among paralinguistic elements, taking up nearly 40% of all paralinguistic elements in the corpus but its frequency goes down with age (from 0.9087 for age 18–30 to 0.3876 for age 55+), while the incidence of sighing increases with age (from 0.0086 for age 18–30 to 0.0426 for age 55+).

The fourth part of the volume, "Music Computing," is concerned with technical aspects of the computational study of both language and music. The opening contribution in this section is by Gleb G. Rogozinsky, Konstantin Lyzhinkin, Anna Egorova, and Dmitry Podolsky, who present a hardware software solution for sonification of complex networks and systems. The suggested solution facilitates the system and allows one to produce the traffic suitable for appropriate audio environment. The second article, by Alexander Kalinin and Anastasia Kolmogorova, describes tools for selecting special music for the "mood" of a given text extract. The main model that underlies this research is Lövheim's Cube emotional model which comprises eight emotional states rather than merely two (positive and negative) as typically used in sentiment analysis. By being able to select an appropriate piece of music to correspond to the emotional state of a text fragment, one is able to create a synergistic effect, making the achievement of the target emotional state by the reader/listener more likely. The third contribution in this section, by Leonid Tereshchenko, Lubov Boiko, Daria Ivanchenko, Elena Zadneprovskaya, and Alexander Latanov, uses a technique of eye–movement recording (without fixating the head) to investigate the so-called eye–hand span: the time from reading a piece of musical text to playback. Their findings reveal that "the eye–hand span depends on the texture of the musical piece perform and inversely correlates with the number of errors as well as directly correlates with the rate of stability in the performance."

The fifth and last part of the volume, "Formalization of the Informality," suggests fresh views on some topics so far non-formalized. The first contribution here, by Basil Lourié and Olga Mitrenina, uses a new logical approach for formal description of poetical tropes and other kinds of indirect meanings, such as humor (and so-called anti-humor), hints, and riddles, which are treated as homogeneous phenomena. The article by Artemy Kotov, Nikita Arinkin, Ludmila Zaydelman, and Anna Zinina describes their attempt to introduce a emotional behavioral pattern to a robot. The following article in this section, by Polina Eismont, suggests a new description that allows one to formalize the syntax–semantics interface in corpus studies. Finally, Anastasia Kolmogorova studies the corpus of 97 Russian verbs to show that *language*, *music*, and *computer* in Russian are living organisms in Lakoff's and Johnson's sense of the term, she proves that in Russian, "music" enters the class of mythic heroes or Demiurges, "language" belongs to the covert class of Humans, and "computer" integrates the class of pets.

The editors are grateful to the Saint Petersburg State University of Aerospace Instrumentation and its leadership, especially to Rector Yulia Antokhina and to Vice-Rector for International Cooperation Konstantin Losev, and to Saint Petersburg State Conservatory named after N.A. Rimsky-Korsakov and its leadership, especially to Rector Alexey Vassiliev and to Vice-Rector for Scientific Research Natalia Braginskaya, for the enormous work that they did to organize the Second International Workshop on Language, Music, and Computing. We are also grateful to Springer, Leonie Kunz, Natalia Ustalova and Avula Nikesh for accepting this book for the series

Communications in Computer and Information Science (CCIS) and their help in publication process; it is a great honor for us. For any remaining errors and short-comings, of course, the editors alone carry the responsibility.

We hope that the publication of this volume will lead to in-depth discussions and continuing research on the topic of interaction between language and music, with a use of formal approaches and modern computing, which is becoming more human every day.

References

Berwick, Robert C. and Noam Chomsky (2016) Why Only Us. *Language and Evolution.* Cambridge, MA: The MIT Press.

Fitch, William Tecumseh (2010) *The Evolution of Language.* Cambridge, UK: Cambridge University Press.

Eismont P., Konstantinova N. (eds) Language, Music, and Computing. LMAC 2015. Communications in Computer and Information Science, vol 561. Springer, Cham.

November 2018

Polina Eismont
Olga Mitrenina
Asya Pereltsvaig

Organization

Program Committee

Olga Mitrenina (Chair)	Saint Petersburg State University, Russia
Polina Eismont (Co-chair)	Saint Petersburg State University of Aerospace Instrumentation, Russia
John Frederick Bailyn	SUNY at Stony Brook, USA
Natalia Braginskaya	Saint Petersburg State Conservatory, Russia
Natalia Degtyareva	Saint Petersburg State Conservatory, Russia
Andrey Denisov	Herzen State Pedagogical University of Russia
Elena Erofeeva	Perm National Research University, Russia
Elena Grudeva	Cherepovets State University, Russia
Simon Holland	The Open University, UK
Olga Khomitsevitch	NTENT, Inc., USA
Andrej Kibrik	Russian Academy of Science, Moscow, Russia
Natalia Konstantinova	University of Wolverhampton, UK
Mikhail Kopotev	University of Helsinki, Finland
Sergey Krylov	Russian Academy of Science, Moscow, Russia
Guerino Mazzola	University of Minnesota, USA
Constantin Orasan	University of Wolverhampton, UK
Eric Reuland	Utrecht University, The Netherlands
Martin Rohrmeier	Technische Universität Dresden, Germany
Rafael Salinas	Escola Superior de Música de Catalunya, Spain
Dmitry Sitchinava	Russian Academy of Science, Moscow, Russia
Akira Takaoka	Tamagawa University, Japan
Daniel Junqueira Tarquinio	Universidade de Brasilia, Brazil
Remi van Trijp	Sony CSL, Paris, France
Partick Zuk	University of Durham, UK

Contents

Music Computing

Formalization of the Informality

The Universal Grammar of Music

Does the Y-Model for Language Work
for Music?

Oriol Quintana[✉][iD]

Centre de Lingüística Teòrica, Universitat Autònoma de Barcelona (CLT-UAB),
Barcelona, Spain
Oriol.Quintana@uab.cat

Abstract. The four main modules of the classic model for the faculty of language postulated in generative linguistics—lexicon, syntax, phonology/prosody
and semantics—have been hypothesized to each have a (more or less abstract)
equivalent module in the faculty of music. This hypothesis suggests that it
should be possible to explain the way these modules interact—represented by
the inverted-Y form of the model—in a similar fashion. I propose a refinement
of Katz and Pesetsky's (2011) hypothesis by suggesting that there are a number
of common properties shared by the lexical systems of music and language, and
it is precisely this that explains some of their fundamental syntactic similarities.
What makes the two systems different is not primitively the properties of their
lexical modules, but rather the radically different nature of their respective
interpretive modules—semantics in the case of language (or, technically, the
conceptual-intentional system), and the Tonal-Harmonic Component (THC) in
the case of music.

Keywords: Language · Music · Syntax · Computational system
Semantics · Harmony · Inverted-Y model

1 Introduction

In recent years, interest in establishing a common framework for the study of the
human faculties of language and music has increased significantly. The fact that both
faculties connect physical temporal realities (both musical and linguistic expressions
are displayed in a linear –i.e., one-dimensional– sequence along time) to mental a-
temporal and hierarchically organized structures has led to the intuition that they might
share some underlying cognitive processes. From this intuition follows the hypothesis
that the underlying cognitive principles that music and language may share constrain
the form of their respective grammatical structures in some common way. If this is the
case, then some aspects of their grammars, which aim to account for the principles
restricting their structure, could likewise have a common explanation.

The main handicap for a common (or at least partially common) grammatical
theory for language and music is that thus far the formal theories of the respective
disciplines have not advanced in a parallel fashion. In the case of linguistics, the
revolution of the paradigm promoted by Noam Chomsky since the 1950s has changed
the way language is conceived as an object of scientific study. It had previously been

© Springer Nature Switzerland AG 2019
P. Eismont and O. Mitrenina (Eds.): LMAC 2017, CCIS 943, pp. 3–21, 2019.
https://doi.org/10.1007/978-3-030-05594-3_1

studied only as a cultural and unrestrictedly variant object. Since Chomsky's contribution, however, linguistic theory has focused on the study of language as a biological capacity of individuals which can be addressed scientifically within the study of human nature. The conditions that govern and constrain the grammar of language can therefore be assumed to be cognitive principles of the human mind.

In the case of music theory, on the other hand, this change in paradigm has never fully taken root. Bernstein (1976)'s speculative attempt to apply Chomsky's ideas to music opened a new way to look at music as a system of the human mind, and its study as a biological faculty has spread across the literature (Peretz 2006), along with its comparative studies with the biological capacity of language (Arbib 2013; Grodzinsky 2015; Patel 2008; Rebuschat et al. 2012), also from evolutionary (Fitch 2006) and developmental perspectives (McMullen and Saffran 2004). But in the field of formal theory, this new view of music has never achieved the kind of revolutionary impact that Chomsky's generative grammar has had on linguistic theory. The only attempt to construct a comprehensive theory of the psychological principles that structure musical expressions is Lerdahl and Jackendoff's (1983) Generative Theory of Tonal Music (GTTM), but there have been few explorations of its implications, empirical implementations and possible reformulations (Giblin 2008; Hamanaka et al. 2016; Lerdahl 2001; Lerdahl and Krumhansl 2007; Rohrmeier 2007, 2011). Therefore, there is no single tradition of studying the formal properties of music from a cognitive perspective as well-accepted as in the case of language, and, when this has been done, only few parallels with language have been drawn (Jackendoff 2009). This is the main reason why at present any proposal for a common grammatical theory of music and language from this viewpoint may appear to be doomed to failure.

My concern is wondering if this failure to connect theoretically language and music could be explained in terms of a set of misunderstandings and prejudices caused more by the methodological mismatching of the various existing theories more than by any real differences between the nature of these two faculties. In this paper, I explore the plausibility of a rapprochement between the theoretical models that the generative tradition has postulated to account for the faculties of language and music, for the purpose of looking for a single overarching model. Such an enterprise has already been attempted by Katz and Pesetsky (2011) in the form of their ambitious Identity Thesis of Language and Music, which claims that the syntax of music and language is identical and all their formal differences come from the different nature of their lexicons. I argue that the four main modules of the classic model for the faculty of language—lexicon, syntax, phonology/prosody and semantics—have their analogues in the faculty of music, which implies that the way these modules interact within each faculty—represented by the inverted-Y form in the linguistic model—should also be analogous. I propose here a refinement of Katz and Pesetsky's (2011) hypothesis whereby the lexical systems of music and language share a number of common properties, and that it is precisely in these common properties that some of their fundamental syntactic similarities lie. What makes the two systems different is not the primitive properties of their lexical modules but rather the radically different nature of their respective interpretive modules—semantics in the case of language (or, technically, the conceptual-intentional system), and the Tonal-Harmonic Component (THC) in the case of music, in keeping with Katz and Pesetsky's (2011) proposal.

2 The Theoretical Models for the Language and Music Faculties

In the 1980s, Jerry Fodor proposed the notion that the mind is by nature modular. This view conceived of the human mind as a plurality of cognitive systems or faculties that are distinguishable by their particular functions and specific operating principles (Fodor 1983). The generative approach to the language faculty takes the modularity of mind as a fundamental assumption, since it conceives of language as a cognitive system with its own constraining principles. But the idea of modularity is applied not only to the status of the language faculty within the global human cognition but also to the internal architecture of the language faculty itself, which is described as a system composed of different modules with their own properties and rules interacting through interface systems.

The human faculty of music is conceived of along the same lines in Lerdahl and Jackendoff's GTTM. This model proposes a system of rules that is highly specific to the human capacity for music, which is in turn described as an interaction between different modules of structural representation. The respective generative theories of language and music are nonetheless conceived of as independent, and no attempt is made to explore any common explanation for any possible similar properties. However, the multi-modular character of both theoretical systems will serve us as a practical starting point for their comparison.

Prior to undertaking this comparison, however, let us proceed to a quick overview of the two models.

2.1 The Inverted-Y Model for Language

Generative theory has been evolving as research has been progressing, and the specific model postulated to account for the linguistic system has changed at different stages. Nevertheless, its assumed fundamental architecture has remained relatively constant. This architecture has traditionally been labelled the *inverted-Y model* because of the shape of its schematic representation, as seen in Fig. 1.

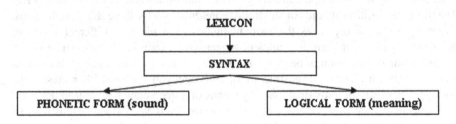

Fig. 1. The inverted-Y model of the language faculty postulated by generative linguistics

As noted above, the language faculty is comprised of four modules: a lexical module, where the basic primitive units of language are stored (the building-blocks of linguistic structure); a central syntactic module, which takes the basic units of the lexicon and combines them, building the hierarchical structure of sentences; and two interfaces to which these syntactic structures are oriented, with one interface to the sensory-motor system, which is responsible for encoding the linguistic expression in a physical/external materialization (the so-called phonetic form), and the other to the conceptual-intentional system, which is responsible for decoding the semantic interpretation of the structure (the so-called logical form).

The syntactic module is given a central status in the architecture of language, as it is considered to be the computational system that makes possible the hallmark of human language: the connection between two arbitrarily-related realities (sound and meaning) in a principled way, by means of a set of general rules that make this relation predictable and creative. The computational character of syntax allows for a direct non-dubious association between utterances and their interpretation at different levels of structural complexity. Most importantly, and as the generative tradition has always emphasized, the systematicity of these rules, along with their property of being recursively applied, is what makes possible the infinite set of sentences that any human being can produce and understand.

2.2 The Generative Theory of Tonal Music (GTTM)

The GTTM is to date the most developed formal theory of music structure, understanding it as the way musical expressions are represented in our mind following psychological principles of hierarchical organization. As noted above, this theory organizes the human faculty of music into a number of modules or domains of hierarchical organization, just as the generative theory of language does with the faculty of language. This does not entail that the two faculties work in a similar way, however. In fact, the two theories have been developed quite independently and treat their respective objects of study as specific cognitive systems with no common operating principles. This has led to two very different theoretical models that at first sight do not seem reconcilable.

Briefly overviewed, the GTTM organizes the faculty of music into two domains related to the rhythmic organization of musical units (*Grouping Structure* and *Metrical Structure*) and two domains related to their organization according to properties of pitch and harmony (*Time-Span Reduction (TSR)* and *Prolongational Reduction (PR)*). The theory uses different kinds of structural representations for these different domains. Grouping Structure organizes the motivic figures of a piece in different levels of hierarchy, by grouping them into units of bigger size at each level; Metrical Structure represents the organization of beats according to the relative prominence of their stress value, very much like the stress structure of language; and TSR and PR represent the harmonic hierarchy of individual tones by means of a tree notation similar to that used by linguistic theory to represent syntactic structure. Figures 2, 3 and 4 illustrate the three kinds of representations applied to the same musical surface, in this case the initial melodic fragment of *Norwegian Wood*, by The Beatles.[1]

---

[1] All three examples are taken from Jackendoff and Lerdahl (2006), p. 41 and 56.

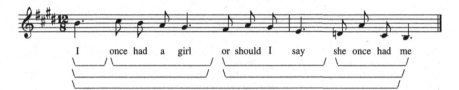

Fig. 2. Grouping Structure of the first sentence of *Norwegian Wood*

Fig. 3. Metrical Structure of the first sentence of *Norwegian Wood*

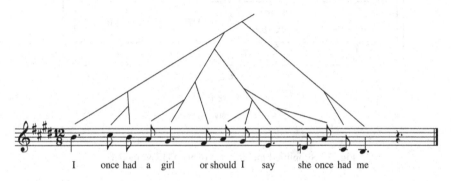

Fig. 4. Pitch structure of the first sentence of *Norwegian Wood*

For reasons of space, I will not detail the differences between TSR and PR. The basic idea behind them is that, while TSR reflects those rhythmic aspects given by Grouping and Metrical Structures that have influence on the pitch structure, PR focuses on the patterns of harmonic tension and relaxation that are unaffected by rhythm. The motivation for their differentiation is that there are some aspects of harmonic structure that cannot be explained without taking rhythm into account, but at the same time there are other harmonic aspects which have priority over rhythm.

One of the characteristics of the GTTM model is the division of the system into two phases of operations, a first phase where well-formedness rules of structure formation are applied and which gives rise to more than one possible analysis of the given musical surface, and a second phase where preference rules are applied over the possible analyses given by the previous rules to yield the one which best fits with the requirements of our mind. The modules of the system do not seem to interact in a very specific directional way, unlike the model for language. A simplified version of the global architecture of the GTTM model is shown in Fig. 5.

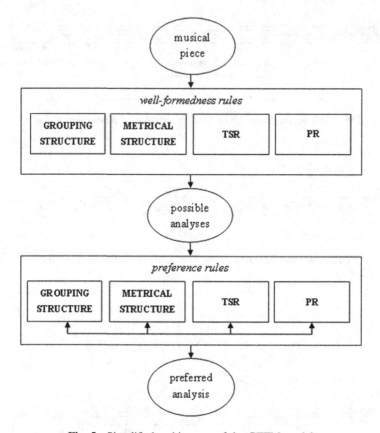

Fig. 5. Simplified architecture of the GTTM model

3   Towards a Reconciliation of Music and Linguistic Theories

At first glance, judging by the overall architecture of these theories (cf. Figs. 1 and 5), it would not seem that language and music systems could have any resemblance at all, since their formal models look very different. However, as noted in Sect. 1, it is reasonable to suppose that these two faculties may have much more in common than what one would deduce from comparing the theoretical models proposed for them. After all, both faculties connect a physical temporal reality to a mental hierarchically-organized reality in a principled way, so it is appropriate that their theories work together to accommodate at least this aspect in a common explanation. As Katz and Pesetsky (2011) point out, it is quite possible that many of the differences that one can perceive between language and music actually derive more from divergences in the methodology of the respective theories than from real natural differences. Part of this theoretical mismatch might be explained by the imbalance between the academic traditions of the respective disciplines: the cognitive perspective is much more fully consolidated in linguistic theory than in music theory, which still conceives of music mainly as a cultural artifact that we humans have created rather than as an internal aspect of our biological nature. This imbalance is not necessarily accidental, however. One of the factors that may explain it is the difficulty involved in applying to musical expressions the same methodological tests used by linguistic theory to evaluate linguistic data (e.g., grammaticality judgements). In this regard, one of the virtues of GTTM as a theory is its claim that music, like language, is formally structured in our minds in a principled way.

One of the main disparities between the two models is that in the GTTM model rules are applied at two levels, well-formedness and preference, while in the model assumed for language rules refer to well-formedness alone. In other words, sentences are structurally well-formed or ill-formed (i.e., grammatical or ungrammatical). This leads us to think that perhaps it would be wise to set aside for the moment the preference rules proposed for the music system and limit our comparison with language to the strictly grammatical rules of music structure, which are those that determine how such structures are properly formed.

Looking at the model as if only grammatical-level rules were involved, we observe that the music system, like the language system, is composed of four main modules. The fact that both models have a modular conception of the faculties to which they refer can be a helpful starting point for the task of reconciling them because it allows us to make comparative observations between the different modules of each system to see whether they share any properties that could reflect some sort of correspondence. Katz and Pesetsky (2011) observe that, although GTTM does not explicitly present it in this way, its four modules interact in a directional way that can be represented in a Y-form. Grouping and Meter Structures are necessarily formed before TSR, as the latter requires some crucial information provided by the former to derive its structure. PR formation, in turn, requires some crucial information provided by TSR. The authors therefore suggest that the interaction between the modules can be schematically represented as in Fig. 6.

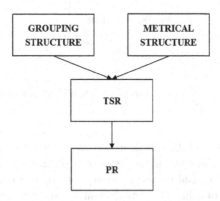

Fig. 6. GTTM's modular mapping (from Katz and Pesetsky 2011, p. 13)

It is clear that the diagram represented in Fig. 6 has virtually nothing to do with the model of language represented in Fig. 1. Firstly, the shape of the Y is not inverted.

More importantly, however, the functional designs of each model show very little correspondence. On one hand, the two modules which converge to the central one in Fig. 6, Grouping and Metrical Structures, do not correspond with the external (materializer) and internal (interpretive) interfaces of language. In fact, both of them correlate with, if anything, the external interface of language, where rhythmic aspects emerge (prosodic grouping and stress structure). Furthermore, although TSR is the central module in Fig. 6, both TSR and PR are formal representations mostly akin to linguistic syntax, while there is nothing similar to a lexical module represented in Fig. 6.

Nonetheless, Katz and Pesetsky suggest that the two models are actually alignable, in other words, that parallels and correspondences can be drawn between them. They say that PR (and not TSR) is the most plausible candidate of the GTTM modules for alignment with linguistic syntax, because they share some fundamental formal properties like binary-branching, headedness and the possibility of establishing non-string-adjacent relations. For its part, the most plausible linguistic parallel to TSR would be prosodic structure, since it involves notions of relative prominence based on the information provided by Grouping and Metrical Structures. Then the interaction between TSR and PR would be alignable to the syntax-prosody mapping in the linguistic system. Thus, in essence, Katz and Pesetsky's idea is that the language and music models could be aligned as illustrated in Fig. 7.

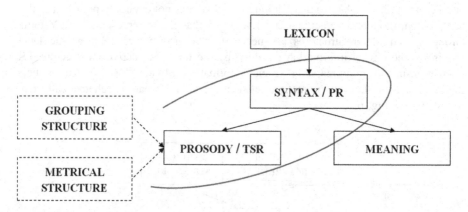

Fig. 7. Integration of the GTTM model with the inverted-Y model for language, following Katz and Pesetsky's (2011) proposal

The question is now whether lexicon and meaning—the modules that do not overlap in the linguistic and musical models—could somehow be incorporated into the latter or not. Although Katz and Pesetsky do not explicitly propose that music could be accounted for by means of a theoretical model with the same inverted-Y shape and with the same (or functionally equivalent) four components, they actually suggest that both a lexicon and a semantic component for music should be considered.

The lexicon is addressed in their Identity Thesis, the central hypothesis around which their proposal is constructed. They suggest that, while the syntax of language and music is identical, the lexicon is the locus to which all their differences can be traced. They assume therefore that music has a lexical system, although it is different from the linguistic one. With respect to the interpretive component, they propose that there is an equivalent to semantics in music, which is the THC. In fact, if music has syntactic structures of the linguistic type, it is reasonable to think that there must be some domain in our mind in charge of interpreting the meaning of these structures, otherwise there would be no obvious meaningful way through which these structures could be built.

In the next section, I will discuss the plausibility of both a lexicon and an interpretive component for music and argue for their integration into a theoretical model that would constitute a step forward in the task of viewing the linguistic and the music capacities through the lens of their common denominators. I will also argue that the differences between the two systems may derive not from the lexicon, as Katz and Pesetsky (2011) claim, but rather from the interpretive component.

4   From the Identity Thesis to a Common Abstract Model

There is no doubt that we humans have a strong intuitive ability to distinguish between what constitutes a piece of language and what constitutes a piece of music, and we hardly ever confuse them in natural situations. We can easily recognize words and phonemes as such, and classify them as linguistic entities, just as we recognize notes and chords as musical entities. Whatever the precise nature of their difference, it must consist of something plain enough to be unmistakable to human understanding.

Katz and Pesetsky (2011) propose that this difference lies in the properties of the minimal units of the respective systems, what we call the *lexicon*. The motivation for their proposal is the evidence that, beyond their categorical differences, language and music share one fundamental feature: the hierarchical organization of their expressions in a non-arbitrary but certainly meaningful way, something which seems truly special to these two systems. This evidence leads the authors to suggest that the two systems share a common underlying syntactic component. Thus, they are differentiated in the nature of their basic units, rather than in the way these elements combine.

(1) and (2) below are examples of a linguistic and a musical expression, respectively, with relatively complex but properly-formed syntactic structures. Despite the powerful combinatorial capacity of both linguistic and musical units, it is obvious that the units of one system and the other are not combinable between them, as shown in (3), which represents an artificially-created hybrid expression which cannot be understood by any cognitive system.

(1)   John told us a nice story this morning.

(3)   *

Equally apparent as the similarity between the units of language and music regarding their combinatorial capacity is the fact that they clearly belong to two separate domains, with no possibility of inter-domain combination. So, for a proper theoretical joint characterization of language and music, the following two questions need to be answered: (1) is there anything common in the lexical units of language and music that allows them to combine in the complex ways they do, and (2) what makes them belong to one or the other domain in such a clear-cut way, preventing them so categorically from being combined with elements from the other domain?

Even if we accept Katz and Pesetsky's (2011) hypothesis that the fundamental distinction between language and music lies in their lexical systems, we need not dismiss the possibility that some of their common properties may also be related with these lexical systems. In fact, it is difficult to think about their respective combinatorial capacities without suspecting that this property has to do with the formal design of their lexical units. In what follows, I argue that it is precisely certain basic formal properties shared by the language and music lexical units that makes them able to participate in the complex combinatorial system of syntax. I also propose that the very primitive origin of their differences is located not in the lexicon but in another module of the system: the interpretive component, which is semantics for language and the Tonal-Harmonic Component for music. This will lead me to claim that the very same abstract inverted-Y model used to characterize the faculty of language may be just as aptly applied to the faculty of music.

4.1 Common Lexical Properties of Language and Music

Discrete Units

The units of music and language share a basic property which is crucial for them to be computable in a syntactic component: discreteness. In both systems, every unit has definite boundaries which let us determine where it begins and ends and where the following unit commences. This is illustrated in (4) below for language, both at the word level (4a) and at the phonological level (4b), and in (5) for music.

(4) a. John told us a nice story this morning.

 b. dʒɒn təʊld ʌs ə naɪs stɔːrɪ ðɪs mɔːnɪŋ

(5)

In the case of language, morphemes and phonemes are two different kinds of minimal units. Phonemes are the minimal units from which phonological and prosodic structure is formed. Morphemes are the minimal meaningful units of language from which syntactic structure is formed to be interpreted at the semantic interface. Morphemes are more abstract and usually smaller pieces than words, which means that sometimes they are not discrete at the surface level. For example, a word like *told* encodes at least two morphemes, the lexical verb *tell* and the morpheme for past tense. But this does not prevent us from understanding that these two morphemes are discrete in an abstract sense. The irregularity occurs at the interface between morphology and phonology, not at the strictly morphological level. Morphemes act as perfectly discrete entities in the syntactic structure and are stored as such in our mental lexicon.

In the case of music, the minimal units are never abstract in principle: they are hearable notes, with a rhythmic nature and a tonal nature (as long as they have harmonic structure and are not simply toneless sounds like drum beats, in which case the tonal nature is absent). The rhythmic character of notes is what generates the rhythmic and metrical structure of music, while their tonal nature is what generates its harmonic structure, which is meaningful in another sense. This dual organization of music into a rhythmic structure and a harmonic one could be quite reasonably argued to parallel the dual organization of language into a prosodic structure and a syntactic one, though we will not pursue this issue in the present paper.

The fact that we can segment linguistic and musical expressions into discrete units is crucial for our mind to assign a particular status to each one of these units and then combine them in hierarchical structures in such a meaningful way as to be interpretable by the respective interpretive components. Without this segmentability, no structural computation would be possible, and these expressions would not have any understandable meaning for the interpretive components. For example, a musical expression like the one tentatively sketched in (6), consisting of a sort of continuous glissando, with no particular notes being recognizable at any point in the expression, could not be processed or understood by the Tonal-Harmonic Component of our mind.

(6) *

By the same token, in the case of language, if we heard not recognizable phonemes but rather a continuous transition between different timbres of sound which we could not segment, we would not be able to process any kind of computable information; and if we could not recognize discrete morphemes in the more abstract morphological level either, no syntactic computation would be possible, thus ruling out any kind of linguistic creativity based on compositionality.

Decomposition into Features

Another characteristic of the lexical units of both language and music, in addition to their discrete nature, is the way they participate in the composition of the syntactic structure, which is considered to be describable as a computational system (Chomsky 1995). It is a traditional convention in generative linguistics to describe the units of language—whether morphemes or phonemes—as bundles of features (from now on, however, we will only consider morphemes, which are the basic units of syntactic structure, which is the one which interfaces with the interpretive semantic component). Some of the features associated with morphemes carry the information about how they must be read at the interfaces, such as the phonological information associated with a morpheme that determines how it will be pronounced, or the conceptual meaning associated with that morpheme that determines how it will be semantically interpreted. But morphemes crucially contain other sorts of features which, rather than being strictly interface-oriented, carry the relevant information for their syntactic treatment. These are called morphosyntactic features. One of the most important morphosyntactic features of morphemes is their syntactic category. Depending on their category, morphemes will carry other kinds of morphosyntactic features, like those which determine the kinds of syntactic entities to which each morpheme must be attached (for example, the features which determine the transitivity of a verb) or those which carry the relevant information for syntactic operations like movement or agreement (gender and number features for nouns, tense features for verbs, etc.).

A rough example of the kinds of features that can be associated with a nominal element like *John* and a verbal element like *told* can be seen in (7) below.

(7)

	John	*told*
PHONOLOGICAL FEATURES:	/dʒɒn/	/təʊld/
MEANING:	"John"	"told"
MORPHOSYNTACTIC FEATURES:	[N]	[V]
	[3rd person]	[ditransitive]
	[singular]	[past]
	[nominative]	[perfective]
	[proper noun]	[indicative]
	[+animate]	[agentive]
	...	...

We will not concern ourselves here with the question of whether the features exemplified in (7) are authentic morphosyntactic primitives or if instead could be better accounted for as the products of operations on simpler elements. What is important is that language structure does not (or does not only) work with the information about how pieces of language sound and what they mean, but requires some extra formal information about these pieces for their proper combination into syntactic structures.

Moving now to music, it would appear difficult on first thought to describe individual musical notes as bundles of formal features. For example, for an individual isolated C, like that represented in (8), we can hardly say more than that it vibrates at around the frequency of 523.25 Hz, which is what makes it a C. But if we regard as basic units of computation not individual notes but the harmonic event into which a note is inserted (what in Western tonal music is normally called a *chord*), then a multiplicity of levels of information emerge. These pieces of information are derived from the internal composition of the harmonic event, but they consist of something more than a mere list of the frequency indices of the individual notes that make up the event. The quality of a chord and its inversion, for instance, are firm candidates to constitute two of the chord's formal properties relevant for computation, and they are independent from, and more abstract than, their specific pitch features. A series of examples of this is shown in (9), with different chords in which the very same C in (8) is involved, having a different status in each case.

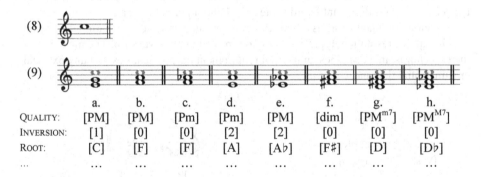

	a.	b.	c.	d.	e.	f.	g.	h.
QUALITY:	[PM]	[PM]	[Pm]	[Pm]	[PM]	[dim]	[PM^{m7}]	[PM^{M7}]
INVERSION:	[1]	[0]	[0]	[2]	[2]	[0]	[0]	[0]
ROOT:	[C]	[F]	[F]	[A]	[A♭]	[F♯]	[D]	[D♭]
...	...	...	...	...	...	...	...	...

The proof that these pieces of information form a consistent abstract category in our mind is that we can recognize them in other units which correspond to completely different acoustic realities. For instance, the chords in (9a) and (9b) share the qualitative property of being perfect major chords, despite being composed of different pitches. In contrast, (9b) and (9c), despite being acoustically much closer, have clearly different qualitative categories in our mind, since the latter constitutes a perfect minor chord.

A discussion about which features might be relevant for the syntactic computation of music requires a detailed exposition which would exceed the scope of this paper. What is relevant here is that minimal harmonic events have their own particular level of analysis, which is describable in terms of formal features in a way that is similar to the way linguistic units are describable. The rest of the section will be devoted to showing that the parallel between the formal content of musical and linguistic units does not end here. The features of the two domains share some basic functions, especially in relation to their role in the syntactic component. These functions are mainly three: guiding the syntactic derivation, determining the asymmetry of the merge operations and being responsible for the success—or crash—of the derivation at the interfaces. This will constitute a crucial argument in support of our claim that there exist some fundamental similarities between the syntax of language and music and, going further, that the same abstract theoretical model may be applied to both faculties.

Guiding the Syntactic Derivation

Mainstream generative grammar regards syntactic structure as being formed derivationally in a bottom-up direction, by merging basic units to form bigger constituents that are hierarchically organized. The features of the minimal units determine the elements with which these units must be merged. For instance, (10) illustrates a possible way of representing the fact that the verb *eat* is transitive and requires a noun phrase as complement (Adger 2003, ch. 3). The feature responsible for this requirement, in this case, is [*u*N]. The noun *apples* satisfies the requirement of the feature [*u*N] in *eat*, so that the two elements can properly merge and form the bigger constituent *eat apples*. This kind of feature is called a *selectional feature*, since it selects the class of element required as sister for the merge operation.

In music, it could also be said that syntactic structure is formed through a merge operation between harmonic entities triggered by the matching of their internal features.

(11) illustrates the typical case of a V^7-I pattern, described as a merge operation between a seventh dominant chord rooted in G and a perfect major chord rooted in C. The seventh dominant chord is a typical harmonic category holding a harmonic tension which requires resolution, typically to a chord rooted in its lower fifth. The matching of the two chords, then, satisfies an internal requirement of their features, not any external circumstantial demand.

(10)

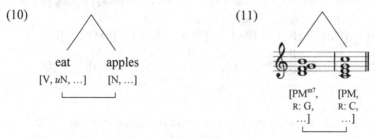

(11)

eat   apples
[V, *u*N, ...]   [N, ...]

[PM^{m7},   [PM,
R: G,   R: C,
...]   ...]

The Asymmetry of Union

A fundamental property of syntactic merge operations is that they are not symmetric, but rather one of the elements labels the syntactic object obtained, in the sense that it determines the categorial status of the bigger constituent that has been formed (i.e. a noun phrase, a verb phrase, etc.). The fact that a complex constituent takes the category of one of its internal elements is called *headedness*. Again, the choice of the head is not aleatory, but determined by the features of the elements being merged. In a verb-complement configuration like the one in (10), the element which projects its categorial label to the bigger constituent is the verb, as represented in (12), since the noun has already been saturated in terms of selection, while the verb still has requirements to be satisfied at upper structural levels, which we will not represent here.

In music, the unions are also asymmetric, and, again, it is not some external circumstance that determines the head. In a V^7-I configuration like the one we saw in (11), the element that resolves the tension (in this case, the C chord) is the one that determines the tonal domain to which the previous chord is inserted, so it is the head of the constituent, as represented in (13).

(12)   V

(13)   C

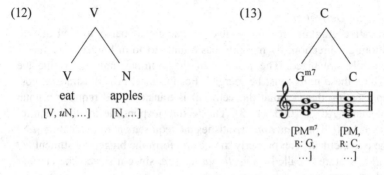

V   N
eat   apples
[V, *u*N, ...] [N, ...]

G^{m7} C

[PM^{m7},   [PM,
R: G,   R: C,
...]   ...]

The Felicity of the Derivation at the Interfaces

As we noted above, lexical features carry the instructions for syntactic derivations. In language, agrammatical objects are obtained if these instructions are not properly followed. Ill-formed structures are said to crash at the interfaces, because they are unable to be interpreted by the conditions imposed on them. (14) shows a syntactic constituent which is not well-formed, because, although we could conjecture as to what the intended meaning might be, the formal selectional properties of one of its internal elements are not satisfied, since the features of the verb *eat* do not accept an adjective as a complement. Note that this does not mean that this verb cannot be followed by an adjective modifying its complement, as shown in (15).

(14)   (15)

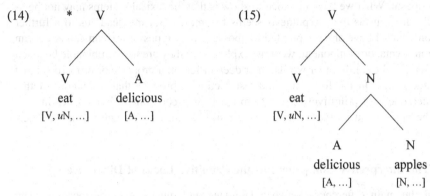

In music, it is difficult to determine categorically if a harmonic construction is not properly formed, but some chord combinations in certain tonal contexts can sound truly odd. For example, the D chord in (16) is not a proper complement of C, provided that this union occurs in the context of a straightforward C major key. This very same chord, however, can be legitimated within a complement of C if the intermediate chord is legitimated by C, as shown in (17).

(16)   (17)

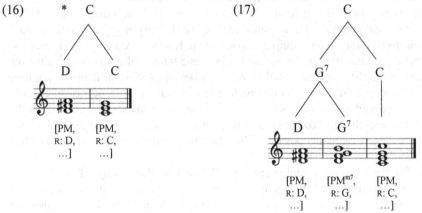

Again, it is due to the internal features of their minimal units that these syntactic configurations might be acceptable or not. Hence, this constitutes another point in common between the minimal units of the formal systems of language and music.

In sum, we have seen that both language and music have a lexical module, and that both lexical modules, despite their different nature, share a set of properties which make them computable at the syntactic component. Our suggestion cannot be considered an argument against Katz and Pesetsky's hypothesis, which postulates the lexicon as the locus of the formal differences between the two systems. Rather, these common fundamental properties of their lexical systems are precisely what allows them to participate in a shared computational component like syntax, which is the central thesis of their proposal. What we have intended to show is that the lexical systems may not be as radically different as their hypothesis seems to predict. But this leads us to a further question which I have already pointed to above: if both types of lexicon can access an analogous syntactic component, we must explain why they are not combinable between them (see (3) above). In other words, their deep differential property or properties must be characterized. In the following and last section, I propose that the nature of this difference does not primitively come from the lexical component, but derives instead from the component of the Y-model which still remains to be addressed: the interpretive one.

4.2   The Interpretive Component as the Primitive Locus of Difference

One of the main differences between language and music concerns meaning. The referential and conceptual semantics of language is clearly absent in music. In the Y-model for language, the interpretive component is the module in charge of attributing meaning to the structures created by syntax. If there is nothing resembling linguistic meaning in music, what is then the 'sense' of musical syntax? Is there any module in our mind which interprets the syntactic structures made up of musical units? In other words, is there any sort of interpretive interface with musical syntax?

It has been proposed that what is equivalent to meaning in music pertains to the field of affect and emotions, but it seems implausible that any emotional content could be read as the *meaning* of any computational system. Katz and Pesetsky (2011) propose a possible equivalent module for semantics in music which falls outside the affective dimension, what they call the *Tonal-Harmonic Component* (THC). If this is so, then music can also be said to have an interpretive module for its syntactic structures, and, thus, it can be said to have the same four components of language according to the inverted-Y model. It then becomes plausible to claim that music can be accommodated to the same theoretical model postulated by generative theory for language, as sketched in Fig. 8.

The fact that linguistic meaning and the THC have fundamentally different natures is obvious. The nature of linguistic meaning is referential and propositional, and involves notions such as event structure, truth conditions and modality. In music we find no such notions whatsoever. The THC involves notions such as principles of

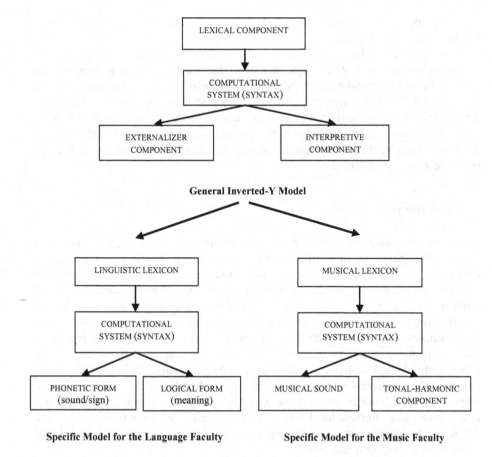

Fig. 8. Language and music as two specifications of the same inverted-Y abstract model

harmonic tension and relaxation, consonance and dissonance and tonal interpretation[2]. The hypothesis is then that the differences which can be observed in the syntax of language and music are due to phenomena related to their interaction with their interpretive components. This would explain, for instance, why we should not expect to find in music a phenomenon typical of language like variable binding, because, although it relies on syntax, it involves notions like referentiality, among other things.

In spite of their different nature, however, both THC and the linguistic semantic module are mental a-temporal realities, quite particular to the human mind, which share the property of being able to compute hierarchical structures created by a similar syntactic component. From this perspective, both language and music appear to be plausibly accommodated in the same abstract theoretical model with the inverted-Y

---

[2] See Katz (2017) for a proposal of what kind of conditions may the THC impose to the syntactic structures of music for a proper tonal interpretation.

shape provided in Fig. 8, with four modules each which are functionally equivalent in this inverted-Y architecture.

This hypothesis offers a new view on the structure of music that is much more similar to the structure of language than what has traditionally been assumed. To explore the accuracy and plausibility of the hypothesis, a proper characterization of how the THC and the syntactic component interact must be posited. Accurately detailing how the interpretive components of each system affect the composition of the respective lexical systems also needs to be explored, in order to justify that the different nature of the respective lexical elements is determined by the nature of the interpretive component they are oriented to.

5 Summary

We have shown that the theoretical model for the human faculty of language postulated by generative theory, the inverted-Y model, is useful to explain also the human faculty of music. It has been our contention that their respective main modules can be mapped and that a similar interaction between them can be posited. Both systems have a central syntactic module, which builds up structures from the units provided by a lexical system through the instructions encoded in their features, and which is connected to two interfaces, one related to the sensory-motor system that materializes and externalizes structures in a sequential form, and the other connected to an interpretive component, which is different for each system. For language, the interpretive component is the conceptual-intentional system, which decodes syntactic structures into linguistic meaning; for music, it is the Tonal-Harmonic Component, which decodes syntactic structures through tonal-harmonic interpretation. We have suggested that the different nature of the interpretive components is what determines the formal differences between language and music.

Acknowledgements. This research has been financed by a public grant from the Ministerio de Educación, Cultura y Deportes of the Spanish government (FPU14/04707) and forms part of subproject FFI2014-56968-C4-1-P, financed by the Ministerio de Economía y Competitividad, and project 2017SGR-634, financed by AGAUR-Generalitat de Catalunya.

References

Adger, D.: Core Syntax. Oxford University Press, Oxford (2003)
Arbib, M.A. (ed.): Language, Music, and the Brain. A Mysterious Relationship. MIT Press, Cambridge (2013)
Bernstein, L.: The Unanswered Question. Six talks at Harvard. Harvard University Press, Cambridge (1976)
Chomsky, N.: The Minimalist Program. MIT Press, Cambridge (1995)
Fitch, W.T.: The biology and evolution of music: a comparative perspective. Cognition **100**, 173–215 (2006)
Fodor, J.A.: The Modularity of Mind. MIT Press, Cambridge (1983)
Giblin, I.: Music and the Generative Enterprise. University of New South Wales, Sydney (2008)

Grodzinsky, Y.: Neural substrates for linguistic and musical abilities: a neurolinguist's perspective. In: Toivonen, I., Csúri, P., Van der Zee, E. (eds.) Structures in the Mind: Essays on Language, Music, and Cognition in Honor of Ray Jackendoff, pp. 325–346. MIT Press, Cambridge (2015)

Hamanaka, M., Hirata, K., Tojo, S.: Implementing methods for analysing music based on Lerdahl and Jackendoff's Generative theory of tonal music. In: Meredith, D. (ed.) Computational Music Analysis, pp. 221–249. Springer, Heidelberg (2016). https://doi.org/10.1007/978-3-319-25931-4_9

Jackendoff, R.: Parallels and nonparallels between language and music. Music Percept. **26**(3), 195–204 (2009)

Jackendoff, R., Lerdahl, F.: The capacity for music: what is it, and what's special about it? Cognition **100**, 33–72 (2006)

Katz, J.: Exceptional cadential chords and the nature of tonic-marking. In: Halpert, C., Kotek, H., van Urk, C. (eds.) A Pesky Set: A festschrift for David Pesetsky, pp. 447–456. MIT Working Papers in Linguistics, Cambridge (2017)

Katz, J., Pesetsky, D.: The Identity Thesis for Language and Music (2011). http://www.sfu.ca/~hedberg/katzEtAl_11_The-Identity-.3.pdf

Lerdahl, F.: Tonal Pitch Space. Oxford University Press, Oxford (2001). https://doi.org/10.1093/acprof:oso/9780195178296.001.0001

Lerdahl, F., Jackendoff, R.: A Generative Theory of Tonal Music. MIT Press, Cambridge (1983)

Lerdahl, F., Krumhansl, C.L.: Modeling tonal tension. Music Percept. **24**(4), 329–366 (2007). https://doi.org/10.1525/mp.2007.24.4.329

McMullen, E., Saffran, J.R.: Music and language: a developmental comparison. Music Percept. **21**(3), 289–311 (2004)

Patel, A.D.: Music, Language, and the Brain. Oxford University Press, Oxford (2008)

Peretz, I.: The nature of music from a biological perspective. Cognition **100**(1), 1–32 (2006). https://doi.org/10.1016/j.cognition.2005.11.004

Rebuschat, P., Rohrmeier, M., Hawkins, J.A., Cross, I. (eds.): Language and Music as Cognitive Systems. Oxford University Press, Oxford (2012)

Rohrmeier, M.: A generative grammar approach to diatonic harmonic structure. In: Sound and Music Computing Conference, Lefkada, Greece, pp. 97–100 (2007)

Rohrmeier, M.: Towards a generative syntax of tonal harmony. J. Math. Music **5**(1), 35–53 (2011)

Is Generative Theory Misleading for Music Theory?

Rafael Barbosa[(✉)] [iD]

CTEL, Côte d'Azur University, Nice, France
rafael.barbosa2606@gmail.com

Abstract. During the decade of the 1960s linguistics entered what can be seen as a paradigm shift following Thomas Kuhn's theory of the *Structure of Scientific Revolutions* (1962). As a result, the discipline steps out of the Cartesian dualism between body and mind. During the 80[th's] analytical musicology was related to the methodological approach of transformational grammars, the best known example being the *Generative Theory of Tonal Music* (Lerdahl and Jackendoff 1983). For musicologist, the motivation to adopt this position is naturally nurtured by the work of Heinrich Schenker (*Der Freier Satz* 1935) in which, as in transformational grammar, a hierarchy of layers going from the actual piece of music to its *Ursatz* (Kernel) is proposed. The hypothesis developed in this article is that the analytical musicology, despite the efforts to link it with modern linguistics, has not yet stepped into the new scientific paradigm led by cognitive sciences. The reason for this is that musicology has not yet adopted a redefinition of its object of study from a non-dualistic and transdisciplinary perspective. With the development of experimental aesthetics, the ontological gap between the object of musicology and that of the scientific approach to music has been growing larger. As a result, if the study of aesthetic meaning in music has become possible today, it seems to be inconsistent with the traditional reductionist methods of analytical musicology, from which the analogy with transformational grammar rely upon.

Keywords: Musicology · Music analysis · Scientific aesthetics
Generative theory · Epistemology · Paradigm shift

1 Introduction

Looking at the evolution of knowledge during the twentieth century, a deep transformation on the nature of the object of many sciences can be observed. An important example is the development of a philosophy of an "embodied mind" that can be traced back from the work of James Williams (1842–1910) and later John Dewey (1859–1952) to the publication in 1999, by Mark Johnson and George Lakoff, of *Philosophy in the flesh,* putting forward the concept of an embodied mind as a *challenge to western thought.* Another meaningful example is the assumption that our faculty for abstract reasoning depends to an important degree on an emotional and somatic basis, challenging western traditional ideas concerning the nature and function of sensation and emotions. That is indeed the position defended by neurologists like Antonio Damasio.

© Springer Nature Switzerland AG 2019
P. Eismont and O. Mitrenina (Eds.): LMAC 2017, CCIS 943, pp. 22–34, 2019.
https://doi.org/10.1007/978-3-030-05594-3_2

On the realm of linguistics, The Chomskian hypothesis assuming the existence of an innate linguistic structure working as a *Universal Grammar*, enabling us to acquire linguistic skills, is another example of what can be described as a *paradigm shift*.

The concept of *paradigm* as it was developed by Thomas Kuhn in his acclaimed book released in 1962, *The Structure of Scientific Revolutions*, embrace two broad meanings: on one hand it represents the total amount of beliefs, standard values, and techniques that belong to the members of a scientific community. On the other hand, it describes a specific methodological procedure to resolve a specific kind of enigmas (problems) that become a reference on the *normal* practice and transmission of that scientific discipline. One of Kuhn's ideas is that the ontological definition of the object of a scientific discipline is dependent on the existence of one or more paradigms. Consequently, paradigms have an indirect – but real – influence on the way scholars conceive the methodologies they employ to resolve new enigmas. Kuhn shows that on the evolution of a discipline over an extended period of time, paradigms become obsolete. Before a new paradigm replace the old one, a "crisis" and a "rejection" of the latter takes place. This is commonly represented in a cycle as shown in Fig. 1.

The recent evolution of the disciplines mentioned above – to which anthropology, ethology and scientific aesthetics should be added –, reveals a common faith. It is of course the overtaking of the old paradigm of duality that defended the existence of an ontological contradiction between body and mind, and consequently, on a larger scale, a disconnection between nature and culture. The contact of musicology with modern – and more precisely Chomskian – linguistics, led to the collaboration between the composer and musicologist Fred Lerdahl, and the linguist Ray Jackendoff who in 1983 published *A Generative theory of Tonal Music* (GTTM). This should not be seen as an isolated initiative since in Europe the Belgian musicologist Celestin Deliege also brought forward an analytical theory inspired by transformational grammar [1].

This methodological proximity has been strongly motivated by the work of the Austrian musicologist Heinrich Schenker [2] who developed an analytical method based on systematical reductions leading from the actual piece of music – the foreground – to a kernel which is common to a vast repertoire of musical pieces; what he calls *"die Meisterwerke"*. This hierarchical representation displays a clear formal resemblance with that of surface and deep structures of transformational grammar. The idea that a given phrases – musical or linguistic –, is the result of a more general abstract principle is also a common feature of both theories. The way musicology relates to modern linguistics let us think that music theory takes part to the paradigm renewal described above. In this article I defend the idea that musicology has not entered what can be called a paradigm of *continuity* between body and mind. Therefore, it's relation to generative grammar is problematic.

From an epistemological perspective, I will question the relevance of a methodological interaction between linguistics and analytical musicology in the particular context of the overtaking of the dualistic paradigm. This concern can be formulated in the following questions: are the objects of generative linguistics and analytical musicology heuristics of related paradigms? And, how is analytical musicology related to the dualistic paradigm?

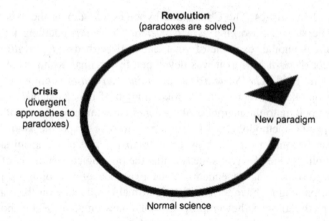

Fig. 1. Kuhn cycle showing the passage from *normal science* to the adoption of a new paradigm.

2   Defining the Objects

2.1   A Call for Transdisciplinarity

The history of sciences and more generally, that of thought, is full of quarrels which seem inevitable when two scholars studying the same objet do not come to an agreement about both the methods to be adopted, and the aims to be fulfilled. It is often some time later, through a retrospective view on history, that the reasons for such disagreements appears clearly: in order to define their object, different scientist may respond to different enigmas and adopt different methods, consequently, their object subscribes to different paradigms.[1] We find a famous example on the critic Chomsky addressed to Skinner's book *Verbal Behavior* in 1959, showing that cognitivism and behaviorism could not share the same idea of what language is. In an interview with the American linguist, Javier Virués-Ortega synthesizes the position against Skinner as follows:

> Behavior is evidence. It's not what you are studying; what you are studying is competence, capacity. If you study man's insight you want to know what is going on in his brain; behavior gives the evidence for that. Nevertheless, in a serious field, you wouldn't identify the subject with the study of the data [3].

In the case of the GTTM, the deliberated application of a common methodological approach to both music and language supposes that the question about their ontological relation has been thoroughly considered. Otherwise we could just be treating one domain as a metaphor for the other. In order to understand those inquires we first have

---

[1] This is also one of the ideas that Kuhn develops extensively on his book. "Men whose research is based on shared paradigms are committed to the same rules and standards for scientific practice. That commitment and the apparent consensus it produces are prerequisites for normal science, *i.e.*, for the genesis and continuation of a particular research tradition." [4].

to make a ontological comparison between a Chomskian definition of *language* as object of research, and *music* as defined by the theoretical apparatus of musicology.

Music, as it is well known, has always call the curiosity of scholars; philosophers like Nietzsche, mathematicians like Leonhard Euler, and physiologists like Hermann von Helmholtz, count among the many thinkers that worked on music before the 20th century. It is possible to assess today, as Delalande [5] does, that an important development of what should be called the "sciences of music" exceeds by far the realm of academic musicology. It is evident that analytical musicology has not made a serious effort to assimilate the discoveries that disciplines like psychoacoustics, cognitive psychology and scientific aesthetics have been accumulating for more 150 years. The excellent work on the physiological basis for the perception of tonal music made by Helmholtz, did not have a real impact on the way tonal harmony is taught in universities and conservatoires. The call for transdisciplinarity that opens Helmholtz's book published in 1863, has not been heard by musicology.

> In the present work an attempt will be made to connect the boundaries of tow sciences, which, although drawn towards each other by many natural affinities, have hitherto remained practically distinct –I mean the boundaries of *physical and physiological acoustics* on the one side, and of musical theory and aesthetics on the other [6].

The study of auditory perception as well as that of music by cognitive psychologists has also been kept sidelined from the development of the 20th century theoretical musicology. This, as well as the achievements of scientific aesthetics – a field that has known a spectacular development in recent decades –, have been considered only by a very small group of musicologist like Michel Imberty and Philipe Lalitte, whose work remain overlooked by the tenants of *normal* musicology. This split between a scientific approach to music and the musicology it self, shows an epistemological disconnection between the way linguistics and musicology have evolved since the late 19th century to the present day. Stressing one of the main features of this distinction we can say that musicology has been refusing transdisciplinarity, while linguistics has been assuming it.

2.2   Scientific Aesthetics, Right Between Body and Mind

With regard to art and particularly to music, special attention should be given to the scientific study of aesthetics, which has undoubtedly contributed to linking culture to nature. This goal has been achieved through the patient development of a scientific approach to sensation, perception and finally, to aesthetic judgement. In contrast with the philosophical tradition of speculative aesthetics, the development of the experimental and empirical approach which started with the publication in 1876 of *Introduction to aesthetics* by the German scientist Gustav Fechner, has remained largely over shadowed to the human sciences and therefore to musicology.

What Fechner started doing was gathering data about the way humans react to specific sensitive stimuli, measuring the hedonic response as pleasant (*Gefallen*) or unpleasant (*Misfallen*). If the complexity of proper art works prevented scientific aesthetics to use them as the basis of experiences for decades, the development of the experimental method and the achievements in the study of perception, have made it possible since the 50's. The French psychologist Robet Francès published a series of experiments on music in 1958, followed in 1971 by Daniel Berlyne who focused mainly on visual Arts [7, 8].

If the tradition of speculative aesthetics conceived beauty as independent of the somatic expression of the agreeable, and as being in disconnection with our rewarding instinct responding to pleasure, from the perspective of scientific aesthetics, the distance between what Kant understood as a *pure aesthetic experience,* and the hedonic experience of pleasurable perceptions, is not impaired by an ontological duality, instead, it implies a challenge of transdisciplinarity and a methodological complexity.[2]

Music has played a prominent role in the development of scientific esthetics as well as on the more general fields of perception and cognition. The question of the perception of time for example, leads inevitably to inquire into the capacity to perceive melodies as coherent entities.[3] The study on the cognitive mechanisms of learning led to a great number of experimental studies that have been measuring our capacity to assimilate and identify violations of expectancies on musical grammars; that has been the purpose of the recent work of Martin Rohrmeier at the university of Cambridge [10]. When it comes to the study of memory, which has been one of the most studied subjects in cognitive psychology during the 20th century, music has also been involved: a series of experiments enquiring the capacity of listeners to judge the effect of the global temporal organization of a piece of music has strongly challenge the traditional ideas of musicology relating to the implication of global structure on the esthetic experience [11, 12]. But *normal* musicology, that is: the academic mainstream of music scholarship, has not take that enigmas into consideration. This lack of overture, as I will try to explain, is the main reasons why the theoretical background of GTTM (namely schenkerian reductionism) remains deeply rooted on the dualistic paradigm.

By giving a scientific status to the hedonic and sensitive aspects of the experience of music, scientific aesthetics has evolved within the paradigm shift that overcomes dualism and embrace an integrated conception of human. Therefore we may recognize the existence of an ontological distinction between the objet of what can be called *sciences of music* on one side, and that of traditional musicology on the other. We can say that the object being studied by the *sciences of music* would be better named, as Michel Imberty puts it, the "human musicality" [13], term that refers to our capacity for aesthetic communication either through the creation, the performance or simply the listening of organized sound. From this perspective, analytical musicology stands out as a rather conservative and isolated discipline, maintaining a representation of it's object inherited from enlightenment music theory, and showing little interest for recognizing a heuristic value to the achievements of scientific aesthetics. This strongly

---

[2] The development of *complexity* as a methodological approach; a kind of *Discours de la méthode* for the 20th century, has been the work of thinkers like Morin [9] who elaborates a theory of complex thinking in order to defend a new epistemological definition of anthropology: what he named *fundamental anthropology.*

[3] Not only the authors of the gestalt theory like Ehrenfelds and Kurt Kofka used melody to explain the effect of grouping laws in time, but Husserl used it as well on his *Lessons on the Phenomenology of Inner Time Consciousness.* Studying time perception, psychologist like Paul Fraisse and John Michon have also reflected both on the nature of melody and musical rhythm.

suggest that an ontological gap persists between analytical musicology and modern linguistics; a gap that remain untold by the literature concerned.

So how it is that music can on the one side encourage scientists to move out of the dualist paradigm, and on the other side leave musicologists indifferent to the implication of such a transformation? The answer I propose is that the modal difference between the score, as a semiotic object, and the aesthetic experience as a phenomenological experience, has not been properly considered as a paradox by musicology, or at least not by a large part of the community of musicologists worldwide. Therefore, most of the enigmas studied by the sciences of music do not resonate with the theoretical construct of analytical musicology.

3 Generative Theory as Temptation

3.1 A "Cartesian" Musicology

The reliance of *normal* musicology on a dualism between body and mind, was already a characteristic of the way music theory was understood in the ancient Greece. If the proportions related to musical intervals placed music among the four sciences of the *Quadrivium* – side by side with astronomy, arithmetic and geometry –, when Plato reflects on the experience of music, the sensitive effect of the same rigorous mathematical proportions could become the target of accusations and even be prohibited. That is the case of the *Ionien* mode[4] in *The republic* where Plato suggests that the music based on this particular mode should be banished. The development of music theory since the 17th century has in deed inherited this ontological duality leaving the aesthetic value of a piece of music beyond the reach of the analytical endeavor. Reductionism appears to be the most constant characteristic in the development of musical analysis of western music. On his excellent book on the history of musical analysis, Bent [14] shows us that Schenker's reductionism inherited a long tradition of German musical theorists starting at least with J. B Logier (1777–1846) and pursued by J. C. Lobe (1797–1881). This trend appears also to be deeply rooted in the fact that the notational system developed in western music allows an abstract representation where sound and musical parameters gain an important degree of autonomy from the acoustic events they signify.[5] The titles of the treatises published by Philippe Rameau show the importance, from a methodological perspective, of proceeding by systematic reduction to reveal the coherence of the whole. The first of them, published in 1722, is suitably entitled *Musical harmony reduced to its natural principles*. In his last treatise Rameau show a position that recalls vividly the place of music among the four sciences of the *Quadrivium*.

---

[4] The *Ionien* mode is one of the musical scales used in the ancient Greece. This mode is known to be used on festivities related to the tribute of Dionysos. Surprisingly, it corresponds very closely to a major scale, which is the basis of tonal music, as developed in Europe from the baroque era.

[5] The sophisticated notation of sound parameters like pitch and duration, played an important role on the evolution of musical style. Theoretical concepts of melodic phrase, harmony, counterpoint and *basso continuo*, are also tightly related to the evolution of notation.

It is in music that nature presents us the physical principles of the pure mathematical notions which are the basis for all sciences. I refer to the harmonic[6], arithmetic and geometrical proportions [15].

This structuralist approach to music has maintained the aesthetic value of music unconcerned, reduced entirely to a matter of subjectivity. Of course, the possibility of a scientific discourse on the affective power of music was not possible before the 20th century. But the segregation between musical analysis and actual perception has continued to grow it's roots to the present day. Even the development of scientific aesthetics through the paradigm shift mentioned above, does not seem to attract analytical musicology, which has remained faithful to it's traditional background. Ultimately, it has led to a situation where, as Pierre Boulez said, "it is possible to make brilliant analysis of music of no interest" [16]. But there is an even worst situation: using the tools of today's *normal* musicology, we can celebrate through a sophisticated and intelligent analysis, a piece of music whose aesthetic value leave us indifferent. The risk is that the analysis becomes a metaphor between the structure it unfolds and the aesthetic content of the piece; a metaphor that does not take into account the value added by perception. This idea is expressed by Nicholas Cook when he argues that musicologists like Allen Forte, Steven Gilbert and Hans Keller[7] "could, if they wished, maintain that the aesthetic value of a piece of music is simply a function of the score's formal structure." [17]. This appraisal applies not only to Shenkerian analysis – which lies at the basis of the analogy between musical analysis and transformational grammar –, but also to theories concerning part of the atonal repertoire of the 20th century like the *Set Theory* developed by George Perle and Allen Forte during the late sixties. Both approaches have been widely taught across conservatories and universities, becoming today an important component of what can be understood as *normal* analytical musicology.

3.2   A Silent Crisis

The growing diversification of compositional techniques that characterizes western music during the last decades of the 20th century, along with the constant and increasing research for new sounds encouraged by new technologies, has pushed the analytical musicology to a "crisis" in the sense given by Kuhn [4]. What this means is that the works of composers like Giorgy Ligeti, Ianis Xenakis and others, could not be properly understood using *Set Theory* or *serial* analysis. This conjuncture was an opportunity for music scholars to broaden the epistemological and methodological template of analytical theory. But did analytical musicology finally dared an alliance with the *sciences of music*? In deed, the study of "human musicality" represented already at that time a new and interesting perspective on music research; it would allow musicologists to face the growing diversity of musical invention through the

---

[6] From antiquity the term *harmony* use to be applied to the study of astronomy. It is still the case during the 17th when Kepler publishes his *Harmonices Mundi* (1619). We can see that it is the same sense used by Rameau on this passage.

[7] Allen Forte and Steven Gilbert are the authors of *Introduction to schenkerian analysis*, New York, Norton & Co, 1983.

universality of the perceptive and cognitive processes that enable the aesthetic experience. This alliance would seemingly open a unifying perspective concerning not only the whole spectrum of western written music, but embracing music as the expression of a communicative skill inherent to human nature. In other words, attention would be driven more on content that on form; more on actual sound perception, and less on music notation.

But engaging on transdisciplinarity would need a huge epistemological endeavor. The need for updating old theoretical concepts in order to fit the enigmas of the new, non-dualist paradigm, would force musicology to build a complex relation between compositional procedures and perceptual capacity. Instead of taking the risk of such a project, the mainstream of analytical musicology engaged on the domain of *sketch studies*, a tendency that was pioneered by Gustav Nottebohm (1817–1882) who worked on the sketches left by Beethoven. This approach consist in trying to understand the genesis of a piece of music, by a cross relation between biographical facts and the analysis of material evidence of the work in progress. If such a method reveals itself as particularly suitable to contemporary music; a repertoire where the standards of notation and traditional instrumentation are constantly challenged by the creativity of each composer, the trend toward a hyper-specialization where each composer or even each piece of music implies it's own theory, becomes inevitable. The dominance of this approach seems to put an obstacle to the transdisciplinary development of the discipline, and therefore to it's epistemological actualization. Lorenz Konrad expresses his preoccupation on this kind of academic development with the following words:

> The specialist comes to know more and more about less and less, until finally he knows everything about a mere nothing. There is a danger that the specialist, forced to compete with his colleges in acquiring more and more specialized knowledge, will become more and more ignorant about other branches of knowledge, until he is utterly incapable of forming any judgment on the role and importance of his own sphere within the context of human knowledge, as a whole [18].

In such a context, the link up between generative grammar and tonal music analysis seems to count as an effort to finally take musicology out of its epistemological isolation. But in fact, it doesn't take it out of the dualistic paradigm. The link between linguistics and music analysis is based on a formal resemblance; an external analogy between transformational grammar on one hand, and Schekerian reductionism on the other. By focusing on this analogy we fail to identify the ontological gap between the object of psycho-linguistics and that of *normal* analytical musicology, which – for the reasons presented above – are rooted in different paradigms. On the basis of the superficial resemblance between the two methods, even respectable musicologists like Jean-Claude Risset, have seen in Schenker's theory a prefiguration of Chomsky's transformational grammar.

> In the course of his analytical study of tonal music, the Viennese musicologist Heinrich Schenker came up with the concept of generative grammar, fifty years earlier than the linguist Noam Chomsky [19].

The authors of *A Generative Theory for Tonal Music* don't make such a statement, but they don't comment either on the hypothesis of a parallel between semantic (linguistic) and aesthetic (musical) meaning; an idea one expect to be the main motivation behind the methodological borrowing of concepts like *transformational rules, span reduction* or the *generative process* it self. This epistemological ambiguity is not apparent to them. The analogy is taken as self-sufficient when they say: "This kind of organization, which in music-theory circles is often called a *pitch reduction* – in the tradition of Schenker –, is notated in *A Generative Theory for Tonal Music* as a tree structure" [20].

Maybe the main difference between Schenker's reductionist approach and transformational grammar is the notion of deep structure, which plays a central role in both cases. In Schenker as in the GTTM, the fact that the different layers keep signifying specific acoustic events placed in time, let us understand them as new *surface* levels. The process of rarefaction of the surface level, which is done by the systematic reduction of harmonic and rhythmic patterns does not imply a process of abstraction, rather it obeys to the application of an external theory of substitution. Therefore we can say that the nature of the reductions is the same as that of the surface structure; they are and remain acoustic statements. In contrast, transformational grammar implies an abstraction from the physical signal of any spoken language, to the computational operations defining *Universal Grammar*. As Chomsky puts it,

> We can thus distinguish the surface structure of the sentence, the organization into categories and phrases that is directly associated with the physical signal, from the underlying deep structure, also a system of categories and phrases, but with a more abstract character [21].

I would suggest that generative theory acted as a temptation for musicology, just in the same way Charles Darwin's theory of evolution was a temptation for linguistics during the late 19th century, when language came to be considered by some as a living organism. In his book *La vie des mots* of 1887, the French philologist Arsène Darmesteter wrote the following statement: "Despite of their intellectual nature, the fact that languages are also living organisms like plants and animals, is today an unquestionable truth" [22]. A statement that could not be defended some 30 years later, under the light of Saussure's distinction between synchronic and diachronic approaches to linguistic in which culture plays an essential part.

4 Differences that Matter

The study of the relation between the sonic structure and the aesthetic meaning of music can certainly benefit from linguistics. Nevertheless, it seems that in order for that relation to be fruitful, the two disciplines concerned should first accomplish a comparative study of the nature of their respective object. In order to prevent false analogies that would cover important discrepancies, there should also be a comparison that lies on the same epistemological context characterized by transdisciplinarity. Both similarities and contrasts may help to identify the convenience or inconvenience of implementing the methodological apparatus of one discipline to the other. The brief comparison on three points that follows seek to underline ontological specificities that dissociate music from language on a basic epistemological level. I suggest that a thorough consideration of these specificities – among others – should point out incompatibilities that question the interest and the aim of sharing specific method-ological tools like the one discussed on this paper.

4.1   Orality vs. Instrumentality

The first comparison concerns the orality of language and the use of manufactured instruments in music. If all the hypotheses on the origin of music propose that singing precedes the use of instruments, the oldest remains of musical instruments go back some 43.000 years in time.[8] Following that fact we can assume that music develops in a close relation to technological acquisitions and material constraints. As a consequence of that, the technical skill of knowing how to play such instruments appears as an specific cultural feature. Another significant consequence is the distinction between the performer and the listener, a feature that will know different variations in different cultures. In contrast, the orality of language is constant from one culture to another. Cultural changes and technological development through time do not seem to challenge the use of inherent vocal capacity as the material means for linguistic communication. As written language depends on a semiotic relation between phonetic units and graphic signs, orality remains a prerequisite. Therefore we can say that while there is a high degree of influence of both ecological and sociological factors on the development of music, what gives language its robustness is it's relation to strong physiological and cognitive constraints.

Both ethnomusicology and psychology of music have shown the existence of music *universals*, which are also related to psychoacoustic and cognitive constraints. It is the case for the preference of harmonic relations such as 2:1 or 3:2, the asymmetric character of musical scales, the prominence of pattern repetition and metric stability. Nevertheless, these characteristics apply in different and renewed ways through different cultures and history. This suggests that universals in music do not imply the existence of a set of rules acting as a generative principle, but are rather a common set of characteristics accessible to direct perception; evident on a *surface level* of the music structure.

4.2   Different Learning Mechanisms

The second aspect I want to briefly consider is the relation of music and language to human innate learning capacity. Cognitive psychology has been studying for more than a century the processes of learning and knowledge acquisition. The use of artificial grammars to that purpose has consistently developed in recent decades [23], and music has been given special attention by researchers. For instances, the acquisition of a competence related to the harmonic regularities of tonal music has been the object of many studies [24]. Other kinds of music, including serial music, have also played an important role concerning implicit learning of artificial grammars [25, 26]. Such studies have shown that the capacity to appreciate a variety of musical styles from different cultural backgrounds can be acquired at any time of life and through implicit

---

[8] It is the case of the well known *Divje Babe flute* found in 1995 in a Slovenian cave by Ivan Turk.

mechanisms of learning. Another feature revealed by the same experiments is the velocity of these processes, which in certain cases need nothing more that a limited number of experiences. In contrast, the acquisition of linguistic skills is strongly related to the biological clock managing the brain's development during the early years of life. Learning a foreign language as an adult requires a great deal of time, and implies an explicit effort of learning.

If the acquisition of a tonal music skill has been proven to take place around the age of 6, this fact does not necessarily point to considering tonality as a natural or universal grammar – which is anyway inconsistent with historical evidence. What is proven is the fact that music, and particularly tonal music, requires a certain state of development of the brain in order to be assimilated. So if the acquisition of language is the consequence of an innate predisposition – *Universal Grammar* –, the acquisition of musical expertise seem to be tightly related to the processes of implicit learning of artificial grammars. That statement alone suggests the necessity of a distinction between the cognitive treatment of linguistic and musical stimuli. Recent research in neurosciences seems to prove that assumption [27].

4.3   Implications of Notational Standards

The last comparison I will comment is the striking difference between the effect of notation in both music and language. Taking the example of western culture – which is not the only one having developed a notational system, but which is in deed a very complex one –, it appears that notation has been tightly linked to the evolution of both stylistic and technological aspects of music [28]. Since the 12th century, when notation became more precise and was systematically adopted by both church and court composers, the history of western music changed dramatically. An example is the apparition of complex polyphonies that encourage the research on rhythmic notation, and ended up challenging the prominent role of the sacred texts in vocal music.[9] Another striking example are the enharmonic relations in tonal music, which become fully practicable only after the adoption of equal temperament. More recently, modern technology has open the possibility for sound wave synthesis, transforming the traditional role of musical instrument, showing once again that when the means for notation evolve, important changes in music aesthetics follow. We can say that meaning in written music depends to some extent on the notational means at hand. This is not the case for language where meaning is embedded in the recursive structure of the generative process, and both the graphic and the acoustic signs remain, as Saussure said, arbitrary.

---

[9] A rapid evolution of polyphonic music takes place following the adoption of the staff invented by Guido de Arezzo during the first half on the 11th century. The music of Léonin (1150–1201) and Pérotin le Grand (1160–1230), using long melismas on each vowel, shows how the understanding of the sacred text became secondary in comparison with Gregorian plainchant.

5 Conclusion

As mentioned in the second point of the last section, the *universals* that ethnomusicological and psychological studies have discovered in music [29, 30] consist on audible features with salient sensitive characteristics. These features are of a very different nature from the "length and complexity of the chain of operations that relate the mental structures expressing the semantic content of the utterance to the physical realization." [21, p. 22]. To consider this and other aspects discussed above when it comes to reflect on the distinction between semantic and aesthetic forms of meaning, should prevent transdisciplinarity from building analogies and methodological bridges that may end-up avoiding or masking some important problematics.

The reductionist theories, conventional to the tradition of theoretical musicology, reflect not only the composite character of written music and the difficulties it engenders to analysis, but also show the influence of a given paradigm on the epistemic priorities that researchers adopt at some point in history. In the context of a redefinition of concepts like body, mind and humanity that concerns both human and natural sciences, it seems to me that the suggested parallel between generative grammar and musical theory can be understood as a reminiscence of the dualistic paradigm.

References

1. Deliège, C.: Fondements de la musique tonale. Lattès, Paris (1984)
2. Schenker, H.: Free Composition, 2nd edn. (trans: Oster, E.) Longman, New York (1979). (original from 1935)
3. Virués-Ortega, J.: The Case Against B. F. Skinner 45 years Later: An Encounter with N. Chomsky. In: The Behavior Analyst, vol. 29, pp. 243–251 (2006). p. 245
4. Kuhn, T.: The Structure of Scientific Revolutions, p. 23. University of Chicago Press, Chicago (1962)
5. Delalande, F.: Analyser la musique, pourquoi, comment?. INA, Paris (2013)
6. von Helmholtz, H.: On the Sensation of Tone as Physiological Basis for the Theory of Music. éd. and trad. A. J. Ellis, New York, Dover, New York, p. 6 (1954)
7. Francès, R.: La perception de la musique. Vrin, Paris (1958)
8. Berlyne, D. (ed.): Studies in Experimental Aesthetics: A Step Toward an Objective Psychology of Aesthetic Appreciation. Hemisphere Publishing Corporation, Washington (1974)
9. Morin, E.: Introduction à la pensée complexe. Seuil, Paris (2005)
10. Rohrmeier, M., Rebuschat, P.: Implicit learning and acquisition of Music. TopiCS 4, 525–553 (2012)
11. Granot, R., Jacoby, N.: Musically Puzzling I: Sensitivity to Overall Structure in the Sonata Form? Musicae Scientiae 15(3), 365–386 (2011)
12. Tillmann, B., Bigand, E.: Global context effect in normal and scrambled musical sequences. J. Exp. Psychol. 27(5), 1185–1196 (2001)
13. Imberty, M., Maya, G. (eds.): Temps, geste et musicalité. L'harmattan, Paris (2007)
14. Bent, I.: Analysis. Macmillan, London (1987)
15. Rameau, J.-P.: Démonstration du principe de l'harmonie, p. viii. Durant-Pissot, Paris (1750)
16. Boulez, P.: Jalons, Pour une décennie, p. 34. Christian Bourgois, Paris (1989)
17. Cook, N.: Music Imagination and Culture, p. 3. Oxford University Press, Oxford (1992)

18. Lorenz, K.: Behind the Mirror: A Search for a Natural History of Human Knowledge, p. 49. Methuen, London (1977)
19. This assumption is made by Jean-Claude Risset, in the forword to: Auriol, Berdard: La clef des sons. Erès, Toulouse (1991)
20. Jackendoff, R., Lerdahl, F.: The capacity for music: what is it, and what's special about it? In: Cognition, no. 100, pp. 33–72 (2006). p. 55
21. Chomsky, N.: Language and Mind, 3rd edn, p. 25. Cambridge University Press, Cambridge (2006)
22. Darmesteter, A.: La vie des mots. Delagrave, Paris (1887)
23. Reber, A.: Implicit Learning and Tacit Knowledge. Oxford University Press, Oxford (1993)
24. Imberty, M.: L'aquisition de structures tonales chez l'enfant. Klincksieck, Paris (1969)
25. Bigand, E., Charles, D.: L'apprentissage implicite de la musique occidentale. In: Kolinsky, R., Morais, J., Peretz, I. (eds.) Musique, Langage, Emotion: une approche neuro-cognitive. Presse Universitaire de Renne, Renne (2010)
26. Rohrmeier, M., Cross, I.: Tacit tonality: implicit learning of context-free harmonic structures. In: Proceedings of the 7th Trennial Conference of the ESCOM, pp. 443–452 (2009)
27. Peretz, I.: The nature of music from a biological perspective. In: Elsevier Cognition, no. 100, pp. 1–32 (2006)
28. Bosseur, J.-Y.: Du son au signe. Alternatives, Paris (2005)
29. Ball, P.: The Music Instinct, How Music Works and Why We Can't Do Without It. Vintage, London (2011)
30. Sloboda, J.: The Musical Mind. The Cognitive Psychology of Music. Oxford University Press, Oxford (1986)

Acoustic and Perceptual-Auditory Determinants of Transmission of Speech and Music Information (in Regard to Semiotics)

Rodmonga Potapova[1]([✉]) [iD] and Vsevolod Potapov[2] [iD]

[1] Institute of Applied and Mathematical Linguistics,
Moscow State Linguistic University, Ostozhenka 38, Moscow 119034, Russia
rkpotapova@yandex.ru
[2] Faculty of Philology, Lomonosov Moscow State University, GSP-1,
Leninskie Gory, Moscow 119991, Russia

Abstract. The paper presents conception regarding speech and music research on the basis of semiotics. The speech and music semiotic systems are examined as special hierarchical subsystems of the common human semiotic interpersonal communication system. And what is more every speech semiotic subsystem has its own subsystems: e.g., articulatory, phonatory, acoustic, perceptual-auditory etc. The speech semiotic acoustic subsystem has its own subsystems, e.g. duration (tn − ms), intensity (I_n − dB), fundamental frequency (F_{0n} − Hz), spectrum values (F_n − Hz). Speech and music are considered as two congeneric phenomena subsystems of the common semiotic interpersonal communication system with regard to semantics, syntactics and pragmatics: semantics as an area of relations between speech and music expressions, on the one hand, and objects and processes in the world, on the other hand; syntactics as an area of the interrelations of these expressions; pragmatics as an area of the influence of the meaning of these expressions on their users. This speech and music semiotic conception includes binary oppositions "ratio-emotio", actual "thema-rhema" segmentation of speech and musical text/discourse, "segmental-suprasegmental items", "prosody-timbre items", etc. In this research was made an attempt to show the progressiveness of using the method of music "score" (composed on the basis of the results of speech prosodic characteristics analysis), which can help to determine the informativeness of parameters used for determining the speakers' emotional state. Creation of music score based on this analysis is viewed as a model for a prosodic vocal outline of the utterance. At the same time the prosodic basis of speech and basic expressive means of the "music language" are connected. Speech as well as music uses the same space and time coordinates representing sound item movements. The height metric grid is based on this principle, which determines sound item in dynamics. Time organization of music and speech creates a common temporal basis. The music score created on the basis of the results of the prosodic features acoustic analysis meets the requirements taking into consideration the restrictions caused by the absence of segmented (sound-syllable) text. Thus, with the help of special music synthesis of speech utterance on the basis of the acoustic and further perceptual-auditory analysis it is possible to conduct an "analysis-synthesis" research.

© Springer Nature Switzerland AG 2019
P. Eismont and O. Mitrenina (Eds.): LMAC 2017, CCIS 943, pp. 35–46, 2019.
https://doi.org/10.1007/978-3-030-05594-3_3

Keywords: Semiotics · Common human semiotic system · Subsystems
Acoustics · Articulation · Phonation · Auditory perception · Music
Speech and music information · Speech and music synthesis

1 Introduction and Research Theoretical Background

The common semiotics of interpersonal communication includes all natural and artificial ways of interaction between people forming a system of signs that serve to
convey information of any kind in a particular society. The study of the common
semiotic system of interpersonal communication is connected with the essences of
various signal subsystems and extends, for example, to psychology, physiology,
sociology, linguistics, etc. At the origins of semiotics were Ch. Pierce (1834–1914),
Ch. Morris (1901–1979) and R. Karnak (1891–1970). In the second half of XX century, there was a shift in the understanding of semiotics: from a theoretical philosophical conception to a more applied concept based on an analysis of the model of
human behavior in communication with the inclusion of all sensory modes of interaction. As applied to Europe, semiotics (semiology, semasiology) has evolved on the
basis of a comprehensive analysis of all aspects of communication, including music,
meals, clothes, dances, etc. [4, 5, p. 431]. It is only natural that various groups of signs,
in our view, form the subsystems of the given system, which carry a semantic load in
the act of interpersonal communication that is different in its volume and "weight".
According to the classical conception of semiotics, the general semiotics usually has
three levels: semantic, syntactic and pragmatic ones, which makes it possible to include
into the semiotic system the significative function of signs, the function of sign
combinatorics and, finally, and their application and influence function.

The consideration of the common semiotic system in the form of a graph makes it
possible, from our point of view, to determine a network (or a graph) of relatively
interdependent semiotic subsystems. Thus, the language subsystem of the common
semiotic communication system includes subsystems of natural and artificial languages. The subsystem of natural language includes, in its turn, subsystems of spoken
language (speech) and written language, each of which has its own subsystems. If the
subsystem of speech is involved within the framework of the language subsystem of
the common semiotic system of interpersonal communication, then this subsystem has
its own hierarchical subsystems: articulatory-phonatory, acoustic and perceptual-
auditory ones having a number of its own features and functions that enable interpersonal communication in both on-line (in real time) and off-line (in delayed time: in
recording and storage systems) modes of the speech signal (Fig. 1).

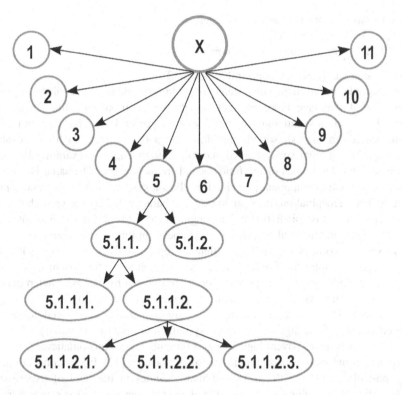

Fig. 1. Fragment of the common semiotic system of human interpersonal communication, which represents an open set.

Some subsystems of the common human semiotic communication system:

1. Tactile
2. Sense of smell
3. Visual
4. Auditory
5. Verbal
6. Musical
7. Hormonal
8. Sexual
9. Locomotion
10. Gustatory
11. Aesthetic

Some hierarchical subsystems of the subsystem "language" (selectively):

5.1.1. Natural language (according to I.P. Pavlov)
5.1.2. Artificial language
5.1.1.1. Written natural language
5.1.1.2. Spoken natural language (speech)

5.1.1.2.1. Articulatory-phonatory subsystem
5.1.1.2.2. Acoustic subsystem
5.1.1.2.3. Perceptual-auditory subsystem

etc. (e.g., perceptual "events", spectral bands etc.)

For example, the acoustic subsystem, which in turn relates to the subsystem of the spoken natural language (speech), includes its own components: fundamental frequency (F_{0n} in Hz), sound intensity level (sound power I_n in dB), duration of the acoustic signal (tn in ms), sound spectrum values (F_n in Hz). Each of the above components has its own subsystem of acoustic components: for example, F_0 can be decomposed into harmonics of the fundamental frequency, etc. The same is observed for such an acoustic component perceived by the subsystems as a timbre and a phase spectrum. The perceptual-auditory subsystem is characterized by the sign characteristics of its subsystems: pitch (in mels), range, voice register (in musical intervals), temporal values (in temporal proportions), loudness (in phons and sones), etc.

Any spoken word, phrase, utterance that are representatives of the sign subsystem of any language within the framework of the common semiotic system of the interpersonal communication with regard to speech are realized by means of heterogeneous subsystems (articulatory-phonatory, acoustic, perceptual-auditory) [12].

The complexity of profound and serious study of speech is aggravated not only by the heterogeneity of the signs of these subsystems, but also by the variety of physiological, organo-genetic, psychological, psycholinguistic, psychosomatic and intellectual features of individuals participating in communication [11]. In this connection, it is hardly possible to believe the results of many studies in the field of experimental speech studies (speechology – science of spoken language), where the researcher does not take into account the factor of sign heterogeneity of the spoken language subsystem, on the one hand, and the factor of intra- and interspeaker variability, on the other hand.

2 Semiotic Subsystems: Music and Speech

The study of the semiotic subsystem of speech is inconceivable without interpreting experimental data from the point of view of the significance of concrete units for concrete subsystems in the act of concrete interpersonal communication. These or other values of acoustic parameters obtained with the help of computer speech analyzing programs that have not been checked for "significance" in the process of perception and influencing in the communication act are unlikely to carry a significative weight and be useful in describing the specifics of interpersonal communication.

At present, digital acoustics is actively developing "… in connection with the creation of a new generation of microprocessor (audio-processor) and computer equipment" [1, p. 15].

The examination of speech as a subsystem regarding the semantic-syntactic-pragmatic "significance" takes on special importance in solving such problems as:

– determination of the influence degree the partner (partners) in communication experiences;
– identification/verification of a person by voice and speech;
– determination of the person's rhetorical potential;
– determination of the speaker's emotional state;
– creation of an individual "portrait" (attribution) of a person by voice and speech;
– determination of the potential for acting;
– establishment of the ratio "norm – deviation from the norm" with reference to:
  • the degree of proficiency in a native language;
  • the degree of proficiency in a non-native language;
  • the presence/absence of speech signs of pathological lesions in the process of speech production and speech perception [14–16].

In various linguistic sources it is usually pointed out that in the field of semiotics the greatest parametric and functional commonality is found between the language and fiction, that is, art that uses language as its primary means [7, p. 440]. A similar analogy also arises for the relation "spoken language and music" ("speech and music").

When asked "What is music?" people will give various replies. The making of music is not restricted to human beings. Many animals, such as whales and birds, appear to use music as a means of communication. French composer, Olivier Messiaen, who used to go out into the countryside to transcribe birdsong, which he incorporated almost note-for-note into his orchestral and piano music. The American composer John Cage believed that the mechanical background sounds of everyday life could be described as music, and other composers have written works requiring all kinds of everyday objects to be used as "musical instruments". Perhaps an easier question would be "What is not music? … Even without understanding, all music has the power to exert an effect on the emotions" [18, pp. 12–13].

In the framework of our concept of the subsystem semiotics architectonics in relation to the common communicative-semiotic system, the subsystem of speech has its own set of subsystems (articulatory-phonatory, acoustic, perceptual-auditory). The greatest commonality is observed between the subsystem of speech and the subsystem of music – the art that uses the above subsystems of speech (in particular, articulatory-phonatory, acoustic and perceptual-auditory). From this point of view, both music and speech can be considered as genetically related subsystems of the general semiotic system of interpersonal communication.

By comparing the subsystems of speech and music from the point of view of the activity approach, one can speak of the presence of parallelism for a number of phenomena for speech and music: e.g., monophony and polyphony, ways of sound formation (legato-staccato), speech melody, rhythm, loudness, temporality, pausation, tonality, femininity – minor, masculinity – major, agogics, theme-rheme, types of speech and music segmentation, phonosemantics, registers, intervalics, etc.

Parallelism in speech and music was also mentioned by Vargha et al. [19, p. 248; pp. 118–119]. But in this case it was a graph of the invention of the notation text, which developed in a variety of ways.

The inseparable connection between the two semiotic subsystems (speech and music) is also evidenced by parallelism in the field of perception, too. "Thus, for anyone listening to music performed by another person, sound representations, that is, representations of physical sounds, must be subjected, the sounds of music must cease to be external... On the other hand, for a musician playing any instrument, music, as a musical power, must be objectified, musical sounds must become physical" [6, p. 211]. Absolutely the same can be said about speech.

"People have been making music for a very long time, probably beginning with the voice and proceeding to simple rhythmic drumming – hitting a log with a stick or banging a rock with a club – and blowing a blade of grass or a conch shell" [18, p. 6].

If one goes further and looks into the past of the history of music, here G. Spencer's opinion seems convincing: "... All music was originally vocal; all vocal sounds are produced by the action of known muscles. These muscles are driven to contract by pleasant or painful feelings. And that is why feelings are expressed by sounds as well as by movements" [17, p. 219]. In this regard, K. Eyges notes that "... Spencer took a big step forward when he began to consider singing not as a purely physical phenomenon, not as physical sounds (air vibrations), but as a biological phenomenon, as the action of a living body" [6, 17].

Speech as a special semiotic subsystem is the foundation of the speechology actively introduced and developed by [14, 15] for many years, since the 80's of XXth century. Veidle wrote about the expediency of studying spoken meanings [20] and speechology as a separate field: "... Linguistics being a science about the language system, has become much more scientific (in the narrow, but magical sense of the word) than before. In the system there are no meanings: they are not considered by the system at all. It takes into account only constituent parts of the signs (phonemes) that mean nothing by themselves; these signs (morphemes, words) that must mean something but do not oblige the "system scientist" to know what exactly they mean; and finally, the rules of their combination into meaningful "unities" (syntagmas, sentences), which are also not required to mean something specific, although preliminary schemes of their meanings are taken into account. ... The system cannot but be a sign system, but the language, in a broad sense, including speech, is not fully described by signs or by the system. ... The Saussure revolution in linguistics persistently ... requires the creation of a new discipline, which would be (in simplest way) called "speechology" in Russian. When it is created, this revolution will be completed, completely justified and will find its full meaning not yet taken now" [21, pp. 590–591].

3 Experiment on the Basis of "Speech–Music Transformation"

In our experiments, the "speech-music" transformation was implemented stage by stage:

– pronouncing of test phrases by speakers in various emotional states;
– perceptual-auditory analysis of phonograms of these experimental phrases in order to determine the emotional state;

– acoustic analysis of the experimental phrases;
– perceptual-auditory analysis of "synthesized" phrases in order to determine the emotional state;
– comparison of the analysis results.

When translating the acoustic analysis data into a musical notation, a table was used to translate the values of the fundamental frequency (in Hz) into semitones (st), according to the tempered scale [10, pp. 244–248]. The values of the "pitch frequency in acoustics/interval in semitones in music" ratio were taken into account, both within a phonetic unit of speech, for example, a vowel in stressed and unstressed positions, and at the boundary between phonetic words, syntagmas, phrases. A fragment of the initial values is presented in Table 1 [10, pp. 244–247]. The **frequency range** in the study of speech intonation is relative and varies from speaker to speaker. It is determined by the volume of values of the fundamental frequency from the minimum to the maximum available in the material under study (sound, syllable, phrase) as a whole. In everyday speech, the fundamental frequency range is about one octave, while in emotional states it expands or narrows depending on the type of emotion. The possible changes in the values of the fundamental frequency range, as a rule, lie within the following octaves: the great octave (65 Hz–130 Hz), the small octave (130 Hz–261 Hz), the one-line octave (261 Hz–522 Hz).

Table 1. Measurement of the fundamental frequency range values and intervals (fragmentary)

1.	$1,059^1$	1,059—minor second
2.	$1,059^2$	1,122—major second
3.	$1,059^3$	1,188—augmented second or minor third
4.	$1,059^4$	1,258—major third
5.	$1,059^5$	1,331—perfect fourth
6.	$1,059^6$	1,411—augmented fourth or diminished fifth
7.	$1,059^7$	1,494—perfect fifth
8.	$1,059^8$	1,582—augmented fifth or minor sixth
9.	$1,059^9$	1,675—major sixth
10.	$1,059^{10}$	1,774—minor seventh
11.	$1,059^{11}$	1,879—major seventh
12.	$1,059^{12}$	2,000—octave

When studying the intonation area, one usually measures the value of the fundamental frequency range by the number of semitones (st) between the boundary fundamental frequencies of the range. The st number, as well as the value of the interval, is determined according to the tempered musical scale. The required st number in the range under study is determined from Table 1, which indicates, firstly, the increase factor of the sound by st of 1.059 and, secondly, the power coefficient, that is, the number denoting the st number, by which this sound should be increased [10].

The **frequency interval in speech** (an interval in music is the ratio of two sounds by their values of fundamental frequencies) is the ratio of two values of the fundamental frequency within any phonetic unit of speech or at the boundary of such units, for example, at the junction of two syntagmas or at the junction of stressed and unstressed syllables. This interval is called a pitch or melodic interval. In music, from which the concept of fundamental frequency intervals is borrowed, all fundamental frequencies values are in strict proportions, whereas in speech the latter can be very approximate. In the analysis of intonation, in most cases one may only talk of an interval larger (>) or less (<) than that indicated in Table 1 [13].

Between the basic steps of the scale the following intervals are formed [8, p. 213]:

- Perfect tonic—0 t
- Minor second—½ t
- Major second—1 t
- Minor third—1 ½ t
- Major third—2 t
- Perfect fourth—2 ½ t
- Augmented fourth—3 t
- Perfect fifth—3 ½ t
- Diminished fifth—3 t
- Minor sixth—4 t
- Major sixth—4 ½ t
- Minor seventh—5 t
- Major seventh—5 ½ t
- Perfect octave—6 t

For example, the ratio of semiotic subsystems "language-music" (but not "speech–music" [11, 12]) was described by M. Bonfeld, who argued that "… every musical work is a semiotic (i.e., sign) system similar to a statement (text) in a natural language" [3, p. 17]. The concept of the musical text as language was developed by M. Aranovsky (e.g., [2]).

Thus, if speech and music are regarded as subsystems related by their nature within the framework of general communicative semiotics (semasiology), then it can be concluded that their common function is the influence function. However, it is here that one can see the difference in the target attitude with reference to speech and music communication. For speech communication, the influence on the recipient can be realized on the basis of purpose regarding both the rationality (informing) and the emotionality. As for music (the musical subsystem of interpersonal communication), in this case the recipient can be subjected to some influence regarding exclusively the emotionality (influence on the recipient's emotional state) [16, 17]. An exception is vocal communication in the presence of text including both the rationality and the emotionality [9].

At the same time, the effect of the influence is achieved with the help of the same material means: articulatory-phonatory, acoustic and perceptual-auditory ones. So, examining emotionally charged speech, we conducted a special experiment, in which prosodic speech characteristics and their parameters obtained as a result of analyzing test phrases in various emotional states without accompanying text formed the basis for a kind of "synthesis" of these phrases with the help of violin and piano music notation. Subsequent listening to the played "synthesized" examples of emotions representing joy, fear, horror, anger showed a high degree of perceptual-auditory identification of the above conditions by listeners (98%) (number of listeners n = 45).

In this research we tried to show the progressiveness of using the method of music "score" (composed on the results of speech prosodic characteristics analysis), which can help to determine the informativeness of parameters used for determining the speaker's emotional state. Creation of music score based on analysis data is viewed as a model for utterance's prosodic vocal outline. Speech as well as music uses the same space and time coordinates representing sound movement. The height-metric grid is based on this principle, which determines sounds in dynamics. Time organization of music and speech creates a common material basis. If we disengage from the segment (sound-syllable) structure of an utterance and concentrate on the prosodic side of an utterance we can, changing various parameters included in the music score, with the help of further perceptual-auditory analysis of music stimulus determine the informativeness of varying parameters and grade of dependence from these parameters of correct recognition of stimulus. Music score created on the basis of results of an acoustic analysis of prosodic features of speech satisfies taking into consideration the restrictions caused by the absence of segmental (sound-syllable) text. Thus, with the help of special music synthesis of speech utterance on the basis of acoustic analysis of parameters and further perceptual-auditory analysis it is possible to conduct "analysis-synthesis-analysis" research.

The next experimental research comprised two parts: the first part was aimed at recognition by listeners of emotional states on the basis of music phrases played on the piano and violin; the second part of the experiment was dedicated to determine the most important prosodic elements for perception of an emotional image. This is the first step in studying important that leveling allowed to transfer speech into music and helped to receive the acoustic data of analysis of emotions. Thus, using music means and excluding segmental structure with the help of the "analysis-synthesis-analysis" method, one can determine and check the informativeness of one or another acoustic characteristic acting while formalizing emotional belonging of an utterance and relativeness of one or another emotive feature marking emoteme (sign of abstract item of emotion). The clarifying of the above mentioned problem is also very important for objective evaluation of emotional speech by forensic phonetic experts in the domain of auditory (subjective) and instrumental (objective) types of analysis of the speech signal [9, p. 12].

The use of prosodic information implies reference to other tiers of the language (syntactic, semantic ones), which provides a relatively self-contained method of acoustic detection of syntactic structures, independent from potentially erroneous sequences of hypotheses of the words derived from the input acoustic information [11, 12, 16].

Modern scholars expand the main prosodic features helping to implement he automatic recognition of continuous speech, including the stress, the F0 envelope of the utterance, rhythm, pausation, tempo, change in the energy configuration and temporal correlation of segments in pre-juncture and post-juncture positions at the boundary of sentences and syntagmas. The task of automatic continuous speech recognition cannot be accomplished without the inclusion of information on macrosegmentation of the text into phrases and minimal semantic fragments extracted from the speech flow – syntagmas. The development of the program for macrosegmentation of continuous speech based on prosodic, syntactic and semantic information requires a series of studies aimed at solving the following tasks:

- identification of prosodic characteristics of continuous speech and music segmentation on the perceptual-auditory level;
- definition of the role (functional weight) of individual prosodic parameters when marking boundaries in continuous speech and music macrosegmentation;
- analysis of the effect of the rhythmic structure of pre- and post-juncture words; syllable type (stressed, not stressed, those in absolutely final positions, non-final positions, etc. …) and the phonetic quality of a stressed vowel on prosodic characteristics of pre- and post-juncture phonetic words at the boundary of syntagmas and phrases regarding speech and music.

Since prosodic information can influence the results of the recognition system, it is assumed that a source of knowledge about prosodic information is needed that would be a module of the recognition system, which can generate hypotheses or produce other knowledge. Since almost all the prosodic algorithms are based on accurate input information extracted from the acoustic signal, the great emphasis is put on the development and organization of prosodic parameter extraction algorithms.

There is a well-known method of interpretation and prosodic stylization. This method allows, on the one hand, to identify the boundaries of prosodic groups and syntactic constituents and, on the other hand, to establish the hierarchy of semantic utterance constituents. The basic principles of this method are as follows: (1) prosody is a multiparameter structure. Selection of a single parameter, usually F_0, can lead to errors in the interpretation, as changes in F_0 may reflect various functions and not be in direct relation with the syntactic and/or semantic organization of the utterance; (2) extraction of prosodic invariants is related to the detection procedure involving transformation of objective data. This transformation allows erasing microvariations and conversion of perceptual data. It is important to properly distribute the relations between prosody and accent, syntax and semantics. Prosody has a demarcation function of the syntactic constituents. It also has a semantic function in the organization of the utterance. To avoid errors, the pitch raise and fall contour should be calculated cyclically from the first detected maximum value [13, pp. 214–215].

A similar experiment for speech and music was carried out with reference to the identification of the basic communicative intonational patterns (intonems) of the Russian language (for a finished narration, unfinished narration, a general question, a special question etc.) with the emotional component completely excluded. The results showed a high degree of identification of intonems in Russian by means of music "synthesis", which also confirms the cognitive conditionality of the sign subsystems in the format of the common semiotic system of the language.

4   Conclusion

It should be emphasized that the paper outlines the concept of the interdisciplinary approach to the study of speech and music. It presents a tree-like architectonics of hierarchical relationships of a number of semiotic subsystems within the common semiotic system of interpersonal communication. The heterogeneous nature is revealed not only for the common semiotic system of interpersonal communication, but also for such an important semiotic subsystem as language and the associated subsystem of speech. At the same time, the general heterogeneity of the entire semiotic system of interpersonal communication presupposes the presence of subsystems that are similar in nature and functions, including subsystems of speech and music, which have similar subsystems for transmitting the form and content of speech and music utterances.

It is entirely possible that both subsystems of speech and music with the hierarchy of their subsystems at the dawn of human development were in a syncretic state, existed in unity and possessed a common sign potential. The further parallel development of these subsystems is evidenced by the ways of conveying verbal and musical information, the terminology used, etc.

In our opinion, it is the semiotic approach to speechology that will "highlight" only those speech signs and sign complexes that are relevant for communication in general, on the one hand, and that mark individual, social, ethnic and other human activities, on the other hand. In connection with this, it is proposed to introduce the name of a new unit of analysis at the "emic" level into the speechology terminology, *semioteme* characterizing an invariant "bundle" of subsystem speech features that determine the outcome of interpersonal communication. Using the *semioteme* apparatus, it is possible to construct paradigms of pragmaphonetic nature for solving various research and practical problems (assessing various types of public speech, acting, diagnosis in the field of psychiatry, criminology, etc.). Thus, language, speech and music are proposed to be considered as a *semiotic triad of meanings, images and emotions*. The paper presents the authors' concept of studying spoken language on the basis of semiotics. Spoken language and music are considered as subsystems of the common semiotic system of interpersonal communication characterized by the heterogeneity of its own subsystems: articulatory-phonatory, acoustic, perceptual-auditory ones. The paper also describes the parallelism of two subsystems: spoken verbal and musical ones.

Acknowledgements. This research is supported by the Russian Science Foundation, Project № 18-18-00477.

References

1. Aldoshina, I., Pritts, R.: Musical acoustics. Publishing House "Composer", St.-Petersburg (2006). (in Russian)
2. Aranovsky, M.: Musical text: structure and features. Publishing house "Composer", Moscow (1998). (in Russia)
3. Bonfeld, M.: Music: Language. Speech. Thinking. Experience of system research for musical arts. Publishing House "Composer", St.-Petersburg (2006). (in Russian)
4. Crystal, D.: A Dictionary of Linguistics and Phonetics, 6th edn. Blackwell Publishing, Hoboken (2009)
5. Crystal, D.: Die Cambridge Enzyklopädie der Sprache. Campus Verlag, Frankfurt/New York (1998)
6. Eyges, K.: Essays on the philosophy of music. In: Spoken Meanings. Publishing House of St.-Petersburg University, St. Petersburg, pp. 175–222 (2007). (in Russian)

7. Linguistic Encyclopedic Dictionary/Yartseva, V.N. (ed.): Soviet Encyclopedia, Moscow (1990). (in Russian)
8. Music Encyclopedic Dictionary/Keldysh, G.V. (ed.): Soviet Encyclopedia, Moscow (1990). (in Russian)
9. Potapova, R.K.: On the possibility of research of identification of emotions (on the basis of method "analysis–synthesis–analysis"). In: Annual Conference of International Association for Forensic Phonetics (IAFP), Wiesbaden, 7–11 July 1996, p. 12 (1996)
10. Potapova, R.K.: Speech driving of robots: linguistics and modern automated systems, 2nd edn. Comkniga, Moscow (2005). (in Russian)
11. Potapova, R.K.: Semiotic heterogeneity of spoken speech communication. In: Neurocomputers: Development and Use. Publishing House "Radiotekhnika", Moscow, no. 1, pp. 4–6 (2013). (in Russian)
12. Potapova, R.K.: Spoken language as a subsystem in the general semiotic system of interpersonal communication. Phonetics: Problems and Perspectives. MSLU, Moscow, pp. 189–196 (2014). (Moscow State Linguistic University Bulletin, № 1 (687). Series of Linguistics). (in Russian)
13. Potapova, R.: Speech dialog as a part of interactive "human-machine" systems. In: Ronzhin, A., Rigoll, G., Meshcheryakov, R. (eds.) ICR 2016. LNCS (LNAI), vol. 9812, pp. 208–218. Springer, Cham (2016). https://doi.org/10.1007/978-3-319-43955-6_25
14. Potapova, R.K., Potapov, V.V.: Kommunikative Sprechtätigkeit: Russland und Deutschland im Vergleich. Böhlau Verlag, Köln, Weimar, Wien (2011)
15. Potapova, R.K., Potapov, V.V.: Language, speech, personality. Languages of the Slavic Culture, Moscow (2006). (in Russian)
16. Potapova, R.K., Potapov, V.V.: Speech communication: from sound to utterance. Languages of the Slavic Cultures, Moscow (2012). (in Russian)
17. Spencer, H.: The origin and function of music. In: Spoken Meanings. Publishing House of St. Petersburg University, St. Petersburg, p. 219 (2007). (in Russian)
18. The Encyclopedia of Music: Max Wade - Matthews & Wendy Tompson. Hermes House, London (2005)
19. Vargha, B., Dimeny, J., Loparits, E.: Language, music, mathematics. Publishing House "World", Moscow (1981). (in Russian)
20. Veidle, V.: Spoken Meanings. New Journal, New York, pp. 103–137 (1973). (in Russian)
21. Veidle, V.: Spoken meanings. In: Spoken Meanings. Publishing House of St. Petersburg University, St. Petersburg, pp. 574–641 (2007). (in Russian)

The Surface of Music and Singing

Synchronization of Musical Acoustics and Articulatory Movements in Russian Classical Romance

Karina Evgrafova$^{(\boxtimes)}$, Vera Evdokimova, Pavel Skrelin ,
and Tatjana Chukaeva

Saint Petersburg State University,
Universitetskaya Emb., 11, 199034 Saint Petersburg, Russia
evgrafova@phonetics.pu.ru

Abstract. The given paper is aimed at investigating synchronization of musical acoustics (pitch, frequencies, durations) and articulatory movements in Russian classical romance. The study employs the method of electromagnetic articulography (EMA) to observe and compare objective data on articulatory characteristics in singing and reading. The genre of romance was chosen as it does not normally employ vocal techniques specific to opera singing (vibrato and etc.) which affect vowel intelligibility significantly. The romance chosen for the experiment is often performed by Russian singers being a part of canonic repertoire at conservatoires. We obtained the samples of singing and read speech and registered the objective data in both types of articulation activities. The recordings can be considered parallel as they were made in succession during one experiment. The calibration and attachment of the sensors was performed once in the beginning of the experiment. That means that the sensor positions were the same for the both recordings which makes them comparable in terms of articulatory data. The obtained material (both singing and reading) is annotated and analyzed in terms of the synchronisation of articulatory movements and pitch in singing as opposed to that in speech.

Keywords: Singing vowels · Intelligibility · Electromagnetic articulography
Vocal tract · Articulation in singing · Acoustics in singing
Perception of singing

1 Introduction

The production and perception of sounds in singing differs from that in speech in a highly significant manner. It especially concerns vowels. Substantial research has been carried out on acoustic and perceptual characteristics of sung vowels. The existing relevant studies analyze different vocal music genres (classical opera singing, musical theater, etc.), vocal techniques (bel canto, vocal jazz etc.) and employ different languages. The problem that has always been focused on is the intelligibility of sung vowels. It has been addressed in many investigations [1–27]. They show that the intelligibility of vowels in classical singing sung by professional singers is relatively low for higher pitches, especially in case of isolated context. The impact of consonantal

© Springer Nature Switzerland AG 2019
P. Eismont and O. Mitrenina (Eds.): LMAC 2017, CCIS 943, pp. 49–57, 2019.
https://doi.org/10.1007/978-3-030-05594-3_4

environment on the intelligibility of the vowels in singing was also studied. It is shown that vowel identification is much better if the vowel is produced in the consonant context. To date, however, there have been no studies that collect and compare articulatory and acoustic data of samples of speech and singing from the same subject.

Although the research on vowel intelligibility in singing has a rich history, it has been mainly done in the fields of acoustic speech science, physiology and vocal pedagogy. There exist numerous reports of research in the field of speech dealing with all of the facets of articulation such as movements of tongue, lips and the soft palate. Nevertheless, the studies focusing on the peculiarities of the articulation as it relates to singing are considered mainly in the literature relevant to vocal pedagogy. However, this literature tends to employ imagery and subjective interpretations rather than scientific terminology and objective evidence.

Obtaining accurate data on the movement and shaping of the vocal tract is crucial for investigations into speech production and singing voice. They afford insights into the execution of speech production goals and the relationship between the mechanisms of articulation and acoustics.

It is well-known that formant frequencies are determined by the specific articulatory configurations of the vocal tract. The modulation of the vocal tract shape is mainly achieved by shifts in tongue positions. F1 is affected both by the vertical position of the tongue (i.e., tongue height), while F2 is affected by horizontal tongue position.

In respect of singing we can suggest that there should be an opening tendency in the articulation of vowels to achieve the formant tuning. Besides, larynx lowering employed to elongate the resonating space above the vocal folds should be associated with somewhat more backward tongue position.

We can also suggest that there should be certain articulatory modifications that accompany pitch transitions in singing.

To understand the interaction between musical acoustics (pitch, frequencies, durations) and articulatory movements, we need to analyse synchronous acoustic and kinematic data.

Thus the aim of the given research is to investigate synchronization of musical acoustics and articulation in the singing of Russian classical romance as opposed to that in speech.

We hypothesized that (1) the tongue should take a lower and more backward position in singing; (2) there should be certain correlation between pitch changes and articulatory movements.

The paper is structured as follows. Section 2 provides a short overview of the technique used and the description of experimental design and procedure.

In Sect. 3 the results of data processing are presented. The discussion of the obtained results and conclusions are given in Sect. 4 and Sect. 5 respectively.

2 Methodology

2.1 Technique

In our study the EMA technology was employed as it ideally suits the purpose of obtaining articulatory data in both speech and singing. The method of electromagnetic articulography is quite popular technology for tracking articulatory movements. It is often used in the study of speech as its high spatial (0.3 mm) and temporal (sampling rate of 200–400 Hz) resolution allows for the measurement of small and rapid articulatory movements. It uses electromagnetic sensor coils which are attached directly to the articulators. These sensors are of a small size (2 x 3 mm), which allows minimizing the physical obstruction to natural speech production [2]. Due to the fact, the period of the adaptation to the sensors is considerably short and subjects maintain natural articulation in both speaking and singing activities. A set of transmitters mounted around the head of a subject produce an oscillating complex magnetic field that induces a current in the sensors allowing their position in space to be calculated. The principles of this calculation are explained in more detail at http://www.articulograph.de/.

2.2 Experimental Design and Procedure

Two types of recording experiments with the use of EMA were conducted. The recordings were made at the recording studio at the Department of Phonetics (Saint Petersburg State University) which houses AG500 system by CarstensMedizinelektronik GmbH (Carstens). The six transmitters of the AG500 are mounted on specific locations of an open clearcube structure that is stationed around the head of the seated subject, as shown in Fig. 1.

Fig. 1. The EMA technician is attaching the coil sensors to the subject.

The AG500 system can support up to 12 sensor channels for tracking positions in the Cartesian dimensions and two angular dimensions. In our experiments 10 coil sensors were employed.

1. Tongue tip
2. Tongue dorsum (5.5–6.0 cm from tip of tongue)
3. Back of the tongue
4. Upper lip
5. Lower lip
6. Head [reference]
7. Nasal bridge [reference]
8. Left ear [reference]
9. Right ear [reference]
10. Lower jaw [stationary]

The goal of the recording was to obtain the samples of singing and reading from the same subject. Four professional female singers (sopranos) were involved in the experiment. The musical genre chosen for the experiment was the Russian classical romance. This is a type of a vocal music composition, usually written for one voice with piano accompaniment, and usually in the classical, art music tradition (similar to the genre of German Lied). The reason for this choice was to focus on a type of classical singing yet does not normally employ the vocal techniques specific to opera singing (vibrato and etc.) affecting the vowel intelligibility in a highly significant manner.

During the first recording the singers were instructed to sing one of the Russian classical romances while they were sitting in the cube with the AG500 coil sensors attached to their main articulators. There was no musical accompaniment. The romance chosen for the experiment is well-known and often performed by Russian singers being a part of canonic repertoire at conservatoires. All of the singers sang the romance in the same key and manner. The audio was recorded by means of Sanken cs-1 condenser shotgun microphone. In the beginning of the procedure the subjects were asked to perform a few vocal exercises to warm up and allow their articulators to adapt to the sensors attached. The adaptation period differed across the subjects, but did not normally exceed ten minutes. At the moment when the subject reported no feeling of obstacle to normal articulation the recording began. No naturalness distortion was perceived during the recording, neither in singing, nor in reading. The duration of the singing performance was approximately four minutes.

The second recording supposed reading aloud the text of the same romance. The duration of reading performance was about two minutes. There was around 30 s break between the first and second recording.

Thus, we obtained the samples of acoustic and articulatory data in singing and read speech and registered the objective data in both types of articulation activities. The recordings can be considered parallel as they were made in succession during one experiment and in the same conditions. The calibration and attachment of the sensors was performed once in the beginning of the experiment. That means that the sensor positions were the same for the both recordings which makes them comparable in terms of articulatory data.

The obtained material (both singing and reading) is annotated and analyzed in terms of the synchronization of articulatory movements and pitch in singing as opposed to that in speech.

3 Results

The recorded acoustic and articulatory dataset (including both singing and speech) includes 588 occurrences of the six Russian vowels /a/, /e/, /i/, /ɨ/, /o/, /u/ presented in the samples of speech and singing of 4 female subjects. The manual segmentation and phoneme boundary labelling was carried out by expert phoneticians. It should be noted that the unstressed singing vowels are not reduced due to the significant increase in duration caused by the necessity to sustain a note. That means that they acquire phonetic quality similar to that of stressed ones and cannot be compared with the same unstressed vowels in speech which are normally reduced. Thus, in the paper it was only stressed vowels that were analysed. The speech data from EMA was processed by Carstens software package and then imported and analysed in EGUANA. It is a free software developed at the Oral dynamics lab at the University of Toronto. The software allows the application of different calculation methods for the head and jaw correction. The data can furthermore be filtered and visualized with a basic visual display within the software. The greatest advantage are the various calculation methods wrapped in a user friendly GUI (www.articulograph.de/?page_id=1089). The software was provided to us by the courtesy of the developers. The movement of each of the 10 coils was plotted separately in three Cartesian dimensions (x, y, and z) for 200 occurrences of the 6 Russian vowels. The movements of tongue tip, tongue dorsum, tongue back, upper and lower lips in singing and speech were of special interest. The plots for the movements of these articulators in x-plane (forth and back) and z-plane (up and down) were obtained and analyzed in terms of the kinematica in singing as opposed to that in speech. Some major tendencies are illustrated in the plots below. The plots present the trajectories and amplitudes of articulatory movements in x-plane (forth and back) and z-plane (up and down) laid over the waveforms of speech and sung vowels. The articulatory and acoustic data in each plot are synchronized in time which allows observing the shifts in the locations of the main articulators during sound production. The horizontal axis shows time (in s), the vertical axis shows the distances of the coil sensor displacements during articulation (in mm).

The acoustic characteristics of the recorded material were also obtained (in Praat). They included pitch, formant values, jitter and duration. Pitch and duration characteristics differ in the singing and speech material. The acoustic analysis shows that the pitch values are consistently higher in singing across all the singers which allows us to expect the difference in articulatory data. However, the pitch values are not as high as in opera singing and relatively close to that of speech. That should mean that the intelligibility is preserved in this singing genre. The duration tends to be two times longer in singing than in reading.

Figures 2, 3 and 4 below demonstrate articulatory and acoustic data for an utterance sung and read by singer 1. They show the dorsum, back and tip of the tongue movements in x-plane (forth and back) and in z-plane (up and down), the waveform and pitch of the initial phrase of the romance in singing.

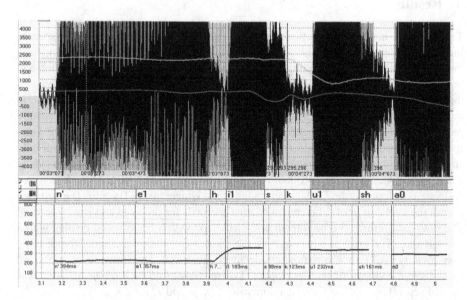

Fig. 2. Tongue back movements in x and z planes and pitch

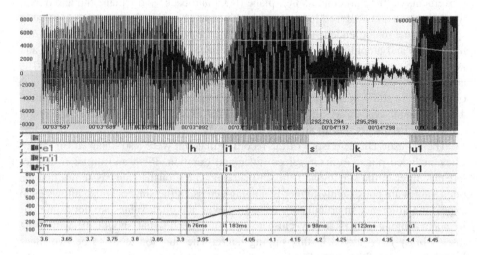

Fig. 3. Tongue tip movements in x and z planes and pitch

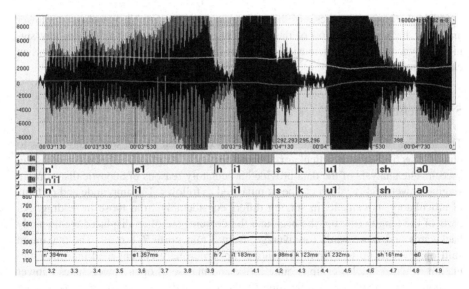

Fig. 4. Tongue dorsum movements in x and z planes and pitch

4 Discussion

The comparison of the movements of the main articulators in singing and reading for the 3 cardinal vowels /a/, /i/, /u/ showed the following. The data for singer 1 demonstrate that in singing the most significant tongue shift backwards is characteristic only for /u/. Yet the formant tracks show the lower values of F2 for all the vowels which is associated with the backward position of the tongue. The abrupt lowering of the tongue at the stationary part is consistent for all the vowels. Besides, the lowering of the tongue is not accompanied with the lower lip lowering. The plots for singer 1 show that in singing for vowel /a/ the tip of the tongue is 7 mm lower than in reading, the tongue dorsum – 7 mm, the back of the tongue – around 6 mm. For sung vowel /i/ the tip of the tongue is 7–8 mm lower, the dorsum of the tongue – 7 mm, the back of the tongue – 5–6 mm. For sung vowel /u/ the tip of the tongue is 3–4 mm lower, the tongue dorsum – 3 mm, the back of the tongue – 3 mm. The data for singers 3 and 4 are similar to those of singer 1. The data for singer 2 show a slightly different tendency for /a/. The tongue tip in singing shifts 2.5 mm forward than in reading, the tongue dorsum – 3 mm forward, while the back of the tongue shifts around 7–8 mm backwards. The position of the tip of the tongue in singing is also 6 mm lower than that in reading, the tongue dorsum – 8 mm, the back of the tongue – 11 mm. The difference in the distances between the upper and lower lips is 1 mm and cannot be considered significant. The formant tracks also show the lower values of F2 for all the vowels which confirms the more backward position of the tongue in singing. As it seen in Figs. 2, 3 and 4, no correlation between pitch changes and articulatory movements is observed.

Thus the initial hypothesis of the study was partly confirmed. We observe a lower and more backward position of the tongue but our material does not show any significant synchronization of musical acoustics and articulatory movements in Russian classical romance.

5 Conclusion

The method of electromagnetic articulography employed in the study allowed us to obtain objective data on articulatory characteristics in singing as opposed to those in speech. The analysis of the data provided articulatory reasons of acoustic distortion in singing vowel quality which can be summarized as follows. The amplitude and patterns of articulatory movements in singing differs considerably from those in reading. All parts of the tongue (the tip, the back and the dorsum) are often displaced significantly backwards and downwards (on average, from 3 mm up to 7–8 mm). The maximum shift observed is up to 11 mm. The upper lip is normally not engaged into the articulation, whereas the lower lip is quite active and in case of open vowels takes a lower position. The unstressed vowels (due to the increased duration in singing) are not reduced and articulated in the fashion of the stressed ones. Despite the radical shifts in the tongue positions at the stationary parts of the vowels, the intelligibility is preserved due to the restoring of the positions specific for the particular vowels at the transitions.

References

1. Andrea, D., et al.: Tongue and jaw movements in high-pitched soprano singing (a case study) (2016). https://doi.org/10.15775/Beszkut.2016.24.7
2. Andrea, D.: Intelligibility of sung vowels: the effect of consonantal context and the onset of voicing. J. Voice 28(4), 523.e19–523.e25 (2014). https://doi.org/10.1016/j.jvoice.2014.01.003
3. Glotova, O.N., Evgrafova, K.V., Evdokimova, V.V.: The perception of sung vowels by the native speakers of Russian. Homo loquens: the studies of XXI century, Ivanovo, pp 59–67 (2012). (in Russian)
4. Galunov, V.I., Garbaruk, V.I.: The acoustic theory of speech production and the system of phonetic features. The 100 years of experimental phonetics in Russia. In: The Proceedings of International Conference. The Philological Faculty, SPSU (2001). (in Russian)
5. Matthias, E., Johan, S., Susan, A., Michael, M., Martin, S.: Richter Bernhard vocal tract in female registers—a dynamic real-time MRI study. J. Voice 24(2), 133–139 (2010)
6. Evgrafova, K., Evdokimova, V.: Perception of Russian vowels in singing. In: Baltic HLT Frontiers in Artificial Intelligence and Applications, vol. 247, pp. 42–9. IOS Press (2012)
7. Fant, G.: Acoustic Theory of Speech Production, The Hague, Mouton (1960) (Second edition (1970))
8. Henriques, R.N., et al.: A comparison of methods for decoupling tongue and lower lip from jaw movements in 3D articulography. J. Speech Lang. Hear. Res. 56, 1–16 (2013)
9. Hollien, H., Mendes-Scwartz, A.P., Nielsen, K.: Perceptual confusions of high-pitched sung vowels. J. Voice 14(2), 287–298 (2000)

10. Hoole, P., Nguyen, N.: Electromagnetic articulography in Coarticulation research. In: Hardcastle, W.H., Hewlett, N. (eds.) Coarticulation: Theory, Data and Techniques, pp. 260–269. Cambridge University Press (1999)
11. Howie, J., Delattre, P.: An experimental study of the effect of pitch on the intelligibility of vowels. National Assoc. Teachers Singing Bull. **18**(4), 6–9 (1962)
12. Calvin, L.: Validation of the Magneto-articulography for the Assessment of Speech Kinematics (MASK) System and Testing for Use in a Clinical Research Setting. A thesis for the degree of Masters of Health Science in Clinical Engineering Institute of Biomaterials and Biomedical Engineering University of Toronto (2013). http://hdl.handle.net/1807/43001
13. Lundy, D.S., Roy, S., Casiano, R.R., Xue, J.W., Evans, J.: Acoustic analysis of the singing and speaking voice in singing students. J. Voice **14**(4), 490–493 (2000)
14. Morozov, V.P.: Intelligibility in singing as a function of fundamental voice pitch. Soviet Phys. Acoust. **10**, 279–283 (1965)
15. Mendes, A.P., Rothman, H.B., Sapienza, Ch., Brown Jr., W.S.: Effects of vocal training on the acoustic parameters of the singing voice. J. Voice **17**(4), 529–543 (2003)
16. Nelson, H.D., Tiffany, W.R.: The intelligibility of song. NATS Bulletin. **25**, 22–28 (1968)
17. Scotto Di Carlo, N., Germain, A.: Perceptual study of the influence of pitch on the intelligibility of sung vowels. Phonetica. **42**, 188–192 (1985)
18. Schutte, H.K., Miller, D.G., Svec, J.G.: Measurement of formant frequencies and bandwidths in singing. J. Voice **9**(3), 290–296 (1995)
19. Strange, W., Verbrugge, R.R.: Consonant environment specifies vowel identity. J. Acoust. Soc. Am. **60**(1), 213–224 (1976)
20. Sundberg, J.: Articulatory differences between spoken and sung vowels in singers. Speech Transmission Laboratory/Quarterly Progress Status Report, vol. 1, pp. 31–42 (1969)
21. Sundberg, J.: Research on the singing voice in retrospective. TMH-QPSR, vol. 45 nr. 1, pp. 11–22 (2003)
22. Sundberg, J.: The acoustics of the singing voice. Sci. Am., 82–91 (1977)
23. Sundberg, J.: The Science of the Singing Voice. Northern University Press, DeKalb (1987)
24. Titze, I.R.: Speaking vowels versus singing vowels. J. Singing, 487 (1995)
25. Toutios, A., Narayanan, S.: Advances in real-time magnetic resonance imaging of the vocal tract for speech science and technology research. APSIPA Trans. Signal Inf. Process. **5**, e6. https://doi.org/10.1017/ATSIP.2016.5. Published online: 31 March 2016
26. Watts, Ch., Barnes-Burroughs, K., Andrianopoulos, M., Carr, M.: Potential factors related to untrained singing talent: a survey of singing pedagogues. J. Voice **17**(3), 298–307 (2003)
27. Westerman, J.G., Scherer, R.C.: Vowel intelligibility in classical singing. J. Voice **20**(2), 198–210

A Comparison Between Musical and Speech Rhythms: A Case Study of Standard Thai and Northern Thai

Chawadon Ketkaew[1][(✉)] and Yanin Sawanakunanon[2]

[1] Chiang Mai University, Chiang Mai, Thailand
chawadon.k@cmu.ac.th
[2] Bangkok, Thailand

Abstract. The nPVI measurement is an empirical tool used for finding phonetics evidence supporting language classification in terms of rhythmic properties. The nPVI can also be used in order to find the influence of a composer's
native language on instrumental music's rhythm (Patel and Daniel, 2003).
However, there is a question as to whether music with lyrics will yield the same
result as instrumental music. Therefore, this study aims to investigate rhythm in
Standard Thai and Northern Thai pop songs. The results show that the nPVI
value for Standard Thai pop songs is lower than the nPVI value of Northern
Thai pop songs and the result of rhythmic property in music obtained from nPVI
calculating is not parallel with speech nPVI value. To illustrate, musical nPVI
value calculated from Standard Thai pop songs is lower than the musical nPVI
value of Northern Thai pop songs. This incongruousness might result from the
influence of Western music and melodies on Standard Thai pop songs and folk
melodies on Northern Thai pop songs.

Keywords: Musical rhythm · Speech rhythm · Pop songs · Standard Thai
Northern Thai · nPVI

1 Introduction

Rhythm refers to periodicity or patterns that are repeatedly arranged and organised in
time. In speech, rhythm may refer to many components that can organise languages in
time, such as syllables, stressed and unstressed syllables, syllable length and pausing
between words or utterances. Rhythm is also an essential element in music. The core
concept for rhythm in music also refers to periodicity and elements that are arranged in
time.

Rhythm may vary when impacted by different cultures. For this reason, many forms
of music with different cultural backgrounds will have unique beats and patterns. For
speech, even in languages that are derived from the same language family, rhythmic
features will vary and have unique rhythmic properties. For example, English and

---

Y. Sawanakunanon—Independent Researcher.

© Springer Nature Switzerland AG 2019
P. Eismont and O. Mitrenina (Eds.): LMAC 2017, CCIS 943, pp. 58–64, 2019.
https://doi.org/10.1007/978-3-030-05594-3_5

French are classified differently in term of rhythmic properties; the former is a stress-timed language and the latter a syllable-timed language.

As for music, there are notable differences in Western and Asian styles. For example, in Western music, beats or rhythms are hierarchically organised with alternation of weak and strong beats. On the other hand, fretless zither called Ch'in played by the Chinese has no reference to the beat but the timing of the note randomly comes from the dynamics of the player's hand [1].

Even though some studies point out a relation between speech and musical rhythm, comparison between the two is surprisingly underdeveloped. This is despite widespread claims of the relation and the similarity between rhythm in music and language and that the prosody of a composer's language can influence their instrumental music [2, 3]. However, [4] used the systematic method to prove that the prosodic or rhythmic properties of a composer's language can be reflected in their music.

1.1   The nPVI Measurement

It is widely accepted that speech rhythm can be classified into three groups: stress-timed, syllable-timed and mora-timed rhythm, according to the units determining rhythm [5, 6]. In his acoustic study of speech rhythm, [7] found that in syllable-timed languages like French, the duration of each syllable in a sentence is roughly equal while in stress-timed languages like English, the intervals between stressed syllables are roughly equal. He also suggested that languages which are classified as stress-timed languages allow complex consonant clusters that will lead to higher variation of vocalic intervals.

In 1999, [8] proposed a new acoustic approach to study speech rhythm. Instead of measuring syllable durations, speech data was segmented into consonantal and vocalic intervals. Successive consonants belonged to the same consonantal interval regardless of their syllable or word boundaries. In the same fashion, successive vowels belonged to the same vocalic interval.

The proportion of total vocalic duration (%V) and the standard errors of consonantal interval durations (ΔC) were then computed and compared among languages. The results clearly show three groups of languages by the values of %V and ΔC. English, Dutch and Polish, which are usually classified as stress-timed languages, have similar values of both parameters which are significantly different from those of Japanese, a mora-timed language, and French, Spanish, Italian, and Catalan, the so-called syllable-timed languages.

[9] adopted the idea of consonantal and vocalic intervals but developed new measurements, raw intervocalic variability index (rPVI_C) and normalized vocalic pairwise variability index (nPVI_V). These indices aim to capture the variability of interval duration from the difference between the duration of two successive intervals. While rPVI_C reflects the complexity of consonant clusters, nPVI_V demonstrates the difference between durations of stressed and reduced vowels. As different speech tempo can directly affect vocalic durations, [9] normalised the durations of vocalic intervals using Eq. (1).

$$nPVI = 100 \times \left[\sum_{k=1}^{m-1} \left| \frac{d_k - d_{k+1}}{(d_k + d_{k+1})/2} \right| / (m - 1) \right], \qquad (1)$$

In Eq. (1), m represents the number of vocalic intervals present in an utterance, while d_k represents the duration of the kth interval. When measuring the nPVI for a given utterance, larger contrasts between neighbouring durations result in higher nPVI values.

The results demonstrate that stress-timed languages tend to have higher values of both parameters due to more complex consonant clusters and the difference between stressed and reduced vowels. On the other hand, syllable-timed languages have lower PVI values due to their less complex consonant clusters and lack of vowel reduction. In the study, Thai, German and Dutch are among languages with higher values of nPVI_V and are classified as stress-timed languages while Mandarin and Spanish are considered syllable-timed for their low nPVI_V values.

[4, 10] then applied the nPVI measurements to compare the variability of musical note duration as a core unit in English and French classical music with vowel durations in speech.

In Fig. 1, the result suggests that the different linguistic rhythm of English, a stress-timed language, and French, a syllable-timed language, is also reflected in music. To illustrate, the nPVI value of English speech is higher than that of French speech. In the same way, the nPVI value of English music is also higher than that of French music.

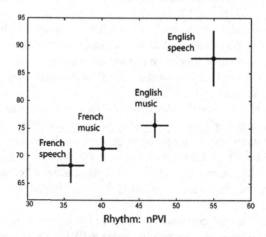

Fig. 1. The nPVI values of English and French musical themes compared to speech [10]

[4] also left the intriguing idea that music with lyrics will unsurprisingly affect speech rhythmic properties in music. Other studies using the same methodology in Japanese [11] and Polish [12] also reveal results supporting Patel and Daniele's hypothesis. In addition, the study of [13] also support the hypothesis proposed in [4] by applying the method to testify the rhythmic characteristics of speech that can influence music in a dialect level.

1.2   Standard Thai and Northern Thai Languages

Politically, Standard Thai is the official language of Thailand and spoken throughout the country while Northern Thai (or Tai Yuan) is considered a dialect and spoken in six provinces in the north. Linguistically speaking, even though the two are members of the southwestern branch of the Tai language family, they are considered different languages. Each has its own writing system and they are also different in terms of lexicon and phonology systems. There are more consonants and more tones in Northern Thai. However, more combinations of consonant clusters are allowed in Standard Thai and this reflects in the higher rPVI_C value of Standard Thai (47.0) compared to Northern Thai (45.57). Greater variability of vocalic durations in Standard Thai reflects in a higher nPVI_V value (54.63) than that of Northern Thai (48.71) [14]. Following the interpretation suggested by [9], it might be possible to say that Standard Thai, with higher values of both nPVI_V and rPVI_C, is a more stress-timed language than Northern Thai.

In this study, we want to examine whether nPVI measurement can capture the similar characteristics, as in Patel and Daniele's hypothesis, between rhythm in music with lyrics in Standard Thai pop songs and Northern Thai pop songs and rhythm in speech in Standard Thai and Northern Thai speech. Even though the genres and forms of music are different, we expect a lower musical nPVI value of Northern Thai pop songs than that of Standard Thai pop songs as found in speech.

2   Data and Method

2.1   Speech Data

The speech data in this study was retrieved from [14, 15]. Spontaneous speech was recorded from three native speakers of each language. Forty-six utterances in Standard Thai and 40 utterances in Northern Thai were segmented and labelled into vocalic and consonantal intervals using Praat. As it was impossible to identify the beginning of the interval boundary where the first syllable starts with a stop consonant, utterance-initial syllables were not included in the analysis for consistency. The last syllables of each utterance were also excluded to avoid lengthening effects.

Vocalic interval boundaries were marked from the beginning of a vowel, where explicit patterns of vowel formants are shown. Durations of 486 vocalic intervals in Standard Thai and 520 vocalic intervals in Northern Thai were obtained and computed into nPVI values using Eq. (1). The average nPVI values for Standard Thai and Northern Thai were 54.63 and 48.71 respectively [14, 15].

2.2   Musical Data

Ten Standard Thai popular songs and 10 Northern Thai popular songs with moderate tempo of 80–118 BPM were randomly selected from various composers. Standard Thai pop songs were randomly selected from the radio chart in Thailand between 2014 and 2015. For Northern Thai pop songs, most of the songs were chosen from 1977 to 2001 because of the limited number of Northern Thai pop songs produced after 2002.

Fig. 2. Example of four musical phrases of the song "หากฉันตาย" by Sixty Miles

While [4] only analysed the chorus, we analysed the whole song as we believed that it would represent the rhythmic characteristics of a song better than only the chorus. Musical phrases of each song were parallel with their syntactic boundaries as shown in Fig. 2.

A total of 212 and 195 musical phrases from Standard Thai and Northern Thai, respectively, were examined. Each note was given a duration according to the time signature of each song. To illustrate, a half note in 4/4 is given a duration of 2 and a quarter and an eighth note are coded as 1 and ½ respectively as illustrated in Fig. 3.

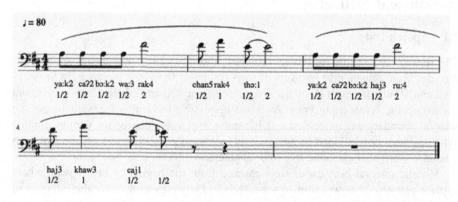

Fig. 3. Example of note duration coding of the song "หากฉันตาย" by Sixty Miles

Note durations that were obtained from converting note value into number were then used in Eq. (1) to calculate the musical nPVI value. Two-sample t-test was used to compare the means with a .05 level of significance.

3   Results

Speech nPVI values for Standard Thai range from 35.64 and 76.85 and from 20.29 to 77.41 for Northern Thai [15]. In Standard Thai pop songs, nPVI values range from 23.58 to 48.31. Northern Thai pop songs have wider range of nPVI values from 23.94 to 80.39.

Average nPVI values of speech and music in Standard Thai and Northern Thai are shown in Fig. 4. It is worth noting that the difference of the average nPVI values in Northern Thai speech and music are smaller than those of Standard Thai.

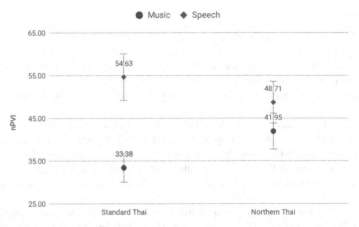

Fig. 4. Speech and musical nPVI values in Standard Thai and Northern Thai

From [14, 15], the average nPVI value of Standard Thai speech (54.63) is greater than that of Northern Thai speech (48.71). However, the average nPVI values of Standard Thai pop songs (33.38) were found to be statistically significantly ($p < 0.05$) lower than that of Northern Thai pop songs (41.95). These results, therefore, disprove our hypothesis that the nPVI values in music should be in the same format as in speech.

4   Summary and Discussion

The songs with lyrics do not yield nPVI format similar to speech as expected in this study. From our observation, music genres might have an influence on nPVI values.

To illustrate, the melodies of some Northern Thai pop songs analysed in this study were adapted from Northern Thai folk song rhythms which could be similar to speech rhythm. For example, the songs "ฮานี่บ่าเฮ็ย" [ha:1 ni:3 ba?2 hə:j3] were adapted from the traditional melody of a well-known Northern folk song called เพลงซอปั่นฝ้าย. As a result, the musical and linguistic nPVI values in Northern Thai are not much different. The average nPVI value obtained from the song "ฮานี่บ่าเฮ็ย" [ha:1 ni:3 ba?2 hə:j3] is 47.29 and it is not much different from the nPVI value of Northern Thai speech (48.71). As for the songs "พี่สาวครับ" [pʰi:3 sa:w5 kʰrap4] and "ไว้ใจได้กา" [wa:j4 caj1 da:j3 ka:1], their melodies are not adapted from Northern folk songs and the result shows that their nPVI values (23.94 and 27.38 respectively) are a lot lower than those of speech.

For Standard Thai pop songs, none of them adapted the melodies from the traditional Thai folk songs but more from Western music. Consequently, musical rhythm in Standard Thai pop music could be different from speech rhythm.

These findings, therefore, do not support Patel and Daniele's claim that "spoken prosody leaves an imprint on the music of a culture". Nevertheless, the songs that are adapted from traditional music can represent the rhythmic property of languages. Links between music genres and adapted melodies should be further investigated.

References

1. Patel, A.D.: Music, Language, and the Brain. Oxford University Press, New York (2010). https://doi.org/10.1093/acprof:oso/9780195123753.001.0001
2. Abraham, G.: The Tradition of Western Music. University of California Press, Berkeley (1974)
3. Wenk, B.J.: Just in time: on speech rhythm in music. Linguistics **25**, 969–981 (1987)
4. Patel, A.D., Daniele, J.R.: An empirical comparison of rhythm in language and music. Cognition **87**, B35–B45 (2003). https://doi.org/10.1016/S0010-0277(02)00187-7
5. Laver, J.: Principles of Phonetics. Cambridge University Press, Cambridge (1994)
6. Pike, K.L.: The Intonation of American English. University of Michigan Press, Ann Arbor (1945)
7. Roach, P.: On the distinction between 'stress-timed' and 'syllable-timed' languages. In: Crystal, D. (ed.) Linguistic Controversies, pp. 73–79. Edward Arnold, London (1982)
8. Ramus, F., Nespor, M., Mehler, J.: Correlates of linguistic rhythm in the speech signal. Cognition **73**(3), 265–292 (1999)
9. Grabe, E., Low, E.L.: Durational variability in speech and the rhythm class hypothesis. In: Gussenhoven, C., Warner, N. (eds.) Laboratory Phonology 7, pp. 515–546. Mouton de Gruyter, Berlin (2002). https://doi.org/10.1515/9783110197105.2.515
10. Patel, A.D., Iversen, J.R., Rosenberg, J.C.: Comparing the rhythm and melody of speech and music: the case of British English and French. J. Acoust. Soc. Am. **119**(5), 3034–3047 (2006). https://doi.org/10.1121/1.2179657
11. Sadakata, M., Desain, P., Honing, H., Patel, A.D., Iversen, J.R.: A cross-cultural study of the rhythm in English and Japanese popular music. In: Proceedings of the International Symposium on Musical Acoustics (ISMA), Nara, pp. 41–44 (2004)
12. Jekiel, M.: Comparing rhythm in speech and music: the case of English and Polish. In: Yearbook of the Poznan Linguistic Meeting, vol. 1, no. 1, pp. 55–71. De Gruyter Open, Warsaw (2014)
13. McGowan, R.W., Levitt, A.G.: A comparison of rhythm in English dialects and music. Music. Percept. Interdiscip. J. **28**(3), 307–314 (2011). https://doi.org/10.1525/mp.2011.28.3.307
14. Sawanakunanon, Y.: Segment timing in twelve Southeast Asian languages. Manusya **20**, 124–156 (2014)
15. Sawanakunanon, Y.: Segment timing in Southeast Asian languages: implications for typological classification. Unpublished Doctoral Dissertation, Chulalongkorn University, Bangkok (2012)

Singer's Performance Style in Numbers and Dynamic Curves: A Case Study of "Spring Waters" by Sergei Rachmaninoff

Gregory Martynenko[(⊠)] [iD]

Saint Petersburg State University,
Universitetskaya nab. 11, 199034 St. Petersburg, Russia
g.martynenko@spbu.ru

Abstract. The paper is devoted to the research of vocalist's individual manners of performance made on audio recordings with use of their acoustic analysis. The research method was tested on recordings of five performances of the famous song "Spring waters" by Sergei Rachmaninoff sung by different vocalists-tenors. Audio recordings were manually segmented into vocal syllables to obtain information on duration of each vocal note. Tabulating data on different performances into a single database allowed to conduct their statistical analysis. As a result, we have obtained time series that reveal tempo dynamics for each singer, composed an averaged profile of all performances under study, and made comparison between tempo characteristics of syllables, vocal lines and performances in whole. It turned out that an average tempo differs significantly for different performers. In "Spring waters", tempo profiles of different individual singers have much in common, going almost in parallel in the beginning of the song, however diverging from each other closer to its end. The greatest variation of tempo was observed in two important points—in the final vocal line and in the point of the golden section, the latter being the break point in the song composition. The proposed method allows to reveal the average style of performance for a particular song and the deviations from it.

Keywords: Russian romance · Song · Sergei Rachmaninoff · "Spring waters"
"Spring torrents" · Fyodor Tyutchev · Singing · Performers · Tempo
Dynamics · Time series · Duration · Trend · Cyclical fluctuations
Climax · Golden section

1 Introduction

The paper is devoted to the research of vocalist's individual manners of performance made on audio recordings of art songs by Sergei Rachmaninoff. Art song is a hybrid genre based on the interaction of musical and poetic components. Its features have been studied in a number of works; see, for example, [3, 7, 10].

Usually, musical notation contains hints on how to perform the corresponding composition proposed by the composer to both the vocalist and the accompanist. Musical notation may prescribe the dynamics, or loudness, between notes or musical fragments (e.g., *f* (*forte*), *p* (*piano*), *mp* (*mezzo-piano*), *crescendo*, *diminuendo*, etc.),

© Springer Nature Switzerland AG 2019
P. Eismont and O. Mitrenina (Eds.): LMAC 2017, CCIS 943, pp. 65–77, 2019.
https://doi.org/10.1007/978-3-030-05594-3_6

accents and different forms of musical articulation (*staccato*, *legato*, etc.). Indications of the manner of singing, or of emotional state are also frequently used (e.g., *tranquillo* (in a quite or calm manner), *espressivo* (expressive), *appassionato* (impassioned), etc.). The list of terms and symbols used in musical notation is quite large.

However, musical notation does not provide strict numerical quantification for dynamics, tempo and emotional tone. Therefore, relative freedom is allowed in these aspects for individual performing manners. Being interpreted by performers in different ways, one and the same original score may result in quite diverse interpretations.

While studying the style of performance, different methods are used, but more often they are of a qualitative nature. In our study, the emphasis is made on mathematical and instrumental methods of research, which have been rarely used for this purpose earlier [6, 14].

2 Approaches to Studying Compositional Dynamics in Songs

In musicology, and to lesser extent, in literature studies, much attention is paid to research on text dynamics, and in particular, to look for formal criteria for identifying the text culmination (for either musical or verbal texts) dividing it into two parts. The choice of such a culmination point (or peak, or climax) is quite arbitrary, however in many cases it is *the golden section* that is referred in this concern. Usually, at first, the place of culmination point is assigned, and then the researcher tries to convince himself and his supporters of the validity of his hypothesis [1, 2, 5, 8, 9, 15].

In the paper [4], a methodology for studying structural interaction between poetry and musical components in art songs by means of time series analysis was proposed. The method is based on analysis of musical notation, which is structured by an index, taking into account pitch and duration of each note in the vocal line of the song. Though it was the musical text in focus of the research, its verbal text has also been taken into consideration by analyzing its rhythmic structure. The resulting dynamic patterns were presented in the form of dynamic curves, representing one or another type of an upward or downward trend (or the combination of the both), on which cyclic variations were superimposed. It was shown that the geometry of these curves providing the important information on the song structure can also indicate its culmination point.

In this paper, the research approach is fundamentally different. Here, the reference point is a poetic text, which is divided into syllables and lines. The study is based on the use of acoustic analysis of audio recordings. The sound wave (or oscillogram) contains data on all relevant acoustic characteristics of the performance—duration, height of pitch, loudness, and timbre. All together they express emotional dynamic tones of individual performances. Having an audio recording of a particular performance, it is possible, for example, to measure the duration of each syllable of the song (as well as each line) by means of instrumental methods. And having obtained the data on each vocal note duration, one can plot the corresponding graphs and compare in this aspect the individual manners of singing.

The research method and the results of the analysis are shown on audio recordings of several performances of one famous song by Sergei Rachmaninoff sung by different vocalists. The proposed approach allows revealing an average style of performance for each particular song and the deviations from it by individual performances.

3 "Spring Waters" by Sergei Rachmaninoff

For this research, we have chosen to take "Spring waters" (or "Spring torrents"), which is one of Rachmaninoff's most popular songs. This song is considered by many musicologists to be one of the greatest songs by Rachmaninoff written in 1890s. As Rachmaninoff's scholar Richard D. Sylvester describes this romance: "After the long, cold Russian winter, the coming of spring is not just a relief, but a liberation, in which dancing for joy, ideally in bare feet, would be a natural response" [13, p. 83].

The romance is characterized by particularly strongly pronounced dynamics. The vocal part of the romance, unfolding against the background of flowing, undulating piano passages, is imbued with active calling intonations, creating a visible impression of a visible flood—an uncontrollable water flow. And almost like a battle cry, the phrase "Spring is coming!" is sounding at the culminating point of the song.

The text was written by the famous Russian poet Fyodor Tyutchev. It was first published in 1832. This poem was set to music by over 30 composers since 1861, including Grechaninov and Tcherepnin [13].

Below is the text of this poem and its translation into English by Yuri Mitelman [12]. The lines of the poem are numbered for easy reference.

Eshche v poliakh beleet sneg,	(1)	*But the streams are already rolling in a spring mood,*
A vody uzh vesnoi shumiat --	(2)	*Running and awakening the sleepy shore,*
Begut i budiat sonnyi breg,	(3)	*Running and glittering and announcing loudly.*
Begut, i bleshchut, i glasiat...	(4)	*The fields are still covered with white snow*
Oni glasiat vo vse kontsy:	(5)	*They are announcing loudly to every corner:*
"Vesna idet, vesna idet!	(6)	*"Spring is coming, spring is coming!*
My molodoi vesny gontsy,	(7)	*We are the messengers of young spring,*
Ona nas vyslala vpered!"	(8)	*She has sent us ahead!"*
Vesna idet, vesna idet!	(9)	*Spring is coming, spring is coming!*
I tikhikh, teplykh maiskikh dnei	(10)	*And the quiet, warm May days,*
Rumianyi, svetlyi khorovod	(11)	*In a rosy, bright dancing circle.*
Tolpitsia veselo za nei!...	(12)	*Follow her, merrily crowded.*

Music was composed by Rachmaninoff in 1896. The song is dedicated to Anna Ornatskaya, who was Rachmaninoff's first piano teacher and his mother's friend. "Spring waters" is one of the twelve songs that constitute Op. 14 (No. 11). Initially it was published with Opus 14 by A. Gutheil in Moscow in 1896. The song is written in E-flat Major with 4/4 time. Tempo is notated as *Allegro vivace* (the beginning of the song), *Meno mosso* (line 9), *Andante* (line 10), *Allegro vivace* (final piano solo). For high voice, it is performed in e^1 flat (or b flat)—b^2 flat [13].

This expressive and optimistic romance has been quite widely performed by various singers in Russia and abroad: Ivan Kozlovsky, Sergei Lemeshev, Nikolai Gedda,

Irina Arkhipova, Galina Kovaleva, Tamara Milashkina, Yuri Gulyaev, Vladimir Atlantov, Elena Obraztsova, Renée Fleming, Ferruccio Furlanetto, Dmitri Hvorostovsky, Lyubov Kazarnovskaya and many others. It is even known that Caruso sang "Spring waters" in French on several occasions, however he did not record it [11].

A long list of recordings of this song by different singers allows to compare individual styles of singing. However, for the given research we decided to limit ourselves to studies of vocal styles by five tenor singers.

4 Research Data and Its Preparation

At the first stage of the study, five recordings of "Spring waters" by five male vocalists-tenors—Ivan Kozlovsky, Sergei Lemeshev, Nikolai Gedda, Vladimir Atlantov, and Grigory Martynenko—were selected. All of them, with the exception of Gregory Martynenko, are world famous singers. The recordings were obtained from YouTube video hosting and other Internet music archives.

The recordings were manually segmented into vocal syllables (i.e., notes of the vocal line). The segmentation was carried out in ELAN multimedia annotation program (see Fig. 1), developed at the Max Planck Institute for Psycholinguistics in Holland. As a result, we obtained information on duration of each vocal note for each vocalist. The piano solo fragments were not specially segmented, but they were marked with the <P> symbol, thus allowing us to consider the duration of these fragments, too. The segmentation was made for each analyzed performance.

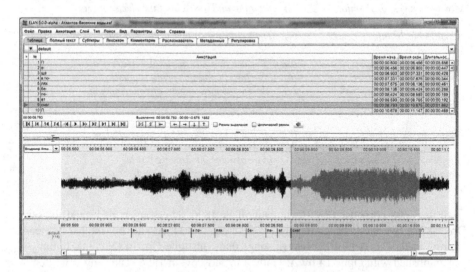

Fig. 1. Segmentation into vocal syllables (notes) in ELAN

The next task was to bring all gathered information together into a database for its statistical comparison. ELAN provides export of segmentation data into a table format compatible with MS Excel, MS Access, as well as specialized statistical programs. It was assumed that the structure of such a database containing information about specific vocal notes should be uniform for all singers, since academic tradition requires from vocalists the necessity to accurately adhere to text of the vocal work prescribed by the composer.

Thus, numerical data were obtained on actual durations of vocal syllables (notes). On the basis of these data, graphs of time series were constructed, on which distinctions between different singers are clearly visible, making it possible to compare the individual style of performing for each particular singer.

However, it turned out that some singers make extra pauses in unusual places either to take a breath or as a means of artistic expression, therefore breaking the common sequence of "vocal syllables" and "piano solo fragments". Below the positions of piano solo fragments are marked by <P>, whereas additional vocal pauses made by individual singers are marked by (P1)...(P4). One may see that there are four positions, in which the singers could "break" the prescribed vocal line. In Table 1 these positions are referred to vocalists.

<P>
Eshche v poliakh beleet sneg, <P>	(1)
A vody (P1) *uzh vesnoi shumiat --* <P>	(2)
Begut i budiat sonnyi breg, <P>	(3)
Begut, i bleshchut, i glasiat... <P>	(4)
Oni glasiat vo vse kontsy: <P>	(5)
"Vesna idet, <P> *vesna idet!* <P>	(6)
My molodoi vesny gontsy, <P>	(7)
Ona nas vyslala (P2) *vpered!"* <P>	(8)
Vesna idet, <P> *vesna idet,* <P>	(9)
I tikhikh, (P3) *teplykh maiskikh dnei* <P>	(10)
Rumianyi, svetlyi khorovod <P>	(11)
Tolpitsia (P4) *veselo* <P> *za nei!...*	(12)

<P>

Table 1. The extra pauses made by vocalists

(P1)	Ivan Kozlovsky, Vladimir Atlantov
(P2)	Grigory Martynenko
(P3)	Grigory Martynenko
(P4)	Ivan Kozlovsky, Nikolai Gedda, Vladimir Atlantov

It is seen from this data that Sergei Lemeshev's performance adheres more strictly to Rachmaninoff's notation—he did not insert any pauses "from himself". Nikolai Gedda takes an additional breath just before the final long note. The most similarity in extra pausing is observed for performances by Ivan Kozlovsky and Vladimir Atlantov. The performance by Gregory Martynenko is unlike other tenors in this aspect: making pauses in unusual places breaks a vocal tradition, however may lead to the expressiveness of the performance.

The database was brought to a common structure by means of inserting additional boxes at the places where one (or more) of the singers took a pause. The initial fragment of the database is presented in Table 2. The element No. 14 is an additional pause made by Kozlovsky and Atlantov (it is marked by an asterisk). The other singers have at this point a zero duration. Here and below, the vocal syllables are given in phonetic transcription. The stressed syllables are noted by an accent mark.

Table 2. The duration of syllables for the first two lines of the song

No	Segment	Duration, ms				
		Kozlovsky	Lemeshev	Gedda	Atlantov	Martynenko
1	<P>	5430	6040	4989	5856	5770
2	je-	400	459	225	447	590
3	schó	646	418	393	428	590
4	fpa-	348	454	396	344	354
5	ljáh	364	374	252	461	523
6	bi-	354	289	288	288	261
7	lé-	267	313	200	169	190
8	jet	231	295	122	192	159
9	snék	1802	1908	1578	1882	2368
10	<P>	424	668	887	469	500
11	a	304	227	238	328	611
12	vó-	788	908	654	856	827
13	dy	370	767	756	417	261
14*	(P1)	349	0	0	336	0
15	uzh	376	460	322	528	287
16	vis-	535	294	150	185	209
17	nój	1749	1210	1593	2100	1314
18	shu-	574	411	460	642	314
19	mját	1912	2024	1380	2999	1531
20	<P>	3030	3319	3180	2155	2544

Such an approach to extra pauses made it possible to bring all vocal performances to a single structure and to perform statistical analysis on the duration of syllables and vocal lines.

5 Statistical Data Analysis on Syllable Duration

Table 3 presents mean values, standard deviations, and variation coefficient calculated for each segment of five performances under study. Mean values help to understand an average tempo dynamics, whereas standard deviation and variation coefficient allow to judge which fragments of the song vary the most.

Total duration of each performance (not including applause) is presented in Table 4. The average tempo for each performer was counted as the total duration of all vocal segments divided by their number (97 syllables).

Table 3. The descriptive statistics of syllables' duration for the first two lines of the song

No	Segment	Mean (ms)	SD	Variation coefficient
1	<P>	5617	414.97	0.31
2	je-	424.2	131.80	0.23
3	schó	495	114.73	0.12
4	fpa-	379.2	46.70	0.26
5	ljáh	394.8	103.19	0.15
6	bi-	296	34.52	0.26
7	lé-	227.8	60.11	0.33
8	jet	199.8	66.74	0.15
9	snék	1907.6	288.28	0.46
10	<P>	589.6	190.12	0.12
11	a	341.6	156.56	0.45
12	vó-	806.6	95.88	0.25
13	dy	514.2	232.77	0.56
14*	(P1)	137	187.65	0.22
15	uzh	394.6	99.08	0.27
16	vis-	274.6	154.95	0.32
17	nój	1593.2	355.64	0.31
18	shu-	480.2	130.19	0.23
19	mját	1969.2	633.63	0.12
20	<P>	2845.6	484.21	0.26

Table 4. The duration of different vocal performances and their average tempo

Singer	Duration, ms		Average tempo
	Total song	Vocal part	
Gedda	1.84	1.05	648
Atlantov	1.95	1.37	844
Lemeshev	2.1	1.41	871
Martynenko	2.18	1.58	976
Kozlovsky	2.31	1.61	993
Mean	2.02	1.35	834.93
SD	0.15	0.22	137.08

Thus, it is seen from Table 4 that an average tempo differs significantly for selected performers. The fastest tempo is observed in the performance by Nikolai Gedda, and the slowest tempo is demonstrated by Ivan Kozlovsky.

Further, we have to bring the duration of each vocal syllable to standardized data, dividing the specific "performance" value by the average value calculated for all five singers (see Table 5). At this stage, we exclude the additional pauses from our consideration. The correspondent graph is shown on Fig. 2.

Table 5. Standardized duration of vocal syllables and piano solo fragments (for the initial two lines of the song)

No	Segment	Kozlovsky	Lemeshev	Gedda	Atlantov	Martynenko
1	<P>	0.97	1.08	0.89	1.04	1.03
2	je-	0.94	1.08	0.53	1.05	1.39
3	schó	1.31	0.84	0.79	0.86	1.19
4	fpa-	0.92	1.20	1.04	0.91	0.93
5	ljáh	0.92	0.95	0.64	1.17	1.32
6	bi-	1.20	0.98	0.97	0.97	0.88
7	lé-	1.17	1.37	0.88	0.74	0.83
8	jet	1.16	1.48	0.61	0.96	0.80
9	snék	0.94	1.00	0.83	0.99	1.24
10	<P>	0.72	1.13	1.50	0.80	0.85
11	a	0.89	0.66	0.70	0.96	1.79
12	vó-	0.98	1.13	0.81	1.06	1.03
13	dy	0.72	1.49	1.47	0.81	0.51
14*	(P1)	0.00	0.00	0.00	0.00	0.00
15	uzh	0.95	1.17	0.82	1.34	0.73
16	vis-	1.95	1.07	0.55	0.67	0.76
17	nój	1.10	0.76	1.00	1.32	0.82
18	shu-	1.20	0.86	0.96	1.34	0.65
19	mját	0.97	1.03	0.70	1.52	0.78
20	<P>	1.06	1.17	1.12	0.76	0.89

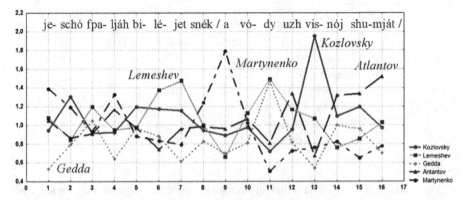

Fig. 2. Standardized duration of vocal syllables for five performers (the first two lines of the song)

It is seen from Fig. 2 that on certain syllables, some performers allow themselves "excessive tempo freedom". This is especially true for Ivan Kozlovsky and Gregory Martynenko. This may be also seen from the values of variation coefficients for the individual syllables (see Table 3). An interesting and unexpected conclusion is that the greatest range of this statistic is observed on unstressed syllables.

6 Time Series of Vocal Line Duration

Summarizing duration of syllables gave the possibility to calculate the duration for each vocal line of the song for each vocalist under study. Thus, we have obtained time series allowing studying tempo dynamics. These data are given in Table 6 along with the main statistics: mean, standard deviation (SD), and variation coefficient (VarC) for each vocal line. In Fig. 3 one may see the mean values marked as dots, the wave-like curve of smoothed data, and the general trend, which is shown by a dashed line and characterized by an upward movement. The smoothing was made using the distance-weighted least squares method.

Table 6. Standardized duration of vocal syllables and piano solo fragments (for the initial two lines of the song)

Line number	Kozlovsky	Lemeshev	Gedda	Atlantov	Martynenko	Mean	SD	VarC
1	4412	4510	3454	4211	5035	4324	574	0.133
2	6608	6301	5553	8055	5354	6374	1072	0.168
3	4817	5128	3990	4476	5330	4748	533	0.112
4	4944	5129	4116	4523	5419	4826	513	0.106
5	7898	7448	6114	6623	7829	7182	783	0.109
6	6135	6081	4599	5218	6071	5621	687	0.122
7	4865	4565	3387	4322	4695	4367	582	0.133
8	8518	6626	4153	8873	7254	7085	1877	0.265
9	16545	10319	6323	8710	10392	10458	3782	0.362
10	11020	8499	7395	8289	9901	9021	1434	0.159
11	6400	6348	5550	5696	6273	6053	399	0.066
12	14151	13579	8196	12918	21121	13993	4630	0.331

Now, let's compare the dynamic curves for different performers. Figure 4 shows time series for the two most contrasting (in terms of tempo) performers—Ivan Kozlovsky and Nikolai Gedda (see Table 4), and Fig. 5 presents three other graphics, for performers, whose dynamic curves are not very different from each other. It is noteworthy that the curves run almost in parallel to each other in the beginning of the song, however moving to the end of the song these curves diverge from each other. This difference is especially dramatic in the pair Gedda-Kozlovsky, who are the "tempo antipodes".

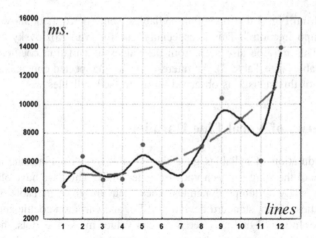

Fig. 3. Time series of average vocal line duration

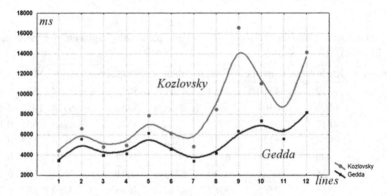

Fig. 4. Tempo profiles for Ivan Kozlovsky and Nikolai Gedda

However, the average values presented in the graphs of Fig. 4–5 give incomplete information. It is also necessary to consider the variability of duration in each vocal line. Thus, in Fig. 6 a time series graph of the generalized variation coefficient calculated for five performers is shown. It can be seen from Fig. 6 that the curve of variation coefficient has two local maxima: (1) in the final (12th line) of the song ("*Follow her, merrily crowded!*"), and (2) in its 9th line "*Spring is coming, spring is coming!*".

It is interesting that it is exactly in the end of 9th line that the "golden section" of all five performances takes place. More precisely, for four tenors the golden section point exactly coincides with the last syllable of the 9th line, whereas in the performance of the fifth singer this point is located in piano solo just after this syllable. The golden section was calculated as 0.618 to the total duration of all segments as the whole.

Thus, we may conclude that the golden section in terms of real duration do correspond to a break point in the song composition.

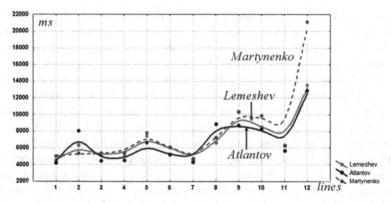

Fig. 5. Tempo profiles for Sergei Lemeshev, Vladimir Atlantov, and Gregory Martynenko

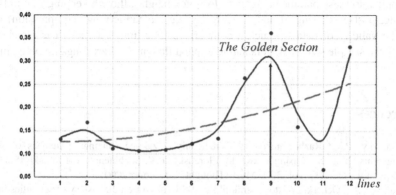

Fig. 6. Time series of the generalized variation coefficient and the Golden section

7 Conclusions

An approach to study vocal pieces is proposed, based on integration of both poetic and musical texts. It implies that the syllabic structure of poetic text is concerned and its interaction with the tempo of individual performances (the duration of syllables, vocal lines and the song as a whole) is analyzed, while the real sounding of song—not its musical notation—being the focus of attention.

Duration of particular vocal fragments as well as general tempo of performance can be used as diagnostic features to identify the performance manner of different vocalists along with other diagnostic signs. It was shown how to construct an averaged tempo profile for different performances of the same song. Comparing an average profile with that of particular singers, their personal performance styles become explicitly clear. The proposed method makes it possible to study tempo deviations on certain song fragments by individual vocalists. These differences may refer to means of musical expression, providing at the same time the individual features of individual performance styles.

As a result of the study, we have made comparison between tempo characteristics of syllables, vocal lines and songs as a whole for different singers and have constructed the averaged profile of all performances under study. It should be mentioned that the cyclic character of this profile (Fig. 3) generally corresponds with music notation by Rachmaninoff. Tempo profiles of individual singers turned out to have much in common, going almost in parallel in the beginning of the song and diverging from each other closer to its end. As for tempo variation in syllables, an interesting conclusion is that the largest range of this statistic is observed on unstressed syllables. The greatest variation of tempo was observed in two important points—in the final vocal line and in the point of the golden section, the latter being the break point in the song composition.

In this article, we confined ourselves to the analysis of tempo variations among different vocal performances. However, apart duration, the sound wave of any song recording contains data on other acoustic characteristics of music performances—height, loudness, and timbre. It seems that in some cases the similar method may be also applied to these parameters (except for pitch height), though keeping in mind that computer post-processing of audio recording (e.g., dynamic range compression) may spoil the validity of data for such a comparison. For future studies, it is planned to increase the sample size of singers and to expand the range of art songs involved in the study.

References

1. Florensky, P.V.: Razbor nekotorykh suzhdeniy o zakone Ceizinga [Analysis of some judgments about the Zeising's law]. In: Florensky, P.V. Sochineniya v 4 tomakh [Selected works in 4 volumes], vol. 3(1). Mysl [Thought], Moscow (2000)
2. Ivanov, V.V.: Ocherki po istorii semiotiki v SSSR [Essays on the history of semiotics in the USSR]. Nauka [Science], Moscow (1976)
3. Martynenko, G.Y.: Korpus russkogo romansa kak osnova issledovaniya verbalno-muzykalnykh tekstov [The corpus of Russian romances for studying poetry and music]. In: Trudy mezhdunarodnoj konferencii "Korpusnaja lingvistika 2013" [Proceedings of the International Conference "Corpus linguistics 2013"], pp. 371–378. St. Petersburg State University, St. Petersburg (2013)
4. Martynenko, G.: Structural interaction of poetry and music components in songs by Sergei Rachmaninoff. In: Eismont, P., Konstantinova, N. (eds.) LMAC 2015. CCIS, vol. 561, pp. 127–139. Springer, Cham (2015). https://doi.org/10.1007/978-3-319-27498-0_11
5. Mazel, L.: Analiz muzykal'nyh proizvedenij [Analysis of musical works]. Muzyka [Music], Moscow (1979)
6. Morozov, V.P.: Kompyuternye issledovaniya intonacionnoy tochnosti [Computer studies of intonation accuracy]. Eksperimentalnaya psihologiya [Exp. Psychol.] 2(3), 35–46 (2009)
7. Jin, P.S.: Vokalnoe tvorchestvo S. V. Rakhmaninova: k probleme evolyucii stilya [Vocal works by S. V. Rachmaninoff: to the problem of style evolution]. The Author's abstract of Ph.D. dissertation. The Herzen State Pedagogical University, St. Petersburg (2002)
8. Rozenov, E.K.: Zakon zolotogo secheniya v poezii i muzyke [The law of the golden section in poetry and music]. In: Rozenov, E.K. Statyi o muzyke. Izbrannoe [Selected works on music]. Muzyka [Music], Moscow (1982)

9. Sabaneev, L.L.: Etyudy Shopena v osveschenii zolotogo secheniya. Opyt pozitivnogo obosnovaniya [Chopin's Etudes and the Golden Section. An Experience of Positive Justification]. Iskusstvo [Art] **2**, 132–145 (1925)

10. Saitanova, N.I.: Nekotorye ritmicheskie sootvetstviya notnoy zapisi i ee ispolneniya [Some rhythmic correspondences of musical notation and its performance]. Issledovaniya po strukturnoy lingvistike [Studies on structural linguistics], pp. 159–168. Nauka [Science], Moscow (1975)

11. Scott, M.: Rachmaninoff. The History Press, Stroud (2008)

12. SINGRUSSIAN homepage. http://www.singrussian.co.uk/wp-content/uploads/2014/09/Rachmaninov-Spring-Waters.pdf. Accessed 3 July 2017

13. Sylverster, R.D.: Rachmaninoff's Complete Songs: A Companion with Texts and Translations. Indiana University Press, Bloomington (2014)

14. Todd, N.: The dynamics of dynamics: A model of musical expression. J. Acoust. Soc. Am. **91**, 3540–3550 (1992)

15. Zeising, A.: Neue Lehre von den Proportionen des menschlichen Körpers. Rudolf Weigel, Leipzig (1854)

Textual and Musical Invariants for Searching and Classification of Traditional Music

Ilya Saitanov[✉]

DSM Group, Moscow, Russia
rslon@mail.ru

Abstract. The goal of this research is to determine whether such properties as tonality, mode, meter and tune title remain similar between different versions of the same melody. A variability in some features makes classifying and searching tasks more difficult. The author uses a corpus of traditional dance melodies on audio recordings from Macedonia (Greece), as a base for analysis.

We show that, in general, none of the features – meter, mode, key and tune title – are invariable on their own, for all versions of a selected tune. At the same time, using linguistic features where the musical ones fail, and vice versa, helps to improve the chances of a correct attribution and an efficient search.

It is possible now to use the examples of invariance violations to assess possible search systems for a corpus of musical works.

Keywords: Traditional Greek dance music · Feature selection
Music information seeking

1 We'll Start with a Small Glossary

Corpus. This term as used in this text means a collection of musical data, organized by a certain criteria. A collection like this requires instruments of classification and search, and, most important, should allow verification of theories regarding musical content assembled within the corpus. A corpus approach has been used in linguistic studies since 1960 (see [1]). Currently this is a developing trend in music studies as well.

Invariant. This text employs a "mathematical" definition of invariant: "a property which remains unchanged when transformations of a certain type are applied". We regard changes in an entire music piece or its fragment occurring between performance versions included in a corpus as such transformations.

Features. In this text we use the word "features" for classification elements of the corpus.

Mode. The author regards mode as a logically differentiated system of sonic relationships within a piece, specifying the primary tone and the scale re-lated to it.

I. Saitanov—Independent Researcher.

© Springer Nature Switzerland AG 2019
P. Eismont and O. Mitrenina (Eds.): LMAC 2017, CCIS 943, pp. 78–87, 2019.
https://doi.org/10.1007/978-3-030-05594-3_7

2   Research Objective

Creation of a musical corpus assumes that tunes and their elements can be attributed and classified in order to provide the possibility of carrying out a search among them. It is therefore important to identify the features and attributes pivotal for a given system. A violation of invariance in some features makes the classifying and searching tasks much more difficult.

The goal of this research is to verify the invariance of linguistic and musical features in the audio records of traditional music from Macedonia (Greece).

This work is based on studying the dancing melodies from one region in Greece – namely Macedonia (Μακεδονία). The author has been analyzing recordings by local performers released on vinyl and CD. The list is available in the Appendix 1.

The author has analyzed by hand a total of 524 records; two or more versions have been found for 102 of them.

As a rule, these are recordings of ensembles; however, it is a monophonic melodic line of a leading instrument that has been a subject for study and attribution.

3   Bibliography Review

A lot of work is focused on classification of audio recordings. For example, in [2] and [5] authors specify features for audio recordings description and classification.

A study by Stanford University professors Christopher D. Manning and Prabhakar Raghavan, with contributions from Heinrich Schutze from Stuttgart [4], covers primarily textual search, but it ignores the titles of music pieces. Textual features of audio albums are covered, for example, in a report [3], where also "140 spelling variations of Pyotr Ilyich Tchaikovsky's name and surname" are mentioned. No sources on music information retrieval known to the researcher cover the meter differences between the versions of the same tune (such as an alternation between 7/8 and 4/4 common for the region specified).

4   Main Part

Let us review the primary features used for musical pieces classification: tonality, meter and mode.

4.1   Primary Tone

Tonality (the key) is a trivial example of a violation of invariance. In many examples different versions of the same tune have different primary tones. A performer presumably selects a tonality comfortable for him or her to perform. Therefore, this feature is not invariable for a search and classification task. We can only speak about a group of tonalities common for the given melody.

4.2   Meter

There is a distinct metric pulsation common for dancing melodies. This allows to assign to a fragment of a given melody a certain meter: 4/4 or 5/8, for example. Selecting a downbeat may vary: for instance the same example can have 4/4, 2/2 or 2/4 m.

Let us take a look at more significant variations. Figure 1 is the researcher's own transcript of a fragment of Παπαράτζα (Paparadzha) tune. Performed by Τα Χάλκινα της Γουμένισσας (Ta halkina tis Goumenissas) ensemble, it has the meter 11/8 (2 + 2 +3 + 2 + 2), while Κυριάκος Γευγελής (Kyriakos Yevgelis) performs it at 7/8 (3 + 2 + 2).

Fig. 1. Παπαράτζα. Τα Χάλκινα της Γουμένισσας vs. Κυριάκος Γευγελής

As we can see, the same melodic formulae can be expressed in performance practice with different rhythmic formulae of different musical meter.

4.3   Mode

Is the mode or, at least, tone series always preserved between various versions of the same melody? Analysis of the corpus produces a negative answer.

Let us show the mode change between versions of a fragment of Pousednitsa tune (Πουσέτνιτσα). These versions have differing third and fourth tonal degrees. One can see (Fig. 2) where Κυριάκος Γευγελής (Kyriakos Yevgelis) plays third and fourth degrees lower than Θανάσης Σέρκος (Thanasis Serkos). See notes marked with arrows.

Fig. 2. Πουσέτνιτσα. Κυριάκος Γευγελής vs. Θανάσης Σέρκος

We used an enharmonic record for Fb (E) tone in the beginning of a glissando above in order to preserve the difference of the same sound's modal functions between performance versions.

Such strong differences are rare in the corpus. Usually they are limited to small variations in the intoning of certain degrees or the addition of passing notes in neighboring tones and melismas.

4.4   Naming

Primary origins of a dance tune's names in Greek Macedonia:

1. *The name of the dance itself performed to this melody.*
   Μπαιντουσκα (Baidouska), Συρτό (Syrto), Καρσιλαμάς

2. *The name of the original song of which the tune is the instrumental version.*
Variations occur here: it may be the first line, keywords (from the Greek or
Macedonian text). The name itself can be Macedonian or Greek. Regardless of the
language, most likely the Greek alphabet will be used there.

Γαλανή γαλαζιανή (Galani galaziani) = Με κάλεσε μια αρχόντισσα (Me
kalese mia archontissa) [keywords/first line]

Βέταρ πουντουϊνάλ (Vetar podouinal) = Αέρας να φυσάει (Aeras na fisai)
[Macedonian/Greek variant of 'wind started blowing' phrase]

3. *Dance movements and tempo specifics*: Γεροντικος (Yerontikos) (old people's
dance), Ζάραμο (Zaramo) (holding each other's shoulders), Αντικρυστός
(Antikristos) (face to face), Πατινάδα (Patinada) (moving along the street) (Fig. 3)

Γεροντικος   Ζάραμο   Αντικρυστός   Πατινάδα

Fig. 3. Dance movements and tempo specifics

4. *Meter*: Συρτός Μακεδονίας 7σημός (Macedonian syrto at 7), Γιώργος 9-8
(Yorgos at 9/8), Συρτός – 4σημος (Syrto at 4)

5. *Assumed geographic origin*: Μπερατσε (Beratche, after the city of Berat),
Τικφεσκο (Tikfeshko, after Tikveš region in Macedonia), Μακεδονικό Συρτό
(Macedonian syrto)

6. *The title can be lacking entirely* – for example, if a recorded version is within
medley of several tunes, and only the first tune's name is used.

For all variations of the title genesis listed above (except 2 and occasionally 5) the
same title can correspond to a multitude of tunes. Exceptions occur in such cases as a
narrowly limited geographical span (when a certain settlement is explicitly referenced)
or a song line. Still, the name of the specific song may become a name of the dance,
and then any melody having this dance's rhythm acquires the same name. This is what
happened to Μπαιρατσε (Beratche, took its name after the city of Berat) – various
melodies with 16/8 (2 + 2 + 2 + 3 + 2 + 2 + 3) meter have the same name.

On the contrary, the same melody might have many names. Here are the various
names from the corpus for the melody with 11/8 (2 + 2 + 3 + 2 + 2) meter:

H1 Σουλειμάνοβο/Σουλειμάν Αγάς/Μολάεβο
H2 Μπουκιτε Ραζβιβατ/Οταν ανθίζουν οι οξυές/Οξιές/Σερβικος
H3 Στάνκενα/Στάνγκαινα/Καρασούλης/Λισσαβω/Μάραινα – Γιδά

H4 Μουσταμπεικο/Μουλαιοβο/Μουλαιβο
H5 Βέταρ πουντουϊνάλ/Βέτερ πουντουινάλο (Μουλάεβο)/Αέρας να φυσάει/Φ
ύσηξε αεράκι
H7 = F8 Παπαραντζα
H8 Μαρία (Τζιαρουδα)/Μαρια/Τι Κλαις Καημενη Μαρια
H9 = T1 Της Κατερίνας

Where H1, H2, etc. are the unique ID-markers of melodies.

In the case of H4, versions of Moulaevo are only different in their spelling (Μουλαιοβο vs. Μουλαιβο). At the same time H3 names differ a lot:

- Stankena
- Karasoulis
- Lissavo
- Marena – Gida

As we can see, the same melody can have many titles, while the same title can correspond to a number of different melodies.

4.5 Melody

What happens to the melody itself? Let us assume we keep the title, tonality, meter, mode and the general recognizability of melody. Can we expect the melody will be searchable by a fragment of consequent notes?

The answer will be negative: there is no invariance here either. The primary mechanisms of the violation of invariance are not region-specific. This is frequent re-use of melodic fragments, common for folklore in various countries as a composition method, and a richly developed variability of a melodic line.

As an example, let us examine Έντεκα (Endeka). We will compare two versions: the one by Θανάσης Σέρκος (Thanasis Serkos) is more ornamented and developed than Xalkina Kozanis' (Χάλκινα Κοζάνης). Therefore, first and fourth bars have more differences than similarities (Fig. 4)[1].

At the same time, Ράϊκο (Raiko) and Τρεχάτος (Trehatos) have identical first four bars, then go separate ways entirely (Fig. 5).

The regional specific shows up in the structure of the piece. Often the main tune is preceded by a lengthy improvised intro, usually untimed. Then we hear the main dance melody, followed by an improvisation based on the melody and its meter. The return to the main melody is an option as well. In extreme cases the fragment of a main tune, common for all versions, is a short-sounding pretext for an improvisation. Best examples include Τώρα τα πουλιά (Tora ta poulia) by Κυριάκος Γευγελης (Kyriakos Yevyelis). The main melody goes for 28 s of the song's total 256 s. The other example is Οσμάν πασάς (Osman pashas) by Θανάσης Σέρκος (Thanasis Serkos), where the

---

[1] Presumably, instead of searching for consequent notes of melody one can use one of the reduction techniques described in GTTM (see [6]) to identify a basic melody first. And then search for this basic version instead of melody itself. For traditional dance melodies of Macedonia (Greece) this could be a subject for further study.

Fig. 4. Έντεκα. Χάλκινα Κοζάνης vs. Θανάσης Σέρκος

primary tune shows up in two fragments, 13 and 14 seconds-long, appropriately, in between the untimed and timed improvisations, as well near the end.

The illustration below (Fig. 6) shows the place of the melody in the general arrangement of this version of Οσμάν πασάς (Osman pashas).

In such cases it is a non-trivial task to extract several bars of the melody from the surrounding improvisation. But it becomes easier if the title is known, as this gives some clues for searching in other versions and variants.

Fig. 5. Τρεχάτος (Ψαθάδες) vs. Ράϊκο (Ψαθάδες)

Fig. 6. Οσμάν πασάς

5 Conclusions

In general, none of the features – meter, mode, name and melodic line – are invariable on their own, for all versions of a selected tune. At the same time, using the linguistic features where the musical ones fail, and vice versa, helps to improve the chances of a correct attribution and an efficient search.

Since none of the studied features is purely invariable, a researcher shouldn't specify them all at once searching the full corpus, but rather should examine the search results with features selected separately and seek desired melody among these partial search results.

An important task – to use such examples of features' invariance violations in order to assess a search system for corpus of musical works. The examples, selected by the author of this work, will be accessible for researchers via this link: http://vigele.info/LMAC2017.

6 Further Developments

The database assembled by the researcher can be used for tutoring or validation of a possible automatic search and comparison algorithm.

The methodology for determination of features' invariance can be transferred to other features not covered in this work.

It would be interesting to see a similar work based on examples from other regions, and to see whether the conclusions which are true for Greek Macedonia, remain true elsewhere.

Finally, in the triad of dance – instrumental – song the researcher omits the dance movements. It would be interesting to have an unequivocal answer: whether the melodies with the same attributes (*a title* or *a melody* or *a meter*) are bound to the dance with specific movements in a given region.

Appendix: Record's References

References to above-mentioned records

Παπαράτζα – Κυριάκος Γευγελης (Κλαρίνο)	CD 1	Track 08
Παπαραντζα – Τα Χαλκινα Της Γουμενισσας	CD 2	Track 10
Συγκαθιστός του γάμου (Πουσεντνιτσα) – Θανάσης Σέρκος (Κλαρίνο)	CD 3	Track 11
Πουσέτνιτσα – Κυριάκος Γευγελης (Κλαρίνο)	CD 1	Track 07
Έντεκα η Αϊβασιλιάτικος – Χάλκινα Κοζάνης	CD 4	Track 06
Έντεκα – Θανάσης Σέρκος (Κλαρίνο)	CD 3	Track 07
Ραικος – Ψαθάδες	CD 5	Track 16
Τρεχατος – Ψαθάδες	CD 5	Track 22
Τώρα τα πουλιά (Χιτζαζ) – Κυριάκος Γευγελης (Κλαρίνο)	CD 1	Track 09
Οσμάν πασάς – Θανάσης Σέρκος (Κλαρίνο)	CD 3	Track 17

List of CD's

1. Τα χάλκινα της Γουμένισσας – Ιστορική μουσικολογική προσέγγιση. Γιώργης Μελίκης. 2001.
2. Τα χάλκινα της Γουμένισσας. Θερμαϊκός, Θερ 166.
3. Χοροί της Γουμένισσας και της Κεντρικής Μακεδονίας. Με την κομπανία του Θανάση Σέρκου. Λύκειον των Ελληνίδων. CD Α΄ LCGW 111
4. Χάλκινα Κοζάνης, με την κομπανία του Δημήτρη Κώτσικα. Κίνησις 329-2. 2002
5. Μακεδονικοι χοροι με την οικογενεια Ψαθα.

References

1. http://www.essex.ac.uk/lin-guis-tics/ex-ter-nal/clmt/w3c/cor-pus_ling/con-tent/cor-po-ra/list/pri-vate/brown/brown.html
2. Peeters, G.. A large set of audio features for sound description (similarity and classification) in the CUIDADO project/Ircam, Paris (2004). http://recherche.ircam.fr/anasyn/peeters/ARTICLES/Peeters-2003-cuidadoaudiofeatures.pdf
3. Kornilina E., Krofto E.: How the musical search works/Yandex, Moscow (2014). https://events.yandex.ru/lib/talks/1809/
4. Manning, K., Raghavan, P., Schutze, H.: Introduction to Information Retrieval. Williams, Kyiv (2011)
5. Mitrovic, D., Zeppelzauer, M., Breiteneder, C.: Features for Content-Based Audio Retrieval, Vienna (2010). http://publik.tuwien.ac.at/files/PubDat–186351.pdf
6. Lerdahl, F., Jackendoff, R.: A Generative Theory of Tonal Music. The MIT Press, Cambridge (1983)

Language as Music

Sound Symbolism of Contemporary Communication: Croatian Imitative Expressions in Computer-Mediated Discourse

Jana Jurčević[(✉)] [iD]

Faculty of Humanities and Social Sciences,
University of Zagreb, Zagreb, Croatia
jjurcevi@ffzg.hr

Abstract. Generally, sound symbolism has been regarded as a marginal linguistic ocurrence because (traditional/structuralist) linguistic theory presupposes arbitrary link between sound and meaning. Phonemes are perceived as the smallest building blocks of language structure whose value comes from (distinctive) relations with other phonemes. These abstract units do not posses nor carry their own meaning, but trough their distribution they make differences in meaning of more complex language units (e.g. morphemes, words). In contrast, sound symbolism presupposes direct, motivated link between sound (consequently grapheme) and meaning, which is the case with onomatopoeic expressions or imitatives. Led by communicative practice and observation of Croatian online vernacular, we have decided to approach this problem from pragmalinguistic perspective. Starting from everyday language-use, in the context of computer-mediated communication (chat analysis), we have noticed employment of large numbers of imitative expressions with various communicative functions (not exclusively poetic). Main objective of this paper is to point out the importance of a language process (sound symbolism) that has a potential of logically connecting two different systems of human communication and expression (language and music) and shed light on developmental, evolutionary and context-sensitive features of signing activities.

Keywords: Pragmalinguistics · Sociolinguistics
Computer-mediated discourse · Chat analysis · Sound symbolism
Croatian vernacular · Phonology · Etymology · Paralanguage
Communication evolution

1 Introduction

As a part of modern-day linguistics, phonology and phonostylistics based upon structuralist tradition, sound symbolism has mainly been regarded as a marginal linguistic occurrence.

Usually observed within poetic language function, sound symbolism has been discussed as a part of stylistics. On the other hand, in the domain of linguistics and language philosophy, sound symbolism has come to focus in discussions on arbitrary

© Springer Nature Switzerland AG 2019
P. Eismont and O. Mitrenina (Eds.): LMAC 2017, CCIS 943, pp. 91–110, 2019.
https://doi.org/10.1007/978-3-030-05594-3_8

nature of linguistic sign, as well as questions concerning origin, natural language evolution and its connections to other semiotic systems (e.g. music).

Despite those tendencies, led by communicative practice and observation, it has been decided to approach this problem from a pragmalinguistic perspective. Starting from Croatian vernacular, in the context of computer-mediated communication, specifically from chat analysis (N = 500, applications used: *Facebook Messenger, WhatsApp, Hangouts*), large production of imitative expressions has been noticed. In their variety, those imitatives carry out different language functions like conative or expressive function in Table 1, where types of sound symbolism [1] have been listed. Adjacent to them, on the right hand side, we have added correspondent examples from our own Croatian corpora and assigned them with phonetic transcription, different language functions and English translation.

Table 1. Types of sound symbolism.

Type of Sound Symbolism	Croatian example with phonetic transcription	English equivalent	Language function
i. corporeal	*AAAAA!!* [aː]	aaarghhh!	Expressive
	auuuuuch [aʊtʃ]	ouuuuch	Expressive
	hihihihi [xixixixi]	hihihihi	Expressive
	iii? [iː]	aaaand?	Conative & phatic
	eeee! [eː]	heeey!	Conative & phatic
ii. imitative	*boooom!* [buːm]	booom!	Referential
	brm brm [br̩m]	vroom vroom	Referential
iii. synasthetic	*daaa* [daː]	yeees	Poetic
	puuuuno [puːno]	a loooot	Poetic
iv. conventional	*kmečati* [kmetʃati]	to whine	Referential & poetic
v. metalinguistic	*khm* [kʰəm]	cough	Metacoumunicational

That led to the following hypothesis:

H1: Use of sound symbolism balances two forces of language use: the tendency for language economy and the redundancy of the system. As a consequence, imitatives proliferate to ensure unobstructed information flow which is again ensured by balance of beforehand mentioned forces.

H2: Dominant usage of a visual channel in online communication led to a formation of compensatory techniques to convey meaning usually transferred by sound (face-to-face communication). That is seen in 'transliteration' of paralinguistic and extralinguistic cues into graphemes by the process of sound symbolism.

H3: Studied as a legitimate part of computer-mediated communication, sound symbolism isn't a marginal but a very fertile process of formation, production and communication of linguistic meaning. That misconception comes from the fact that its use is most prominent in the beginnings of signing activities until it gives to the social forces of conventionalization.

Goal of this paper is to point out to language creativity as a driving force of language development and evolution. To indicate that there are vast possibilities in the times we live in, because new communication technologies are giving us a chance to change perspective and look at the old problems from a different angle. On the other hand, diachronic research can also be employed effectively, since it is possible to observe ever faster language change fueled by quick advances in (communication) technology and context of living in general (globalization, multilingualism, heteroglossia).

In short, this paper will address the relevance of the topic of sound symbolism by using examples from Croatian online vernacular. As follows, its nature, classification, history as well as contemporary findings on sound symbolism will be discussed. Finally, imitatives will be distinguished on the bases of their origin, syllable structure and sound symbolism of their consonants.

2 Sound Symbolism

Since the classical period of the ancient Greece and Rome, a controversial topic of the arbitrariness of linguistic sign has been strongly discussed [2: 383a].

Many have followed in giving their views on the topic: from the very father of modern-day linguistics Ferdinand de Saussure, philosophers like Ludwig Wittgenstein (language games), Saul Kripke and Jean-Jacques Rousseau, all the way to writers and mathematicians, where one of the most famous would certainly be Lewis Caroll (nonsense literature). Each of the above mentioned authors have tried to grasp the very nature of natural language from their own perspective, but the axiom of linguistic structuralism became and remained an understanding of a phoneme as the smallest component of language structure which shapes meaning through its relations with other phonemes in the system, but does not have a specific meaning on its own.

Sound symbolism has been closely tied to beforehand mentioned problem of the arbitrary nature of linguistic sign, since it is in essence opposed to that idea. According to Nuckolls [3: 228] sound symbolism is a phenomenon in which an item like phoneme, syllable or a feature of prosody overcomes borders of making difference in meaning, but directly carries and has meaning (content). In other words, sound symbolism represents direct connection between sound and meaning which has generally been seen as an exception to the rule and has been a subject of interest in very narrow and specialized subfields of language production (e.g. poetry). Standing on ontological grounds, some authors like Friedrich [4] go that far in saying that language without sound symbolism would be as impossible as existence without a culture. Today, more and more studies appear on the topic of sound symbolism and they have reopened some old questions (e.g. [5–8]), on the other hand the rapid growth of communication technologies has given a new perspective on the yet unsolved puzzles.

Taking into account both sides of the previous debate, Hinton, et al. [1: 2] suggest a scalar representation of language utterances concerning the degree of motivation. If their assumption is correct, one pole of the scale will represent utterances formed in the process of sound symbolism, which will then travel to the opposite pole of arbitrariness through everyday usage and social convention. This inspired authors to think of a classification of different types of sound symbolism, in which corporeal sound symbolism would be the most motivated type, then comes imitative, synaesthetic, conventional and most arbitrary would be metalinguistic (see Fig. 1).

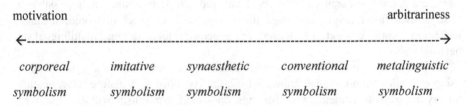

Fig. 1. Scalar representation of symbolism

Considering that this classification will be taken into account during the analysis, later it will be explained in detail and underpinned by examples from our original corpora in Croatian. Furthermore, each example will be joined with its language function during communication exchange, as well as the description of phonetic characteristics of imitatives in Croatian language used in online communication.

3   Contemporary Research and Theoretical Study

Practical research as well as the heuristic theorizing on the topic of sound symbolism can be divided into several different categories.

First group of research compiles studies of intonation patterns in languages. Their main concern is the fundamental frequency (F0) which determends the perception of a voice pitch (tone), and if changed it makes distinctions in meaning of an utterance. As many authors have noticed [9, 10], a wide variety of languages employ increasing of the fundamental frequency to transform statement into a question. It has also been proven that high F0 is being used to express politeness and sympathy towards one's interlocutor, or quite the opposite: by lowering the pitch of F0, people express aggression, anger or threat [11].

The second group of research deals with language patterns used to express size, magnitude or scope, for that very reason sometimes it's been referred to as *Magnitude Sound Symbolism* [3: 231]. The main idea in the background of this type of research lies in the assumption that languages categorize sounds accordingly to the size of what they represent. Following that strain of though, Ohala [12, 13] provides the examples of words and morphemes from various languages which convey the meaning of 'big' (usage of low, back vocals and of grave, voiced consonants with a low pitch) or the ones which represent 'smallness' (usage of high, front vocals and acute, voiceless consonants of high(er) pitch).

More general linguistic approaches have aimed to fathom whether there is an universal sound symbolism or is it a language-specific phenomenon. Final answer hasn't yet been agreed upon, but arguments for sound symbolism as a linguistic universal [14–16] as well as the ones against it [17, 18] have been introduced.

Fourth group of research in sound symbolism deals with synaesthesia. The very word synaesthesia comes from Greek σύν + αἴσθησις, which literally means 'joined perception'. In other words, stimulation of one specific sense (e.g. smell) will activate another or various other sensory experiences (e.g. hearing). Simply put then, synaesthetes can see sound (apart from only hearing it) or can taste colours and so on. First legitimate research concerning this topic has begun in the 19th century, but only with the rise of modern technology have the scientists managed to successfully prove its objective existence (PET scan, fMRI). Nowadays it has been widely accepted that synaesthesia is a sensory and perceptual process caused by enhanced and atypical communication among specific brain regions and not by memory (which was previously hypothesized). Majority of authors agree that the most common type of synaesthesia is triggered by lexical stimuli such as numbers, letters and words [19–23], and that brings us into the domain of psycho and neurolinguistics, semiology and cognitive studies. For instance Jakobson and Waugh [24] debate on evidence for intersensory compatibilities and overlap between acoustic characteristics of spoken sounds and chromatic differences (light vs. dark). They've proven that acute sounds are correspondent to light, whereas grave join with dark. This topic will be addressed later on in more detail while discussing a synaesthetic type of sound symbolism.

Finally, from all of the above listed subtypes of research on sound symbolism, one key and quite eternal question emerges: does sound symbolism have any connection to natural language origin, and if it does: what is the nature of this relationship? Today there is relatively small amount of general theories on sound symbolism in that sense, but one of the exceptions would certainly be Ohala's *Frequency Code Hypothesis* [13]. In it the author suggests biologically grounded theory according to which each pronounced sound has a fundamental frequency (F0) that is (inversely) connected to the expression of size of communicator.[1] This theory also suggests the relationship among sound symbolism and types of vocals, consonants, tones and intonation and it presupposes innateness which is activated by the environment and is not limited to human species exclusively.

4 Imitatives

Imitative words, also known as onomatopoeic, expressive or echoing expressions make up a separate group of words, which (in Croatian language and many others) does not have clearly defined borders. This vagueness of imitative word category is a result of beforehand mentioned (epistemological) circumstances and is typical for many other languages in the Indo-European family, especially those spread in the West. Nevertheless, some of the languages do lexicalize imitative expressions and they are recognized under the name of ideophones[2]. Doke [25: 118] defined them for the first time

---

[1] For more details see Ohala [13: 340, 341].

[2] Largest corpora of work concerning ideophones as a discrete word category can be found in studies on African languages [3: 239]. Also, there are studies on ideophones in some Asian languages (Dravidian, Sanskrit, Bengali, Korean, Viatnamese, Japanese), South American (Caribean, Ge, Tupi-guarani, Quetchua), Australian and North American.

as colourful realizations of ideas in a form of sounds. In languages where ideophones are well developed word category, their use can be seen in many different contexts (e.g. emotional, colloquial), mostly they can be compared with adverbs, but sometimes they are more similar to modal particles, nouns or adjectives. According to Oswalt [26: 293] imitative is an approximate realization of some non-linguistic sound which has been adjusted to a phonological system of a particular language. He goes further by suggesting the division of imitative expressions into three subcategories (which will be employed in the following analysis): animate, inanimate and expressive. Animate/inanimate distinction refers to the origin of imitated expression (e.g. human, mammal, bird vs. sound of glass cracking or an explosion), whereas expressive imitatives convey emotional states and attitudes.

After introducing the domain of new media in the following passage, as it is a context and a channel of contemporary communication, the goal will be to provide a clear picture of the case of imitatives in Croatian online vernacular.

5 Computer-Mediated Communication as a Context of Research

Defined quite broadly, communication can be perceived as transference of messages from one person to another [27: 69]. In addition, communication processes can unroll on various different levels: intrapersonal, interpersonal, public (communication between social groups, institutions and individuals in public sphere), mass communication (one-way, monologic communication with large auditorium but unique source, e.g. tv or radio) and hyperpersonal[3] (a type of interpersonal communication characteristic for CMC which provides its users with more opportunities for strategic identity development through manipulation of self-presentation).

Computer-mediated discourse is a form of communication which emerges when people interact via networked computers. This type of discourse (defined in regards to the channel and the medium) gathers all types of interpersonal as well as public[4] communication performed online: from e-mails, chats, statuses, commentaries, blogs etc. Research in CMD is a part of a wider interdisciplinary field of Computer-mediated communication. Susan Herring [29: 612] defines it as any type of communication exchange realized by means of two or more networked computers. Studies in this field mainly deal with influences of computer-enhanced technologies on sign systems (like language) and on social relations.

---

[3] Term introduced by Joseph B. Walther [28: 3–43] designating a type of communication which appears to be more desirable than face-to-face communication and which is radically different than other forms of communication in four main characteristics: idealization of the sender's perceived image, easier and meticulously elaborated identity performance, easier impression manipulation as a result of asynchronous communication channels and direct feedback which increases a feeling of closeness in interaction.

[4] Borders between different levels of communication have been blurred by the 3rd revolution of literacy, in other words by the uprise of computer technologies and digital media.

Applying methods and theoretical models from various disciplines, this area of research has shown that it is profoundly multidisciplinary in its character. For instance, from a sociopsychological point of view, authors have investigated ways in which individuals use computer technologies in interpersonal relations and everyday interaction (e.g. identity formation, obtaining, maintainingand performing social rolesetc.) On the other hand, investigations have been made concerning the use of paralanguage (e.g. emoticons), phonology, morphology, syntax and pragmatics in this type of communicative practice, as well as employing Computer-mediated discourse analysis.

As it is obvious from previous subheadings and introduction, this paper won't step merely into the domain of phonetics and phonology, language philosophy and pragmatics, but also into the context of computer-mediated discourse in a form of chat and into the realm of semiotics.

6 Differentiae Specificae of Online Communication

Some of the tools of computer-mediated communication are necessary (*conditiones sine quibus non*) for its proper functioning and are exclusively attached only to it (as a specific subtype of communicative action). These mechanisms come into existence if the information they convey comes only from that source (without any help of context, co-text, possible interpretation, etymology and so on). Following that strain of thought, Kalman and Gergle [30: 187] defined them as adjustments of online messages which subsequently change the meaning of those messages inside a social sign system, leaving the form and the rearrangement of the very expression intact. Furthermore, literature as well as practice clearly shows that there are three main types of interest in the area of online communication: first one deals with the topic of chronemics[5], second with emoticons and the third one with paralanguage of the Internet. First two groups of research have been given a lot of attention in the last decade, but in this paper we shall be dealing with a less explored the topic of paralanguage.

Carey [31] was the first scientist, one of the pioneers in paralinguistics of computer-mediated communication, who singled out and defined its main characteristics/mechanisms listed in Table 2. The examples in brackets have been taken from our own corpora.

If one should employ Carey's categorization in the following analysis of imitative words (as we shall), attention should be steered in the way of vocal surrogates, vocal spelling (which conveys rhythm, speed and intonation) as well as manipulation of grammatical markers (volume, intonation, attitude).

---

[5] Studying the function, perception and the role of time in communication.

Table 2. Characteristics of computer-mediated communication (according to [31])

i. vocal spelling	*pliiiiiz* [pli:z]	pleaseee
ii. lexical (like stage directions in a play) & vocal surrogates	*hmmmm* [xə:m]	hmmmm
iii. spatial arrays (using extra spaces between graphemes in order to 'spell it out', arranging letters into a picture)	*n e ž e l i m i ć i*	I d o n' t w a n t t o g o
iv. manipulation of grammatical markers (excessive use of question/exclamation marks, unusual use of capitalization)	*ZAŠTO?!?!*	WHY?!?!
v. minus features (absence of some features of the text)	*not correcting spelling errors*	

7   Method and Analysis of CMC – Sound Symbolism and Its Functions

Analysis has been made on chat history logs which can be defined as saved, static notes of exchanged messages in their original form and order [32]. Recorded conversations came in a form of a dialogue and occurred between male and female interlocutors, from 26 to 36 years of age. All the participants have known each other in their personal lives, and the type of their relationships can be defined in terms of friendship.[6]

Corpora for the analysis is comprised from five hundred (N = 500) dialogues, but because of the spatial/temporal constraints of the paper and nature of qualitative types of researches, here we will show only the most representative examples. All dialogues in the corpora have occurred completely spontaneously and were not influenced in any way by the observer and/or analyst. During the message interchange, the participants of the ongoing conversations did not know that their chat logs will subsequently undergo this analysis.[7]

Criteria which led us to properly choose between large amounts of material are typical for qualitative type of research. Instead of probabilistic and convenient sampling which undergo statistical analysis as a whole, in this study we have employed purposive (deliberate) sampling led by formal and functional criteria that needed to be satisfied and which are discussed in the following text.

---

[6] Participants gave their consent for the subsequent analysis of those dialogues for the purposes of this study. But to ensure their anonimity, in the examples we have used only initials of their nicknames.

[7] This is also applied to the author of this text, as one of the participants of analysed conversations, who only subsequently decided to take a role of an analyst and an interpretor of data.

7.1 Formal Criteria

Formal criteria have been taken from Carey's classification of paralinguistic mechanisms of computer-mediated communication, and are as follows
    vocal spelling (e.g. *pliiiz, boooom*)
    vocal surrogates (e.g. *hmm, khm*)
    manipulation of grammatical markers (e.g. *AAAAAA!!!*)[8]

7.2 Functional Criteria

Functional criteria include all subtypes of sound symbolism and language functions which correspond to those types. The list is as follows

i. *Corporeal sound symbolism*
   Its main language function is expressive because these types of utterances usually refer to emotional and physical state of a speaker. This category includes non-intentional, non-volatile (symptomatic) sounds like coughing or hiccups, intonation, sound quality, exclamations, vocatives (cry for help, crying) and turn taking signals.

ii. *Imitative sound symbolism*
    Its primary language function is referential, because it is associated with onomatopoeic words or expressions which represent sounds from an extra-linguistic context (environment). Languages often use this type in order to express movement (rhythm is transformed to rhythmical movement/dance and vice versa) and are very frequently using the strategy of linguistic reduplication.

iii. *Synaesthetic sound symbolism*
     It is a subtype of sound symbolism with poetic or aesthetic function as its primary one. Simply put, it is an acoustic representation of a non-acoustic event.

iv. *Conventional sound symbolism*
    Its primal role is referential. It is based upon analogy made between certain phonemes or phoneme clusters with specific meanings (phonesthemes[9]): e.g. *klimati (*wobble*), klizati (*slide*), klecati (*totter*), klatiti (*dangle*), klonuti (*droop, languish*)*, where phoneme cluster [kl-] points to a feeling of instability, uncertainty. Phonoesthemes in English would for example be: *glint, gleam, glow, glance, glare*, wherein [gl-] represents a phonoestheme which pertains to light and vision. This type of sound symbolism can be often observed in the naming process of commercial products, because it can successfully make a connection between sound and meaning even though it hasn't really existed before (by employing association and analogy).

---

[8] For translation and phonetic transcription look in Tables 1 and 2.

[9] Phonesthemes are defined as phonemes or phoneme clusters which are thought to be appropriate to convey a specific content. Research concerning the topic of phonaesthesia is most plentiful in the domain of English language. Then again, English as a language with quite humble morphology puts into question the very existence of phonesthemes, as well as the possibility of their classification under a special class of morphemes.

v. *Metalinguistic/metacommunicative sound symbolism*

A subtype of sound symbolism with metacommunicative function as primary, where choices of phonemes and intonation patterns point to different aspects of language structure and function. One of the most famous examples of this subtype is usage of phonemes, neutralization, abstract structural forms and accents to distinguish borders between words [33]. In Croatian language, metacommunicative type is very prominent and can be seen in the examples of shouting (capital lettering) where the acoustic form of speech got adjusted to its (expressive) communicative function. There are also examples of elongation of final vocals in vocatives (conative function).

7.3 Criteria of Syllable Structure and the Source of Imitated Sound

For our final criteria we have chosen the distinction of imitative words and expressions on the basis of their origin and canonical syllable structure. These criteria are the following:

i. animate – imitated sound has originally been produced by a living entity and its canonical syllable structure is (S_1)-VV^{10},

ii. inanimate – imitated sound has originally been produced by a non-living object (very often with a help of a living being) and its syllable structure comes in the form of $C_1V(V)C_2$,

iii. expressive – imitated sounds expresses emotional state, attitude and often comes in a form of an exclamation: VV-(C_2).

Examples which allowed it have been supplemented with dimension of diachrony by employing etymology. All data has been collected from personal chat history logs. Conversations analyzed have been conducted via three different applications: *Facebook Messenger*, *WhatsApp* and *Hangouts*.

Example no 1

First example shown is (1) meets the following criteria.

Manipulation of grammatical markers manifested in terms of excessive use of punctuation (exclamation marks) and unusual use of capital lettering in order to convey loudness.

Vocal spelling is manifested as continued repetition of the same vocal (as if put on a string) to convey the unobstructed flow and lasting duration of a sound or a tone.

Example shows a corporeal subtype of sound symbolism, whose primary language function is expressive.[11]

---

[10] S-sonant, C-consonant, V-vocal.

[11] Caveat lector: every subtype of sound symbolism, as well as their corresponding language functions are ideal types. In practice we can usually see hybrid forms of messages which include all functions of language and a mixture of different subtypes of sound symolism. Nevertheless, the most pominent type is considered to be dominant.

This is an example of an expressive imitative with its characteristic syllable structure: complex vocalic nucleus (VV) [a:] which can sometimes be followed by one consonant.[12]

(1)

Croatian original	English version
J: kak je bilo sinoć	**J:** how was it last night
T: tak da sam gladan	**T:** it made me hungry
jako	seriously
i sad ću pizdit!!!! AAAAAA	and now I'm gonna lose my mind!!! AAAAAA

Example no 2

In this example it is possible to analyze several different traits.

Manipulating grammatical markers can be seen again in unusual usage of capitalization in order to convey loudness (shouting).

In this case we have an example of metacommunicative sound symbolism which employs expressive imitatives because its purpose is to communicate an attitude or emotional state of the speaker.

In the final line of the dialogue one can again notice vocal spelling (*uuu*), which is an expressive imitative, has expressive language function and is an example of corporeal sound symbolism (vocalization as a result of pleasure) which gradually got conventionalized and transformed itself into imitative and finally into metacommunicative symbolism. Vocalic nucleus here is also complex: VV, in other words we have an elongated vowel [u:]

(2)

Croatian Original	English version
T: najbolji je	**T:** he's the best
joj kako razvaljuje	oh he's killin' it
SVAKI PUT!!	EVERY SINGLE TIME!!
J: uuu da, on je izvrstan	**J:** ooooh yes, he's marvelous

Example no 3

Word *boom* [bu: m] shown is (3) is an example of vocal spelling (very frequent and typical for comics), also there is an excessive use of exclamation marks (manipulation of grammatical markers). Besides that we can see lexical surrogates which are used to describe the surrounding context of communication and its modality (e.g. "…sad je evo sunce došlo…").

According to Oswalt's classification of imitative expressions, *boom* should be categorized under the inanimate imitative expressions, nevertheless it is not the case here. Here we actually have a case of an animate imitative which is based upon a metaphor with an inanimate type.

---

[12] See example 5.

Inanimate imitatives are usually monosyllabic, but their canonical syllable structure radically differs from the ones of animate and expressive imitatives. It is comprised from consonantal onset, vocalic nucleus (complex or not) and consonantal coda: $C_1V(V)C_2$. Consonants comprising the onset usually come from the group of obstruents (fricatives, affricates, plosives), whilst the onset of animate and expressive imitative (if there is any to begin with) is made out of sonorants (or resonant such as nasals, semivowels and liquids). Finally, coda of inanimate imitatives can be constructed with both obstruents as well as sonorants and the latter has been depicted in our example.

Etymological dictionary of Croatian language [34: 96] instructs us to consult foreign literature such as the Oxford English Dictionary [35: 391]. It informs us that *boom* is a loud, low frequency sound with very strong resonance or a murmur sound effect, at times resembling the sound of a cannon coming from afar. In much more rare occasions *boom* is used to imitate the sound of an Eurasian bittern, a bird belonging to a subfamily of herons.

(3)

Croatian original	English version
T: eksplodirat ću!	**T:** i'm gonna explode!
sad evo i sunce došlo	even the sun started to show now
kuham leću s patlidžanom!	i'm cooking lentils with eggplant!
boooom!	boooom!
J: ja tu kao neš čitam i zapisujem,	**J:** i'm like reading something and taking
ajme eksplodirat ćeš od te leće i patlidžana	notes, oh man, you're really gonna explode
T: boooooooooom!!!!	from lentils and eggplant
	T: boooooooooom!!!!

Example no 4

Imitative expression in (4) bring about several novelties. Besides vocal spelling (repetition of a vowel i) and excessive use of punctuation (question marks) with phatic and conative language function, there is an example of a vocal surrogate (*hihihihi*). This example clearly shows a subtype of imitative sound symbolism which evolved from a corporeal type (human laughter), its language function is expressive and the source of imitated sound is animate but also expressive. The strategy of syllable [xi] reduplication has been used. At times, this imitative comes in an inverted form [ixixixix] whose syllable structure corresponds to a prototype representative of animate and expressive imitative category.

Etymologically we can connect this imitative with a verb *to giggle* (cro. *hihotati*) which has been derived from beforehand mentioned imitative. Etymological dictionary of Croatian language [34: 324] also suggests that it is a matter of an onomatopoeic word similarly formed in Russian *xoxot*, Slovenian *hihitati se*, *hohotati se* in a sense of thunderous laughter.

Finally the expression *brm brm brm* exemplifies imitative subtype of sound symbolism with an inanimate origin, an expressive language function and a strategy of (syllable) reduplication. Syllable structure of the expression comes in prototypical form of C_1VC_2, comprised from a plosive in the onset, vocalic nucleus formed by vocalic r and a sonorant in the coda.

(4)

Croatian original	English version
J: iii??	**J:** aaaand??
kaj radiš	what ya doin'?
T: tu neš po kompu	**T:** something on my computer
J: kupuješ neš	**J:** are you buying something
hihihihihi	hihihihihi
ili kamione gledaš	or browsing the trucks
T: naručujem mladenku	**T:** i'm ordering a bride
J: mladenku s kamionom iz istočne Europe	**J:** a bride with a dowry in a form of a truck
al taj bi mogo trošit	but be careful, they could both spend too much
T: to bi bilo brm brm brm	**T:** that would be vroom vroom vroom

Example no 5

In the following example shown in (5), you can notice the expression *auch* [aʊʧ] as a great representative of its category of corporeal sound symbolism. Although we can infer from the context that here we actually have a more conventional type of sound symbolism, an imitative sound symbolism which evolved from the previous type and has absorbed some metacommunicative functions.

Its source of origin is animate and expressive, while its spelling is partially borrowed from the English language (*ch* instead of *č*). Syllable pattern of this word is comprised from complex vocalic nucleus (VV) in a form of a diphthong [au] and consonantal coda made out of an affricate [ʧ]. Presupposition that it has historically evolved out of more rudimentary exclamation *au* connects it to the scalar nature of sound symbolism.

Furthermore, the lengthening of a vowel *o* in a word *nešto* is a result of its conative language function and usually it can be found in vocatives and exclamatory expressions. Besides from that, from this expression one can decode an emotional state of his/her interlocutor, which is attenuated by an expressive language function.

(5)

Croatian original	English version
T: zrezo sam se, i čekam da prestane	**T:** i cut myself and now i'm waiting
J: kaj	for it to stop bleeding
na šta, gdje?	**J:** what how, where?
T: nožem	**T:** with a knife
J: opet	**J:** again
T: prst	**T:** a finger
J: kad si ga tak nabrusio luđački	**J:** because you sharpened it
auch	like a crazy person ouch
i kaj onda, ak ne odem van? oćeš da dođem k tebi?	so, if i don't go out, should
oćeš bit doma? daj reci neštoooooooo!!!!!	i come at your place?
T: neznaaaaaaaaaaaaam!	are you gonna be at home?
	say somethiiiiiing!!!
	T: i don't knoooooooooow!

Example no 6

Imitative expression *buuuuuuu* shown in (6) again brings about an opportunity for diachrony. It was (and still can be) an exclamation used for scaring someone or to evoke an ominous, eerie, frightening atmosphere. Later on it obtained an additional meaning. Etymology suggests that it has first appeared in the early 15th century as a part of English language (*booh* or *boo*), as a combination of bilabial voiced plosive and close (high) back, rounded vowels [u:]. Some authors suggest[13] a connection between beforehand discussed exclamation and a Latin word *boare* meaning to roar, shout, whose etymology is in turn related to Greek word Βορέας: the northern wind, in Croatian known as *bura*. That brings us to a suggest that the exclamation could have emerged from imitation of surrounding sounds, such as the sound of the wind howling and with it carrying the sense of dread and discomfort. On the other hand, some presume the existence of a noun **búrja* in Proto-Slavic language [34:94], meaning severe weather, a storm, and its origin is connected to one of anger or *furor* in Latin.

At the beginning of the 19th century, *bu!* has entered use as a form of disagreement, disapproval. For that reason it has excessively been employed in the sphere of public communication: in theatres or political gatherings in order to hoot the ones of different opinion, ideological stance or to express discontent. Here we have a change in etymology, some presume it is related to the vocalizations (lowing) of oxen [35:391].

Considering sound symbolism typology, this example can be seen as an imitative subtype which has gradually evolved into a more conventionalized type.

In the analysis as well as the interpretation of the syllable structure of this imitative, it is necessary to etymology again. In the case of *buuuu* it is a matter of an imitative of inanimate origin (e.g. the wind howling) which has an onset comprised from a plosive, nucleus is vocalic, but the coda is non-existant, and that doesn't coincide with the

---

[13] **For detailed information consult** *Oxford Dictionary of English* **[36], Kindle edition and** *Oxford English Dictionary (1989)*, **Oxford: OUP [35].**

syllable pattern of C_1VC_2. Nevertheless it is possible that at some point in history the deletion of the final sound could have occurred, but to make that claim further investigation is needed. If we would to rely on a later version of this very word, as well as its usage and origin, it would be possible to categorize it under the animate imitative which usually have sonorants (resonant) in their onset. That would indeed be correct if the word in question would be [mu:] as a sound which a cow makes, but it is food for thought in the least since both phonemes [b] and [m] are produced in a different manner but at the same place (both are bilabial) of articulation.

(6)

Croatian original	English version

T: e
    kaj briješ?
J: prepao si me
T: buuuuuuuu
J: ostao mi komp iz nekog razloga ful glasno,
    tu sam se zabuljila u neki papir :P
	T: hey
	    what you're up to?
	J: you startled me
	T: booooooo
	J: for some reason the volume on my pc was
	    left pumped while my mind wandered off
	    staring at some piece of paper :P

Example no 7
In the final example seen in (7), in all of the highlighted places vocal spelling is present as well as elongation of the final vowel (characteristic of vocatives and their phatic, sometimes expressive language function).

The most interesting piece of this example would certainly be the imitative word *kme*. The expression is a more conventional form of an imitative sound symbolic subtype, with an animate origin and an expressive language function. Following the logic of the scalar nature of sound symbolism leads to an inference that the imitative subtype developed out of corporeal one: a sound of human crying which has adjusted to a phonological system of Croatian language. Also, reduplicated versions of this expression are quite common (e.g. *kme kme*).

Syllabic pattern of this word is atypical for imitatives of animate origin because the onset is complex, it is formed from a consonant and a sonorant: C_1S_1-, or [km]. On the other hand complex vocalic nucleus is present as it should be: -VV or [e:].

Etymological dictionary of Croatian language does not mention the word *kme*, but it records the verb *kmečati* [34: 454] highlighting its onomatopoeic origin, its wide spread usage from coastal regions (Brač) to the continental ones (Varaždin), as well as the first registred usage of the verb in the 17th century.

(7)

Croatian original	English version
J: komarci me napadajuuuuuu!!	J: mosquitos are attackiiiiiing meeeee!!!
nevjerojatno	unbelieveable
T: for real?	T: for real?
J: daaaaa	J: yessss
tu mi je u sobi	it's here in my room
T: tak ti i treba!	T: serves you right!
nek te pika	you should get stung
J: a da sad	J: yeah right, easy for you to say
kmeeee	sob sob

8 Symbolism of Croatian Consonants and Resonants (Sonorants)

As you could have observed throughout the previous examples, symbolism of consonants and sonorants is very important. Their manner of articulation causes their acoustic and consequently symbolic properties: that is why we have different types of phonemes used in different types of imitative.

When speaking about consonants it is necessary to consider fricatives, plosives and affricates.

Plosives or occlusives [p, t, k, b, d, g][14], defined by Jelaska [37: 47] are sounds formed by blockage (occlusion) of the airflow, which is then suddenly and completely released in the way that the articulatory organs get widely separated. The result of this manner of articulation is a short and abrupt sound representing short, discontinuous, intermittent, quick sounds and actions when present in the syllable onset (e.g. *tup, brm, kuc* meaning *thump, vroom, knock*).

Fricatives (in Croatian language) [z, ʒ, s, ʃ, f, x] are sound formed in a manner that articulatory organs make a narrow passage for the airflow, which goes through by making friction (hence the name). Because of the nature of their formation they are sounds that vividly convey the impression of friction and turbulence and consequently symbolize that type of actions or emotions (e.g. *fiju, hihihihi*).

Affricates are [ts, tʃ, tɕ, dʒ, dz] sounds begin as plosives but end as fricatives (at first the airflow is completely blocked but sudden release of the airflow happens by only narrow, not wide separation of the articulators. Although they are similar to plosives, the murmur in the affricates is so short that it is usually considered a part of the occlusion. As well as the other subtypes of consonants, sound qualities they produce convey the qualities of actions, states and occurrences they represent (e.g. *ccc*[15], *šuć-muć, čin-čin* translated to English *skimble-scamble, chin-chin*).

---

[14] Consult the IPA chart with sounds for pronounciation.

[15] Expression typical for online discourse, representing clucking sounds made with a tongue in a sense of disapproval, criticism, ridicule or irony. It is the same as in English, from which it probably originated.

Resonants or sonorants can be devided into two subtypes in Croatian language: nasals [m, n, ɲ] and approximants [v, r, l, ʎ, j]. Jelaska [37: 42] says that they are extremely resonant and are formed in a manner of closely approaching or gently touching speech organs, so that the airflow has a partial passage.

Nasals are formed by lowering of a soft palate (velum) which makes the passage for the airflow through the nasal cavity, whilst the passage through the mouth is closed completely. Their resonance and nasality convey sounds, actions and emotions of the similar qualities (e.g. *kme, hnje, mu, njam* translated to English *sob, blah, moo, nom*).

Approximates are formed by narrowly placed speech organs, slightly or more, so that the airflow has enough space not to produce any noise. As a very prominent representative of this group is a semivowel *j:* formed by sliding of the tongue from one position to another (e.g. *jao, ej, ijuijuiju* translated to English *yikes, hey, yeey*) and because of that it is used in imitative of an animate and expressive origin. Labiodental sonorant *v* is quite rare in computer-mediated communication imitative, and usually gives way to another semivowel *w*, although here it is possible to suggest the influence of English language (e.g. *mua → mwa, vau → wow*).

Liquid consonants are yet another subgroup of sonorants and can be divided into lateral approximants [l, ʎ] and trills [r]. These are sounds formed by the tip of a tongue lifted towards the gums (e.g. alveolar ridge for *r*), but the airflow is unobstructed. The fact that these sounds are known as liquid consonants corresponds to the meaning of what they usually represent (e.g. *pljas, bljak, mljac* conveying *the sound of splatter, sensation of disgust –ew!, and the munchies* as the opposite). Finally, Croatian trill *r* is formed by vibrating of a tongue or an uvula due to the difference in the surrounding air pressure. Because of the impression of vibration this sound usually conveys similar meanings or sensations (e.g. *brm* or *brrrrm, arrrrgh*). In cases like *brm*, trill *r* functions as a syllabic/vocalic consonant [r̩].

9 Future Prospects and New Possibilities

This paper has aimed to show and interpret data which is qualitative in its nature, but it can additionally be supplemented with quantitative research. These informations can be gained with the help of corpus linguistics which could provide a statistical analysis on a larger corpora like Croatian national corpus, or smaller ('do-it-yourself') corpora made by sampling history logs of past communication. That would give an insight into frequency of use of various types of sound symbolism in different spheres and levels of human communication.

Diachrony of sound symbolism also has a potential for more detailed inspection, but it demands a multidisciplinary approach (e.g. cooperation between dialectology, linguistic anthropology, phonetics, semiology etc.) This type of research could bring about, reopen the debate on the origins of natural language, its fundamental properties and connection to other sign systems as it was sketched previously. Moreover, comparative studies on imitatives amongst Croatian and other (Balto-) Slavic languages would be of great value if they would provide us with data on similarities, differences and their causal connections.

Finally, domination and growing influence of English language as a contemporary *lingua franca* is especially visible in global and online communication, so it mustn't be overlooked. Here it is possible to gain more data with the help of contact linguistics studying so called *croenglish* (a mix of Croatian online vernacular with English), for which some of the examples have been shown in the article (e.g. Croatian *auč* + English *ouch* fused into *auch*). And last, but certainly not the least is a possibility for cooperation with the IT experts which could result in improvement of communication technologies (e.g. word recognition softwares), while linguists could get more information on the ever changing nature and pragmatism of language.

It can open a space for transdisciplinary study of music and language with both linguistic as well as musicologist contributions.

10   Conclusions

Internet as a communication media reveals new information on language-in-use. It doesn't necessarily cause them, but it highlights them because of the change in perspective provided by new technologies. Detailed inspection of sound symbolism has exemplified the phenomenon of language creativity, elasticity/plasticity and lively character of language, especially in the domain of everyday language use and the examples in Croatian language which are still quite scarce.

On the basis of conducted analysis it is possible to claim that main characteristics of Croatian imitatives are: differences in canonical syllable patterns and acoustic properties between imitative words of different origin (animate, inanimate, expressive). Also the capacity to carry out every type of language function (expressive, conative, phatic, poetic, metalinguistic and referential) and their pragmatic value seen in paralinguistics of CMC (because of the limitations of specific communication channels). That confirmed the H1 because successful use of sound symbolism balances the tendency towards language economy and the necessity for redundancy. As a result of those forces there is a proliferation of imitative expression in discourse which ensure better information flow.

Etymology supports the theses on the scalar nature of linguistic sign, in regard to the level of arbitrariness (suggested by [1]). Dominant thoughts on the main traits and functioning of contemporary languages suggest that in the majority of cases the link between signifier and signified is arbitrary, but (a big one!) the nature of that link is a result of *consensus social* which emerged from a pragmatic necessity: successful and effective communication. Moreover, examples have suggested that origins of (surprisingly) many expressions have sound symbolic background, which is supported by evidence form etymological dictionaries and their morphonological investigations. It could easily be inferred that sound symbolism emerges at the beginnings of signing activities (be it evolutionary, developmentally (children) or contextually induced (new technologies and social structures) but later on it gets conventionalized through time and usage. If we look at it that way, online communication can be seen as a new type of signing activity induced by changes in the context which started of in a very libertarian way, just like the Internet itself. With time it is getting more conventionalized, which can be noticed in efforts to compile netspeak dictionaries or in ever growing multimodality (combining pictures, melodies and writing) in order to make communication easier. Besides from that, it has been shown that imitatives compensate for paralinguistic features absent in solely visual channel which supports our second hypothesis (H2).

Furthermore, hypothesis 3 (H3) was also confirmed because sound symbolism has been exemplified as a very fruitful process of meaning formation and transference. Etymology has supported that by accentuating the evolutive dynamics of social semiotic systems. In order to support these findings, statistical analysis of data collected through a wider stretch of time would be helpful.

There is a choice to be made between semiotic systems in which we wish our ideas to get realized and communicated. But that choice depends on the semantics and the intention behind the message. If we bear in mind that language and music do have some similarities, we believe that studying sound symbolism makes a great starting point for music-language interface.

References

1. Hinton, L., Nichols, J., Ohala, J.J.: Sound Symbolism. CUP, Cambridge (1994). https://doi.org/10.1017/cbo9780511751806
2. Platon: Kratil. Translated by Vladimir Filipović. Zagreb: Studentski centar (1979)
3. Nuckolls, J.B.: The case for sound symbolism. Ann. Rev. Anthropol. **28**, 225–252 (1999). Birmingham, Alabama: Annual Reviews. https://doi.org/10.1146/annurev.anthro.28.1.225
4. Friedrich, P.: The symbol and its relative nonarbitrariness. In: Friedrich, P. (ed.) Language, Context, and Imagination: Essays by Paul Friedrich. Stanford University Press, Stanford (1979)
5. Reichard, G.A.: Prayer: The Complusive Word. Monographs of American Ethnological Society, vol. 7. University of Washington Press, Seattle (1944)
6. Witherspoon, G.: Language and Art in the Navajo Universe. Michigan University Press, Ann Arbor (1977). https://doi.org/10.3998/mpub.9705
7. Feld, S.: Sound and Sentiment: Birds, Weeping, Poetics, and Song in Kaluli Expression. University of Pennsylvania Press, Philadephia (1982). https://doi.org/10.2307/40240027
8. Feld, S.: Waterfalls of song: an acoustemology of place resounding in Bosavi, Papua New Guinea. In: Basso, K.H., Feld, S. (eds.) Senses of Place. School of American Research advanced seminar series, Santa Fe (1996)
9. Hermann, E.: Probleme der Frage. Nachrichten von der Academie der Wissenschaften in Göttingen. Philologische-Historische Klasse, nr. ¾ (1942)
10. Bolinger, D.: Intonation across languages. In: Greeberg, J.H., Ferguson, Ch.A., Moravcsik, E.A. (eds.) Universals of Human Language, Phonology. vol. 2. Stanford University Press, Stanford (1978)
11. Ching, M.K.L.: The question intonation in assertions. Am. Speech **57**, 95–107 (1982). https://doi.org/10.2307/454443
12. Ohala, J.J.: An ethological perspective on common cross – language utilization of F0 of voice. Phonetica **41**, 1–16 (1984). https://doi.org/10.1159/000261706
13. Ohala, J.J.: The frequency code underlies the sound-symbolic use of voice pitch. In: Hinton, L., Nichols, J., Ohala, J.J. (eds.), Sound Symbolism. CUP, Cambridge (1994). https://doi.org/10.1017/cbo9780511751806.022

14. Brown, R.W., Black, A.H., Horowitz, A.E.: Phonetic symbolism in natural languages. J. Abnorm. Soc. Psychol. **50**, 388–393 (1955). https://doi.org/10.1037/h0046820

15. Gebels, G.: An investigation of phonetic symbolism in different cultures. J. Verbal Learn. Verbal Behav. **8**(2), 310–312 (1969). https://doi.org/10.1016/S0022-5371(69)80083-6

16. Miron, M.S.: A cross-linguistic investigation of phonetic symbolism. J. Abrnomal Soc. Psychol. **62**, 623–630 (1961). https://doi.org/10.1037/h0045212

17. Taylor, I.K.: Phonetic symbolism reexamined. Psychol. Bull. **60**(2), 200–209 (1963). https://doi.org/10.1037/h0040632

18. Taylor, I.K., Taylor, M.M.: Another look at phonetic symbolism. Psychol. Bull. **64**(6), 413–427 (1965). https://doi.org/10.1037/h0022737

19. Baron-Cohen, S., Burt, L., Smith-Laittan, F., Harrison, J., Bolton, P.: Synaesthesia: prevalince and familiarity. Perception **25**, 1073–1079 (1996). https://doi.org/10.1068/p251073

20. Cytowic, R.E.: The Man Who Tasted Shapes. Putnam, New York (1993)

21. Day, S.: Some demographic and socio-cultural aspects of synaesthesia. In: Robertson, L.C., Sagiv, N. (eds.) Synaesthesia: Perspectives from Cognitive Neuroscience. Oxford University Press, New York (2005)

22. Rich, A.N., Bradshaw, J.L., Mattingley, J.B.: A systematic, large-scale study of synaesthesia: implications for the role of early experience in lexical-colour associations. Cognition **98**, 53–84 (2005). https://doi.org/10.1016/j.cognition.2004.11.003

23. Simner, J., et al.: Synaesthesia: the prevalence of atypical cross-modal experiences. Perception **35**, 1024–1033 (2006). https://doi.org/10.1068/p5469

24. Jakobson, R., Waugh, L.: The Sound Shape of Language. Indiana University Press, Bloomington (1979). https://doi.org/10.1515/9783110889451

25. Doke, C.M.: Bantu Linguistic Terminology. Longmans, Green, London (1935)

26. Oswalt, R.L.: Inanimate imitatives in English. In: Hinton, L., Nichols, J., Ohala, J.J. (eds.) Sound Symbolism. CUP, Cambridge (1994). https://doi.org/10.1017/cbo9780511751806.022

27. Abercrombie, N., Hill, S., Turner, B.S.: Dictionary of Sociology. Penguin Books Ltd., London (2006)

28. Walther, J.B.: Computer-mediated communication: impersonal, interpersonal and hyperpersonal. Commun. Res. **23**, 3–43 (1996). https://doi.org/10.1177/009365096023001001

29. Herring, S.C.: Computer-mediated Discourse. In: Schiffrin, D., Tannen, D., Hamilton, H.E. (eds.). Handbook of Discourse Analysis. Blackwell,Oxford (2005). https://doi.org/10.1002/9780470753460.ch32

30. Kalman, Y.M., Gergle, D.: Letter repetitions in computer-mediated communication: a unique link between spoken and online language. Comput. Hum. Behav. **34**, 187–193 (2014). https://doi.org/10.1016/j.chb.2014.01.047

31. Carey, J.: Paralanguage of computer mediated communication. In: 80 Proceedings of the 18th Annual Meeting on Association for Computatonal Linguistics. ACL (1980). https://doi.org/10.3115/981436.981458

32. Beißwenger, M.: Situated Chat Analysis as a Window to the User's Perspective. Language@Internet, 5, article 6 (2008). Retrieved from urn:nbn:de:0009-7-15329

33. Trubetzkoy, N.S.: Principles of Phonology. Univrsity of California Press, Berkley (1969)

34. Matasović, R. (ed.): Etimološki rječnik hrvatskoga jezika, sv. 1 (2016)

35. Simpson, J., Weiner, E. (eds.): Oxford English Dictionary (OED), vol. II (1989). https://doi.org/10.1111/j.0079-1636.2004.00140.x

36. Soanes, C., Stevenson, A. (Eds.): Oxford Dictionary of English. 2nd edn. Oxford University Press (2003)

37. Jelaska, Z.: Fonološki opisi hrvatskoga jezika. Zagreb: Hrvatska sveučilišna naklada (2004)

Slips of the Ear as Clues for Speech Processing

Elena I. Riekhakaynen$^{(\boxtimes)}$ and Alena Balanovskaia

Saint-Petersburg State University, St. Petersburg, Russia
e.riehakajnen@spbu.ru, alenaball1994@gmail.com

Abstract. The aim of the paper is to show how slips of the ear can contribute to the understanding of spoken word processing be native speakers and second language learners and to the description of the structure of the mental lexicon for native and second languages. In our experiment, 30 native Russian speakers and 30 Chinese students learning Russian as a second language listened to 100 Russian words and had to write them down. We analyzed the mistakes in the answers of the both groups of participants checking different linguistic and psycholinguistic parameters (phonetic factors, part-of-speech, priming and frequency effects). We found out that the native language of a listener influences the recognition of spoken words both in native and non-native language on the phonetic level. The processing on higher levels is less language specific: we found evidence that the word frequency effect and priming effect are relevant for processing Russian words by both native and non-native speakers.

Keywords: Slips of the ear · Spoken word recognition · Russian
Second language acquisition

1 Introduction

This research is inspired by a small footnote in the paper by Polivanov [1] first published 90 years ago. While describing his experience of transcribing Japanese dialects, Polivanov provides several examples of his own slips of the ear as the evidence for the sounds that substituted each other in these examples to be phonologically connected. This remark by Polivanov is interesting from the (1) theoretical and (2) methodological points of view.

(1) Slips of the ear (misperceptions, mishearings), when "a listener reports hearing clearly something that does not correspond to what a speaker has said" [2], is a type of "negative linguistic data" (together with slips of the pen/misprints, slips of the tongue, and "slips while reading"). As these mistakes occur while processing speech, they should reveal the mechanisms of speech production and recognition. Thus, the analysis of mistakes in spoken word recognition can help to describe the activation and competition in spoken word recognition. Linguists normally describe slips of the ear that occur while perceiving native speech [3–5, etc.]. Polivanov was probably the first to regard the mistakes in second language processing as slips of the ear. We believe such an approach to be promising for comparing the processing of the first and second languages and the structure of the mental lexicon of a native speaker and a second language learner.

© Springer Nature Switzerland AG 2019
P. Eismont and O. Mitrenina (Eds.): LMAC 2017, CCIS 943, pp. 111–121, 2019.
https://doi.org/10.1007/978-3-030-05594-3_9

(2) The method that allowed Polivanov to detect slips of the ear can be classified as introspection. The other method that has been used for studying slips of the ear since the beginning of the 20th century is the "paper-and-pencil" method when a researcher writes down any misperception he/she notices in his own speech processing or in the processing of other people and tries to classify them [3, 4]. This method has at least two disadvantages: it is time consuming and does not allow to check what exactly was pronounced. Thus, a researcher cannot be sure that every example in his/her database is a slip of the ear and not just the result of an inaccurate pronunciation of a word or word combination by a speaker.

The development of the corpus linguistics allows to overcome the latter disadvantage. Large spoken corpora can be used to study slips of the ear occurring in natural communication or while transcribing natural speech [5, 6]. If we have one and the same text transcribed by several people, we can learn how one and the same data is processed by different listeners. However, these listeners usually are professional phoneticians.

In order both to be able to check the acoustic signal processed by a listener and to get the data about how one and the same acoustic signal is processed by different participants, Chiari in [7] conducted a dictation task experiment. This method, although being an offline one, has been used in many psycholinguistic studies [8–10] and showed to be effective as its experimental conditions are "quite close to the situation of natural communication" [10].

2   Experiment

2.1   Aim of the Study

We regarded our research as one of the first attempts to compare the mechanisms of word recognition in Russian as a native and as a second language using systematically controlled data.

2.2   Material

We used 100 frequent Russian words (according to http://dict.ruslang.ru/freq.php) as stimuli in our experiment. The words were divided into 5 lists (20 words in each; see Appendix 1). We formed the lists in such a way that there were all possible Russian consonants and 18 perceptual variants of Russian vowels described in [11] within each list. We also controlled the stimuli for the number of syllables and part-of-speech distribution so that the distribution of words according to these parameters was similar in different lists (see Figs. 1 and 2).

As not only native speakers, but also second language learners participated in the experiment, we had to check whether the words are familiar to the second language learners. We controlled this parameter twice: while choosing the words and after the experiment took place (see Sect. 2.4.). According to [12, 13], 91 out of 100 stimuli correspond to the basic dictionary of the B1 level of Russian as a foreign language, 7 – to the B2 level and 2 – to the C1.

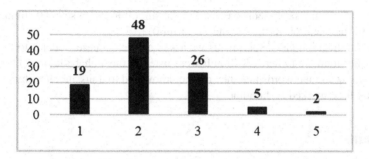

Fig. 1. Stimuli: Number of syllables distribution (from 1 to 5)

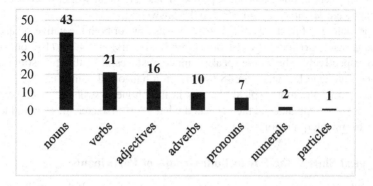

Fig. 2. Stimuli: Part-of-Speech distribution

All words were read aloud one by one by a native Russian speaker (45 years old, male, from St. Petersburg, Russia) and recorded in WAV format (44 100 Hz, 16 bit).

2.3 Participants

30 native speakers of Russian (between 20 and 24 years old, 15 m. and 15 fem.) and 30 Chinese students who study Russian at Saint-Petersburg State University (14 m. and 16 fem., 24 with B1 and 6 with B2 level of Russian as a foreign language) took part in the study. The experiment was carried out in accordance with the Declaration of Helsinki and the existing Russian and international regulations concerning ethics in research. All participants provided informed consents for their participation in the experiment.

2.4 Procedure

The experiment was conducted with each participant individually. Every participant read a written instruction. The experimental procedure was a classical dictation task: participants listened via headphones to words presented one by one and had to write down what they heard. Each stimulus was presented only once. The inter-stimulus interval for the Russian participants was 4 s., for the Chinese students – 10 s. The Russian participants listened to all words in one stimulus set that lasted for 8 min, whereas for the Chinese students we divided the stimuli into two sets (40 stimuli in the first one (7 min) and 60 in the second (10.5 min)).

After the dictation task experiments we asked all the Chinese students to mark in a separate questionnaire (where all stimuli were listed in the alphabetic order) the words that they knew and the words that they did not know and to translate into Chinese those words that they marked as familiar.

3   Results

3.1   General Overview

All native speakers in our experiment provided answers to all words whereas from the second language learners we got 66 "blank" answers.

The percentage of mistakes in the answers was low for both the native speakers and second language learners: 2.0% (61 out of 3000 answers) and 4.7% (137 out of 2934 answers) respectively. The native speakers made mistakes in 21 different stimuli, while the second language learners – in 48 (almost in a half of all stimuli).

We compared the most typical changes in the phonetic structure of the stimuli in both groups of participants and then checked what word characteristics can influence its exposure to misinterpretation.

3.2   Typical Slips of the Ear in Both Groups of Participants

We found the substitutions of initial consonants in 34 out of 61 slips of the ear in the answers of the native speakers (*bol'she* 'more' –> *Pol'sha* 'Poland', *den'* 'day' –> *ten'* 'shadow', etc.). Among other changes, there were also non-initial consonant substitutions, vowel substitutions, extra syllable, final substitutions, and sound metathesis.

The Chinese students who took part in our experiment most often substituted final sounds (33 examples; *kazhdyj* 'every' –> *karty* 'cards', *nachalo* 'beginning' –> *nachat'* 'to begin', *verit'* 'to believe' –> *vera* 'faith', etc.). We also found 21 examples of stress shifts in our data (*tjót'ja* 'aunt' –> *teátr* 'theatre', *pjátnitsa* 'Friday' –> *pjatnádtsat'* 'fifteen', *zhénschina* 'woman' –> *tishiná* 'silence', etc.). Unlike in the results of the native speakers, there were several examples of syllable omissions in the answers of the Chinese students. The most typical sound changes were $[l^{(j)}] \mathbin{<}\!\!-\!\!\mathbin{>} [r^{(j)}]$ (firma 'company' –> *fil'ma* 'film.GEN', *daljokij* 'distant' –> *dorogi* 'roads', *region* 'region' –> *legion* 'legion', etc.).

3.3   Linguistic Factors Influencing Slips of the Ear

Number of Syllables. We presumed that the longer the word is the easier it is for a listener to identify it (if the word is pronounced not in the context, but in isolation). The data we got from the native speakers of Russian support this hypothesis: the more syllables there were in a word the less often slips of the ear occurred, whereas for the second language learners we did not find such a tendency (see Table 1).

Table 1. Percentages of incorrect answers depending on the number of syllables in stimuli

Number of syllables	Native speakers		Second language learners	
	Percentage of words with at least one wrong answer	Percentage of all incorrect answers	Percentage of words with at least one wrong answer	Percentage of all incorrect answers
1	**36.8**	**3**	31.6	2.5
2	**20.8**	**2.4**	45.8	4.8
3	**15.4**	**1.3**	42.3	6
4	**0**	**0**	20	1.4
5	**0**	**0**	100	15

Part-of-Speech. As we included in the experiment words of different parts of speech, we could check whether different parts of speech are equally exposed to misinterpretation while spoken word recognition. Figure 3 shows the percentage of words with at least one slip of the ear in our experiment for both the native speakers and second language learners. We can see the similar tendencies in the distributions of slips of the ear between different parts of speech for both groups of participants (there is a significant correlation according to the Spearman test: $r_s = 0.96$, $p < 0.01$).

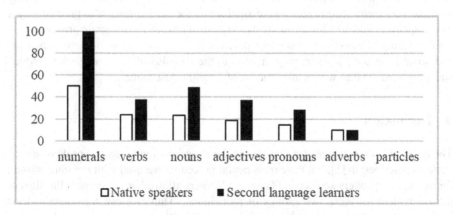

Fig. 3. Percentages of words with at least one slip of the ear

Word Frequency. Almost all models of spoken word recognition admit the role of word frequency in spoken word processing. It means, among others, that frequent word forms are activated in the mental lexicon faster and stronger than less frequent ones. There are at least two aspects of this factor that can be discussed in a study of slips of the ear: (1) whether slips of the ear occur more often when processing less frequent words, and (2) whether there is a tendency that while misperceiving a word a listener substitutes it for a more frequent competitor (neighbour). We could not check the first assumption as we had chosen only frequent words for our experiment. The second one we also could not check systematically, but the results do show that both the native speakers and second language learners tend to substitute less frequent words for more frequent ones than vice versa (e.g., *firma* 'company' (32.9 ipm) –> *forma* 'form' (45.7 ipm), *sfera* 'sphere' (7.6 ipm) –> *vera* 'faith' (19.5 ipm), *znat'* 'to know' (133.5 ipm) –> *znachit* 'so/it means' (385.5 ipm)). At the same time, we found one vivid example contradicting this tendency in the answers on the native speakers: 15 participants substituted the adverb *bol'she* 'more' for the noun *Pol'sha* 'Poland' (we did not find any such substitution in the answers of the Chinese students). In seems that the latter slip of the ear is an example of the part-of-speech-frequency effect. Nouns are more common than adverbs in general and they are more likely to appear in a dictation task experiment (and were the most frequent in our experiment as well, see Fig. 2). Thus, 50 per cent of all participants in the experiment with native speakers preferred the word referring to the more frequent part of speech (although the word *Pol'sha* 'Poland' itself being a proper noun is much less frequent in the Russian language than the adverb *bol'she* 'more').

Priming-Effect. The priming effect means that the previously processed information can somehow influence the following one [14]. We were not going to check this effect systematically in the experiment as we worked with separate words, but as we presented them in a row, we did notice several examples of the priming-effect in the answers of the native speakers and second language learners. The morphological priming can explain the fact that the adjective *gotovyj* 'ready' presented immediately after the verb *ljubit'* ('to love') was recognized as the verb *gotovit'* ('to prepare') by 4 native speakers and 10 Chinese students. As an example of the semantic priming effect we can regard the answers *otchestvo* ('patronymic') (4 and 12 for the native speakers and second language learners respectively) to the stimulus *obschestvo* 'society' which was presented several words after the word *familija* 'last name'.

4   Discussion

The types of sound changes we revealed in the experiment with native speakers are the same as described in [5], but the experimental procedure we used with the same stimuli for the native speakers and second language learners allowed us to compare the slips of the ear typical for these two groups of participants. Thus, we can formulate at least preliminary assumptions on whether there are any differences between spoken word recognition in the first and second languages.

Native Russian speakers tend to substitute consonants more often than vowels while misperceiving spoken words. Number of syllables and stress pattern usually stay intact (occasional exceptions in our material are several slips of the ear with additional syllables). These tendencies can be easily explained by acoustic and physiological reasons, as our auditory system perceives better low frequencies that contain the information about the quality of Russian vowels whereas high frequencies containing the information about the quality of many consonants is perceived worse. However, we did not find out any typical sound substitutions for the native speakers of Russian.

The second language learners in our experiment often interchanged $[l^{(j)}]$ and $[r^{(j)}]$ sounds. The most probable explanation of this tendency is the transfer from their native language – Mandarin Chinese – where there is no l/r-distinction [15]. The transfer from the native language seems to be a plausible reason for the stress shifts in the answers of Chinese students, because their native language is tonal. The causes of other differences from the tendencies observed in native speakers (i.e. substitutions of final vs. initial elements of a word; syllable omissions vs. extra syllables; no number of syllables influence on the percentage of incorrect interpretations for the second language learners) are not that evident. They can be either specific for the native speakers of Mandarin Chinese who learn Russian or common for all second learners of Russian. To answer this question we require additional experiments with the native speakers of other languages learning Russian as a second language.

Our data also revealed some common tendencies in processing spoken words in native and non-native languages. For example, we did find the similar tendencies for native Russian speakers and Chinese students in the distribution of the words referring to different parts of speech among the stimuli that were misperceived at least by one participant in our experiment. Thus, we can conclude that the intrinsic characteristics of certain parts of speech (or even single words) make them perceptually weaker than other words both for the native speakers and second language learners of Russian.

According to our data, the word frequency effect and the sematic and morphological priming effect can influence spoken word recognition in Russian as native and second language. We found the examples of the influence of the part-of-speech frequency effect only in the answers of the native speakers. These results, although being very interesting and promising for the understanding of spoken word recognition in the first and second languages, can be regarded only as preliminary, because we did not control for these factors in the experimental design. But the methodology we described in the paper can further be used for checking these preliminary results.

5 Conclusion

In the paper, we described a study aimed to compare the processing of Russian spoken words by native speakers of Russian and second language learners. We analyzed the mistakes 30 native Russian speakers and 30 Chinese students learning Russian made in interpretation of 100 Russian words presented one by one in isolation.

Although the overall percentage of mistakes was low for both groups of participants, we revealed some interesting common tendencies and differences in the recognition of spoken words by native and non-native Russian speakers. We found out that the native language of a listener influences the recognition of spoken words both in native and non-native language on the phonetic level. The processing on higher levels is less language specific: we found evidence that the word frequency effect and priming effect are relevant for processing Russian words by both native and non-native speakers.

From the methodological point of view, the experiment is not complicated as we used a classical variant of the dictation task paradigm, but for all we know such a method has never been used before to compare the processing of spoken word by native and non-native speakers.

Our experiment has two strong limitations as we used only isolated words as stimuli and recruited only native speakers of Chinese as the second language learners of Russian. Therefore, the further development of the research requires both (1) more second language learners with other native languages as participants as well as (2) new sets of stimuli including not only isolated words but also phrases and aimed to systematically check the frequency and priming effects.

Acknowledgements. The study is supported by the research grant No 16-18-02042 from the Russian Science Foundation. We would like to thank our colleague Tatiana Petrova who helped us to organise the experiment with second language learners.

Appendix

Lists of stimuli (in the order they were presented in the experiment)

#	Stimulus and translation	Number of syllables	Part of speech	#	Stimulus and translation	Number of syllables	Part of speech
1	chelovek 'man/person'	3	noun	51	pogibnut' 'perish'	3	verb
2	ljubit' 'to love'	2	verb	52	ves' 'whole'	1	pronoun
3	gotovyj 'ready'	3	adjective	53	familija 'last name'	4	noun
4	fil'm 'movie'	1	noun	54	khotet' 'to want'	2	verb
5	skazat' 'to tell'	2	verb	55	obshchestvo 'society'	3	noun
6	zhenschina 'woman'	3	noun	56	ijun' 'June'	2	noun
7	vmeste 'together'	2	adverb	57	snjat' 'to take off'	1	verb
8	porjadok 'order'	3	noun	58	ljogkij 'easy, light'	2	adjective
9	pervyj 'first'	2	numeral	59	nazad 'back'	2	adverb
10	stikhi 'poems'	2	noun	60	uspekh 'success'	2	noun
11	vzjat' 'to take'	1	verb	61	region 'region'	3	noun

(*continued*)

(continued)

#	Stimulus and translation	Number of syllables	Part of speech	#	Stimulus and translation	Number of syllables	Part of speech
12	khorosho 'well'	3	adverb	62	verit' 'to believe'	2	verb
13	forma 'form'	2	noun	63	tjotja 'aunt'	2	noun
14	den'gi 'money'	2	noun	64	kljuch 'key'	1	noun
15	daljokij 'distant'	3	adjective	65	srazu 'at once'	2	adverb
16	protsess 'process'	2	noun	66	predlozhenie 'sentence, offer'	5	noun
17	poluchit' 'to receive'	3	verb	67	byt' 'to be'	1	verb
18	russkij 'Russian'	2	adjective	68	gazeta 'newspaper'	3	noun
19	yescho 'more, else'	2	adverb	69	belyj 'white'	2	adjective
20	ljuboj 'any'	2	pronoun	70	vspomnit' 'to remember'	2	verb
21	bereg 'coast, shore'	2	noun	71	khimicheskij 'chemical'	4	adjective
22	poetomu 'that is why'	4	pronoun	72	veshch 'thing'	1	noun
23	kazhdyj 'every'	2	pronoun	73	pjatnitsa 'Friday'	3	noun
24	dom 'house'	1	noun	74	bol'she 'more'	2	adverb
25	umet' 'to be able to'	2	verb	75	chjornyj 'black'	2	adjective
26	shirokij 'wide'	3	adjective	76	firma 'company'	2	noun
27	revoljutsija 'revolution'	5	noun	77	kriknut' 'to shout'	2	verb
28	vkljuchat' 'to switch on'	2	verb	78	vsjakij 'any'	2	pronoun
29	gde 'where'	1	pronoun	79	vykhodit' 'to go out'	3	verb
30	namjoki 'allusions'	3	noun	80	bjudzhet 'budget'	2	noun
31	sfera 'sphere'	2	noun	81	nachalo 'beginning'	3	noun

(continued)

(*continued*)

#	Stimulus and translation	Number of syllables	Part of speech	#	Stimulus and translation	Number of syllables	Part of speech
32	nastojashchij 'real'	4	adjective	82	glava 'head, chapter'	2	noun
33	brat' 'to take'	1	verb	83	vsjo 'everything'	1	adverb
34	tikhij 'quiet'	2	adjective	84	mjagkij 'soft'	2	adjective
35	model' 'model'	2	noun	85	sjuda 'here (direction)'	2	adverb
36	khozjain 'host'	3	noun	86	byvshij 'former, ex-'	2	adjective
37	vid 'view'	1	noun	87	znat' 'to know'	1	verb
38	pisat' 'to write'	2	verb	88	khoroshij 'good'	3	adjective
39	general 'general'	3	noun	89	odin 'one, single'	2	numeral
40	ser'joznyj 'serious'	3	adjective	90	zhizn' 'life'	1	noun
41	zemlja 'earth, ground'	2	noun	91	shchjoki 'cheeks'	2	noun
42	nabljudat' 'to observe'	3	verb	92	schema 'scheme'	2	noun
43	luchshij 'the best'	2	adjective	93	neuzheli 'really?'	4	particle
44	tsel' 'goal'	1	noun	94	fakt 'fact'	1	noun
45	rebjonok 'child'	3	noun	95	ljubimyj 'favourite'	3	adjective
46	ochen' 'very'	2	adverb	96	teper' 'now'	2	adverb
47	zhit' 'to live'	1	verb	97	geroj 'hero'	2	noun
48	drugoj 'another'	2	pronoun	98	uvidet' 'to see'	3	verb
49	tserkov' 'church'	2	noun	99	soobshchit' 'to inform'	3	verb
50	den' 'day'	1	noun	100	ofitser 'officer'	3	noun

References

1. Polivanov, Ye.D.: Factors of the phonetic evolution of a language as a workflow. In: Papers in General Linguistics, p. 64. Nauka, Moscow, (1928/1968). (in Russian)
2. Shockey, L., Bond, Z.: What slips of the ear reveal about speech perception. Linguistica Lettica **22**, 107 (2014)
3. Bogoroditskij, V.A.: Lectures in General Linguistics. Printing-office of the Caesarean University, Kazan' (1911). (in Russian)
4. Bond, Z.S.: Slips of the Ear: Errors in the Perception of Casual Conversation. Academic Press, San Diego (1999)
5. Stepanova, S.B.: Slips of the ear and echo-questions as the basis for speech perception research. In: Problems of Phonetics, pp. 102–113. Russian Language Institute, Moscow (2014). (in Russian)
6. Scharenborg, O., Sanders, E., Cranen, B.: Collecting a corpus of Dutch noise-induced 'Slips of the Ear'. In: 15th Annual Conference of the International Speech Communication Association, 14–18 September 2014, Singapore, pp. 2600–2604 (2014)
7. Chiari, I.: Slips and errors in spoken data transcription. In: Proceedings of 5th International Conference on Language Resources and Evaluation. Università La Sapienza di Roma Dipartimento di Studi Filologici, Linguistici e Letterari (2005). http://www.alphabit.net/PDF/Pubblicazioni/chiari2_LREC2006.pdf
8. Taft, M.: Exploring the mental Lexicon. Aust. J. Psychol. **36**, 35–46 (1984)
9. Ernestus, M., Baayen, H., Schreuder, R.: The recognition of reduced word forms. Brain Lang. **81**(1–3), 162–173 (2002)
10. Nigmatulina, J., Rajeva, O., Riechakajnen, E., Slepokurova, N., Vencov, A.: How to study spoken word recognition: evidence from Russian. In: Anstatt, T., Gattnar, A., Clasmeier, Ch. (eds.) Slavic Languages in Psycholinguistics: Chances and Challenges for Empirical and Experimental Research, pp. 175–190. Narr Francke Attempto Verlag GmbH + Co. KG, Tübingen (2016)
11. Bondarko, L., Verbickaja, L., Gordina, M.: Basics of general phonetics, 4th edn. Philological faculty of Saint-Petersburg State University, St. Petersburg (2000). (in Russian)
12. Andrjushina, N.P., et al.: Program of Russian as a foreign language. The first certificate. General proficiency, 5th edn. St. Petersburg, Zlatoust (2006). (in Russian)
13. Andrjushina, N.P., et al.: Program of Russian as a foreign language. The second certificate. General proficiency, 3d edn. St. Petersburg, Zlatoust (2011). (in Russian)
14. Meyer, D.E., Schvaneveldt, R.W.: Facilitation in recognizing pairs of words: Evidence of a dependence between retrieval operations. J. Exp. Psychol. **90**, 227–234 (1971)
15. Aleksakhin, A.N.: Theoretical phonetics of Mandarin Chinese. AST: Vostok-Zapad, Moscow (2006). (in Russian)

Phrase Breaks in Everyday Conversations from Sociolinguistic Perspective

Natalia Bogdanova-Beglarian[✉]

Saint Petersburg State University, 7/9 Universitetskaya nab.,
St. Petersburg 199034, Russia
n.bogdanova@spbu.ru

Abstract. This study was made on the base of the ORD corpus of everyday spoken Russian, containing the rich collection of audio recordings made in real-life settings. Speech transcripts of the ORD corpus imply mandatory indication of word and phrase breaks, self-correction, hesitations, fillers and other irregularities of spoken discourse. The paper deals with speech breaks in oral discourse (word breaks, phrase breaks, intraphrasal pauses, etc.). Quantitative analysis performed on the subcorpus of 187 600 tokens has shown that 7,56% of all phrases in everyday communication are not finished. If word breaks can be referred to word search/choice or self-correction, phrase breaks affect the text level and result in ragged, rough, and poorly structured syntactic sequence. Sociolinguistic analysis has revealed that phrase breaks are more frequent in men's speech than in the women's (8.16 vs. 7,12%). Seniors have significantly more speech breaks (10,76%) than children (6,78%), youth (6,08%) and middle-aged people (7,37%). As for status groups of speakers, the highest share of breaks is found in speech of unemployed and retired people (10,75%), whereas the lowest percentage of breaks is observed in speech of managers (4,50%) who care, apparently, more about their speech quality than others.

Keywords: Speech disfluencies · Phrase breaks · Spoken Russian Sociophonetics

1 Introduction

The paper deals with speech breaks in oral discourse (word breaks, phrase breaks, intraphrasal pauses, etc.). Speech organized in a corpus, providing the explorer with a big amount of empirical data, shows many phenomena that allow, firstly, to take a look at the mechanism of speech production, and, secondly, by special transcription marks recognize spots that would help to make automatic annotation and/or processing easier. Word and phrase breaks indicating hobbles and hesitation are one of them.

The investigation has made on the annotated part of the corpus "One Speaker's Day" (ORD corpus, [1–5]) counting 27 069 phrases, 125 000 word usages, or 187 000 tokens. The subcorpus consists of speech from 100 speakers and 154 their interlocutors [6].

Speech transcripts of the ORD corpus imply mandatory indication of word and phrase breaks, self-correction, hesitations, fillers and other irregularities of spoken discourse.

© Springer Nature Switzerland AG 2019
P. Eismont and O. Mitrenina (Eds.): LMAC 2017, CCIS 943, pp. 122–130, 2019.
https://doi.org/10.1007/978-3-030-05594-3_10

2   Definition of the Concepts

Phrase breaks of various kinds are the typical manifestation of speech disfluency, which is an inherent feature of everyday conversations. Moreover, the break in spoken discourse is most often one of hesitation phenomena (HP), a distinctive feature of oral speech: "*Spontaneous speech usually includes redundant information such as disfluencies, fillers, repetitions, repairs, and word fragments*" [7: 401]; "*unprepared oral speech organizes itself while being produced, unlike written speech that appears pre-arranged and permanent. Speech is delivered in throes – slips of the tongue, self-interruptions, self-repairs, breaks, repeats*" [8: 27]. It's the breaks that are the main subject of the current paper. There are word breaks (unfinished and self-interrupted words: *s...*, *pri...*) that may be classified as a kind of "stuttering" caused by different reasons and phrase breaks, interrupting the fluency on text level and marking boundaries between utterances and fragments of a monologue.

The break may occur in any spot of the utterance, bringing about hesitation pauses and other hesitation phenomena; after this the speaker goes on with his speech:

- *ne s'uda konechno / nam nado ... / on zhe treugol'nyj / a my jego mozhem obojti prosto* [*we shouldn't go / here... / it's triangular / but we can just walk it around*];
- *no ja ne khochu s... (...) imenno vot (...) <pause> chego tam po ulicam *N ?* [*but I don't want s... (...) just this (...) <pause> for what outdoors *N ?*];
- *a bochki / po 200 litrov / oni vs'o ravno potom tam / pro... propzhavejut / i prochee i prochee potom* [*and barrels / to 200 L / it's all the same they after just / will become rusty / and so on and so forth*];
- *kak ty perevodish' ? # net / ja ne mogu koroche (...) eto samoe ... <pause> ja ne mogu s'uda jego postavit' / u men'a (...) netu (...) kr'aka* [*how do you transfer ? # no / I can't in short (...) how is it ... <pause> I can't install it here / I haven't got a crack*].

In addition, the break naturally result from the generation of natural dialogue, when each participant play its own role in conversation and may interfere the initial intent of the previous speaker:

- *takoe misticheskoe ... # potom tak pojd'om von // do(:) etogo samogo / <pause> khot' do Pr'azhki$ / khot' dokuda* [*so mystical ... # after we will go here // to(:) how is it / <pause> even to Pryazhka% / even to anywhere*];
- *tak / teper' nam ... # da net / so mnoj ne zabludims'a* [*so / now we should go ... # no / I sure we won't get lost*];
- *zdes' letom voda brodit / ona prosto bul'kaet vot tak vot // <pause> to jest' () takoe oshchushchenie / chto s'uda priezzhajut ... # a chto ty khochesh' ? <pause> s armejskikh skladov zdes' ... # vysypajut ...* [*in summer the water ferments here / it's just gurgles like this // <pause> that is to say () it seems like / that some people come here ... # so what do you want ? <pause> here is the stuff from the army depots ... # pour out*].

Types of Phrase Breaks

Breaks are also accounted as self-broken constructions, which are divided into the following types

- Unfinished phrases,
- Restarts (*l'u*... *l'ubimye peredachi* [*fa*... *favorite broadcasts*]),
- False starts (*to est' ne dl'a pu*... *ne predlagaets'a dl'a obsuzhdenija* [*that is not for the pu*... *not suggested for the discussion*]).

It is clear that the breaks in oral discourse is observed in both phrases and individual words.

3   Phrase Breaks from Sociolinguistic Perspective

Statistics of breaks are possible to draw using the whole block of speech data recorded from different groups. The whole amount of the annotated and examined data is 27 069 phrases; 7,56% of them has appeared to be unfinished for different reasons (Table 1).

Table 1. The top zone of frequency list of ORD tokens

Token	Count	Percentage
//	19176	10,22
/	17486	9,32
?	4789	2,555
nu	3565	1,90
ja	3514	1,87
ne	3334	1,78
P <pause>	2973	1,58
da	2971	1,58
*N	2808	1,50
a	2696	1,44
vot	2682	1,43
chto	2575	1,37
i	2402	1,28
v	2367	1,26
eto	2078	1,11
...	**2048**	**1,09**
tam	1812	0,97
u	1568	0,84
tak	1517	0,81
na	1514	0,81
()	1480	0,79

(*continued*)

Table 1. (*continued*)

Token	Count	Percentage
ty	1447	0,77
(...)	1380	0,74
kak	1262	0,67
to	1182	0,63
!	1056	0,56
vs'o	1055	0,56
s	1035	0,55
on	1024	0,55

3.1 Phrase Breaks and Gender

Men's and women's speech are represented almost equally in the data, but the "women's subcorpus" exceeded the men's one in every parameter (number of phrases, word usages, tokens), which supports the observation that women talk more than men in average [6]. However, it emerged that there are a few more breaks in the men's speech than in the women's: 8,16 vs. 7,12% (Table 2).

Table 2. Phrase breaks and gender

	Phrases	Phrase Breaks (%)
Men	10 785	8,16
Women	16 284	7,12

It can be supposed that women pay more attention to their speech in this respect than men do.

3.2 Phrase Breaks and Age

The middle age group (Age 2, from 25 to 50) has turned out to be the most talkative of all age groups: their subcorpus counts 10 557 phrases (Table 3). The amount of data from the younger speakers (Age 1, from 17 to 24) is slightly lesser: 9 906 phrases, and significantly fewer recordings were collected from the older speakers (Age 3, from 50): 4 985 phrases. Nonetheless, the amount of breaks is the biggest in the older group: 10,86 vs. 7,37% in the middle age group and 6,08% in the younger. Children (Age 0), who were only interlocutors to adult speakers, hold middle position: with the data of 1 621 phrases the number of breaks has been 6,78% (Table 3).

It can be seen that younger speakers are the most accurate in this respect while the older speakers are the least so.

Table 3. Phrase breaks and age

	Phrases	Phrase Breaks (%)
Age 0	1 621	6,78
Age 1	9 906	**6,08**
Age 2	10 557	7,37
Age 3	4 985	**10,86**

3.3 Phrase Breaks and Profession/Social Status

Though the biggest amounts of data belongs to the groups SP (specialists, 13 985 phrases), SR (service, 3 639 phrases) and OF (office workers, 3 002 phrases), the "break leaders" in this section are unemployed speakers, including pensioners (UN; 10,75% out of 1 627 phrases). The speech of managers has turned up to be the poorest in breaks (MN; 4,5% out of 1 266 phrases) (Table 4).

Table 4. Phrase breaks and profession/social status

	Phrases	Phrase Breaks (%)
SP	13 985	8,55
SR	3 639	7,45
OF	3 002	7,80
UN	1 627	10,75
MN	1 266	4,50

It can be assumed that the speech of unemployed people is the most abundant in breaks and the speech of managers has the smallest number of them.

4 Reasons of Word Breaks

Word breaks can be caused by various matters:

(1) normal hestitation (*nemalo // *P vot vot takikh vot () otkrytykh l'udej da vot kotorye u kotorykh () nu(:) druzhba da / muzhskaja takaja znaezh' / u nix podkhod / ne to chto sr... (e) sredi etikh jevropejcev zan'ukhannykh* [*a lot of // *P just exactly () exactly these overt people yeah that that have () we(:)ll friendship yeah / men's friendship you know / they have a kind of approach / **un...** (e) unlike these scuzzy Europeans have*] (on the peculiarities of the spelling of the materials of the ORD corpus: [6: 242–243]);

(2) «perfectionism»: the speaker, having already begun to pronounce the word, decides to spread it; in fact, it's like a disguise of the hesitation (*a ja-to () ponimaesh' / ja dumaju chto tvoi **gorazd...** rasskazy byli gorazdo luchshe*) [*and for me () you know / I think that yours is **bet...** your stories were much better*];

(3) selection of a word from a pair:

- synonyms, including contextual ones (*a chem on zanimaets'a / Tan'a% / chem on zanimaets'a ? ne pomni... zabudesh' ? @ mebelju / @ pomnish' ? [what is his business / Tanya% / what is he doing ? do you rememb... forget? @ furniture / @ do you remember ?]*),
- words that are semantically related (*starsh... – pozhiloj; zasunu... – pricepil [elde... – senior; put in... – hooked on]*),
- antonyms (*nachi... – perestajot; v sv... – v teni [begi... – stops; in the lig... – in the shadow]*),
- phonetic variants (*nu / kakoe-to vs... vospominanie ob etom sokhranilos' / ja chto-to pomnil [well / some memor... remembrance I keep about it / I remembered something]*),
- grammar variants (*ve... – s vechera; jeshcho russkie nichego / a vot ukraincy () eto gorazdo khuzhe / eto na klass / kla... nizhe klassom [eveni... – from the evening; Russians even not bad / but Ukrainians () it's much worse / it's lower on a class / cla... lower class]*),

(4) using an idiom or other non-trivial unit (*ja gotov ubr... ubrat' svoi naza... da slova nazad; i ja eto ja khodil (e-e) s etoj () takoj *N / # ma... nu(:) ja ponimaju da / khrenovinoj / # kal... kalosbornikom [I'm ready to ge... get my bac... yeah words back; and I'm so I was walking (e-e) with () such *N / # ma... we(:)ll I understand yeah / stuff / # col... colostomy bag]*);

(5) mistake in the previous word: *zazhal xv... / podzhal khvost; ivy razro... / lipy razroslis' [pinched ta... / drew in tail; willow gr... / lindens grew]*;

(6) a slip of the tongue (*vy chto-to / govorit / ishchete(:) (...) a da moi devki is... priseli otdykhajut [are you / saying / looking for somethi(:)ng (...) well my chicks is... chilling]*);

(7) breaks on the part of the interlocutor (*vy u nikh # Tan'a% ! # sprosite u etikh / davajte ! # podo... # *N / # a mozhno u etikh () devok von sprosit' ! [you ask # Tanya% ! # you ask these / come on ! # wai... # *N and you can ask () these girls !]*).

It is clear that in most cases when the speaker find himself in a "disfluency spot" he tries to overcome it immediately (on-line correction) and either just repeats the broken word, or somehow improves it. Therefore, word breaks can be accounted as a means of control over one's speech, an urge to correct the emerging disfluencies or just pause to revise the chosen words and grammatical forms.

4.1 Word Breaks and Gender

As mentioned above, the "women's subcorpus" is significantly richer in word usages than the men's one (almost 1,7 times: 78 304 vs. 47 135). But the difference in word breaks is not striking: 1,07% in women's speech and 0.88% in men's (Table 5).

Still one can suppose that women are not only more careful in their speech (see Sect. 4.1) but also watch their speech more closely, because breaks usually speak about dissatisfaction on the part of the speaker and an urge to correct. The research has shown that in everyday speech repaired or completed breaks prevail, emerging right after a disfluency (on-line) (see [9]).

Table 5. Word breaks and gender

	Words	Word Breaks (%)
Men	47 135	0,88
Women	78 304	1,07

4.2 Word Breaks and Age

Concerning age groups in the annotated subcorpus, word breaks are more frequent in the speech of the older group (1,00% out of 23 475 word usages) (compare to phrase breaks in Sect. 4.2) and children (1,30% out of 4 203 word usages). They are the fewest in the speech of the middle age group – 0.67% out of the biggest block of 57 431 word usages (Table 6).

Table 6. Word breaks and age

	Words	Word Breaks (%)
Age 0	4 203	**1,30**
Age 1	46 330	0,85
Age 2	57 431	**0,67**
Age 3	23 475	**1,00**

It is hard to draw a firm conclusion out of these data. The numbers may indicate either that middle-aged speakers make less mistakes, or that they have weaker control over their speech and just ignore disfluencies. A context analysis would give a realistic image, but it is quite challenging on such a big data.

4.3 Word Breaks and Profession/Social Status

The biggest amount of word breaks has been found in the speech of the unemployed, including pensioners (1,20% out of 7 635 word usages) and in the speech of managers (1,12% out of 5 958 word usages) (Table 7).

Table 7. Word breaks and profession/social status

	Words	Word Breaks (%)
SP	68 960	0,75
SR	18 746	1,02
OF	15 161	0,75
UN	7 635	**1,20**
MN	5 958	**1,12**

Considering that the very same groups stood out in the statistics of phrase breaks (see above 4.3) two preliminary conclusions can be made. Pensioners, having an altogether least fluent syntax, still pay attention to their speech on the lexical level and correct disfluencies. Managers possess a high "speech quality control": they speak more carefully than others and try to fix all disfluencies.

5 Conclusions

It is evident that approaching the break as a hesitation phenomenon allow to see both what causes disfluencies (colloquial speech studies) and how the speaker gets out of communicative difficulties (psycholinguistics and cognitive studies).

It seems necessary to distinguish between *phrase break* and *word break* for they differ both in quantitative and qualitative respects. *Phrase break* is a product of unpreparedness (a general feature of spontaneous speech) and negligence (an individual trait of a speaker or a whole sociolect). Frequent phrase breaks make the syntax abrupt and indistinct and handicaps speech perception and understanding. Such breaks are surely unfavorable.

Word break, on one hand, is also a result of unpreparedness, but it can be treated differently. As most word breaks end with either repeating or correcting the word (both mainly on-line), and the part of unfinished words is minimal, it is possible to consider word break a sign there is a "speech quality control" on the part of the speaker. It doesn't handicap perception and should be seen as positive.

From sociolinguistic point of view the women's and manager's speech should get high marks: they have few phrase breaks and many repaired word breaks.

Generally, the break indicates not only carelessness in speech, resulting in a rather "uneven" syntax and shaping features of spoken discourse on all levels (word breaks, phonetic reduction, repeats, unintelligible parts, unfinished phrases, etc.), but also a kind of "speech quality control" carried out by the speaker along with spontaneous utterance.

Acknowledgements. The research was conducted within the framework of the project, supported by the Russian Scientific Foundation, # 14-18-02070 "Everyday Russian Language in Different Social Groups".

References

1. Asinovsky, A., Bogdanova, N., Rusakova, M., Ryko, A., Stepanova, S., Sherstinova, T.: The ORD speech corpus of Russian everyday communication "One Speaker's Day": creation principles and annotation. In: Matoušek, V., Mautner, P. (eds.) TSD 2009. LNCS (LNAI), vol. 5729, pp. 250–257. Springer, Heidelberg (2009). https://doi.org/10.1007/978-3-642-04208-9_36
2. Bogdanova-Beglarian, N., Martynenko, G., Sherstinova, T.: The "One Day of Speech" corpus: phonetic and syntactic studies of everyday spoken Russian. In: Ronzhin, A., Potapova, R., Fakotakis, N. (eds.) SPECOM 2015. LNCS (LNAI), vol. 9319, pp. 429–437. Springer, Cham (2015). https://doi.org/10.1007/978-3-319-23132-7_53

3. Bogdanova-Beglarian, N., Sherstinova, T., Blinova, O., Ermolova, O., Baeva, E., Martynenko, G., Ryko, A.: Sociolinguistic extension of the ORD corpus of Russian everyday speech. In: Ronzhin, A., Potapova, R., Németh, G. (eds.) SPECOM 2016. LNCS (LNAI), vol. 9811, pp. 659–666. Springer, Cham (2016). https://doi.org/10.1007/978-3-319-43958-7_80

4. Bogdanova-Beglarian, N., Sherstinova, T., Blinova, O., Martynenko, G.: An exploratory study on sociolinguistic variation of Russian everyday speech. In: Ronzhin, A., Potapova, R., Németh, G. (eds.) SPECOM 2016. LNCS (LNAI), vol. 9811, pp. 100–107. Springer, Cham (2016). https://doi.org/10.1007/978-3-319-43958-7_11

5. Bogdanova-Beglarian, N., Sherstinova, T., Blinova, O., Martynenko, G.: Corpus "One Speaker's Day" for studies of sociolinguistic variation of russian colloquial speech, analysis of conversational Russian speech (AC^3-2017). In: Skrelin, P., Kocharov, D. (eds.) Proceedings of the 7th Interdisciplinary Seminar, pp. pp. 14–20. Polytechnica-Print, Sankt Petersburg (2017)

6. Bogdanova-Beglarian, N. (ed.): Everyday Russian Language in Different Social Groups, Collective Monograph. LAIKA, 244p, Sankt Petersburg (2016)

7. Furui, S., Kikuchi, T., Shinnaka, Y., Hori, Ch.: Speech-to-text and speech-to-speech summarization of spontaneous speech. IEEE Trans. Speech Audio Process. **12**(4), 401–408 (2004)

8. Bogdanova-Beglarian, N. (ed.): Speech Corpus as a Base for Analysis. Collective Monograph. Part 1. Reading. Retelling. Description. Philology Department Publ., Saint-Petersburg (2013)

9. Bogdanova-Beglarian, N.: Word break in the "disfluency spot" and ways of reacting to a communicative difficulty (2017). http://conference-spbu.ru/backend/36/reports/5145/

Audible Paralinguistic Phenomena in Everyday Spoken Conversations: Evidence from the ORD Corpus Data

Tatiana Sherstinova[1,2]([✉]) [iD]

[1] Saint Petersburg State University,
Universitetskaya nab. 11, 199034 St. Petersburg, Russia
t.sherstinova@spbu.ru
[2] National Research University Higher School of Economics,
190068 St. Petersburg, Russia

Abstract. Paralinguistic phenomena are non-verbal elements in conversation. Paralinguistic studies are usually based on audio or video recordings of spoken communication. In this article, we will show what kind of audible paralinguistic information may be obtained from the ORD speech corpus of everyday Russian discourse containing long-term audio recordings of conversations made in natural circumstances. This linguistic resource provides rich authentic data for studying the diversity of audible paralinguistic phenomena. The frequency of paralinguistic phenomena in everyday conversations has been calculated on the base of the annotated subcorpus of 187,600 tokens. The most frequent paralinguistic phenomena turned out to be: laughter, inhalation noise, cough, e-like and m-like vocalizations, tongue clicking, and the variety of unclassified non-verbal sounds (calls, exclamations, imitations by voice, etc.). The paper reports on distribution of paralinguistic elements, non-verbal interjections and hesitations in speech of different gender and age groups.

Keywords: Paralinguistics · Audible paralinguistic phenomena
Vocalizations · Everyday conversation · Spoken interaction · Speech corpus
Russian language · Laughter · Interjections · Hesitations · Fillers
Gender · Age

1 Introduction

We would like to begin this article with a quote by David Abercrombie which, from our point of view, perfectly grasps the main features of paralinguistic elements and the importance of their research:

"Paralinguistic phenomena are non-linguistic elements in conversation. They occur alongside spoken language, interact with it, and produce together with it a total system of communication. They are not necessarily continuously simultaneous with spoken words. They may also be interspersed among them, or precede them, or follow them; but they are always integrated into a conversation considered as a complete linguistic interaction. The study of paralinguistic behaviour is part of the study of

© Springer Nature Switzerland AG 2019
P. Eismont and O. Mitrenina (Eds.): LMAC 2017, CCIS 943, pp. 131–145, 2019.
https://doi.org/10.1007/978-3-030-05594-3_11

conversation: the conversational use of spoken language cannot be properly under-
stood unless paralinguistic elements are taken into account" [1, p. 55].

Paralinguistic elements are used in conversation either consciously or uncon-
sciously. It is generally accepted that they help to convey speaker's feelings, emotions
or state, they make the speech more descriptive and may considerably modify the
meaning of spoken words [17]. Moreover, there is a hypothesis that "almost anything
can be communicated linguistically, and almost anything paralinguistically" [1]. This
communicative potential of paralanguage explains a growing interest in these phenomena in the last 50 years.

In one of the first works in the field by Henry Lee Smith [39] two types of
paralinguistic phenomena—*kinesics* and *vocalizations* (i.e., movements and sounds)
which accompany conversations—have been distinguished. The first classification of
audible paralinguistic phenomena was proposed by Trager [41], who defined three
kinds of vocalizations: (1) *vocal characterizers* are laughter, giggling, yelling, whis-
pering, moaning, etc.; (2) *vocal qualifiers* imply a variation of voice intensity, pitch
height and extent; (3) *vocal segregates* are segmental sounds (such as *uh-uh, ooh,
hmm*), fillers, and other hesitation phenomena [17]. Trager was also the first who
designed a system of notation for vocal paralinguistic behaviour [23]. Since that a large
number of research papers on paralinguistic phenomena has appeared, among which
we shall mention, in particular [9–11, 17, 20, 25, 30–32, 43].

However, starting from the origin of current paralinguistic tradition, there was no
agreement in opinion between researchers which phenomena should be considered as
paralinguistic and which should not (e.g., [1, 43]), and different classification scheme
categories have been proposed by different authors. For example, some researches do
not consider gestures and facial expressions to be paralinguistic elements preferring to
refer them to kinesics [25]. The other claim that to be considered as paralinguistic, the
vocal element should "enter into conversation" [1]. Following such approach, the
sounds like "wolf whistle", though being communicative but not entering into conversation should not be considered as paralinguistic [ibid.]. Then, there is no clear
borders between some paralinguistic and linguistic elements (e.g., between some vocal
segregates and lexicalized interjections) [29]. Many researchers agree that not all vocal
sounds beyond language belong to paralanguage [1, 23] and consider that many
physiological sounds like sneezing or cough should not be taken into consideration.
However, in recent years it turned out that for many practical tasks (e.g., for speech
recognition) it is important to distinguish all kinds of vocal phenomena, irrespective of
whether they are important for conversation or are just physiological. Because of that in
many modern resources pure physiological sounds are treated like paralinguistic
phenomena [33].

In recent decades, the study of paralinguistic phenomena has reached a qualitatively
new level. This happened due to the fact that, firstly, it became easier to collect and
process digital audio and video recordings, which are the main sources for paralinguistic studies [18]; secondly, the research on everyday discourse as well as multi-
aspect conversation analysis both inevitably involved to treat paralinguistic phenomena
are rapidly developing [12, 13, 16, 34]; and thirdly, new opportunities and challenges
connected with speech technologies tasks have emerged (in particular, the need for
developing systems of natural-sounding speech synthesis and increasing the

requirements for speech recognition systems [6, 19, 21, 31, etc.]). Besides, we should mention the growing interest in studies of emotions, affect and personality as well as their automatic detection and processing [17, 31, 43]. The importance of research on paralinguistic features is understood by other interdisciplinary studies as well [26].

There has always been a difficulty in devising a proper notation for paralinguistic phenomena. For example, there is a tradition of designating the common interjections by words (e.g., in English, *tut-tut, whew, humph, uh-huh, ahem, sh, ugh,* etc.), though it is quite impossible to pronounce them from the spelling unless you already knew them [1]. There may be several variants of spelling paralinguistic sounds (e.g., in Russian two spelling variants are used for designating *humph*-like sound—*hm* or *gm*, and more than that, in real conversation these interjections may be pronounced with a variety of intonation contours implying quite different meanings.

Because of complexity of paralinguistic phenomena, three different kinds of their notation are usually used: (a) normal phonetic transcriptions, (b) verbal transcriptions, and (c) auxiliary use of measurement of acoustic parameters and their visualization. Most frequently, combinations of these three modes of transcription are used [44].

A number of notation systems for paralinguistic phenomena has been already proposed—either for paralinguistic elements by themselves, or within wider transcriptions and codings for spoken speech [3, 12, 13, 16, 24, 28, 34, 41]. However, until present there are no common standards in this aspect, and many researches—as well as resources—use the notation of their own.

Currently, most paralinguistic studies are based on either audio or video recordings of conversations—collections of recording are examined. Usually, "the examples of the recurrent form chosen for study are noted and then extracted as 'specimens' so that they then be compared with one another in terms of the interactional and discourse context in which they are seen to occur" [18, p. 226]. For compiling such collections different approaches are used [29].

For linguistic studies, audio and video recording are usually organized into specially designed multimedia corpora—TIMIT [15], JST ESP corpus [8], Aibo Emotion Corpus [40], TUM AVIC corpus [32], Speaker personality Corpus [22], and many others. In this article, we will show what kind of paralinguistic information may be obtained from the ORD speech corpus containing long-term audio recordings of everyday conversations.

2 Paralinguistic Notation in the ORD Corpus

The "One Day of Speech" corpus is the largest linguistic resource of present-day spoken Russian. The corpus is being created with the aim to study Russian spontaneous speech and everyday spoken conversations in natural communicative situations [2]. For collecting data for this resource, individuals-volunteers of both sexes between the ages of 16 and 83 and of different occupations were asked to spend a day with active audio recorders aiming to record all of their spoken interactions. As usual, the respondents made recordings throughout a whole day. Because of that the title *"One Day of Speech"* has appeared, being abbreviated as the ORD corpus.

Audio recordings were made in St. Petersburg in 2007, 2010 and 2014–2016. The last series of recordings was made within the large sociolinguistic project "Everyday Russian language in different social groups" supported by the Russian Science Foundation [4]. At present, the corpus contains 1242 h of recordings made by 127 respondents (66 men and 61 women).

All recordings gathered from the participants have been annotated in detail in order to facilitate data retrieval from the corpus and their further linguistic, sociolinguistic and pragmatic analysis. The recordings are segmented into 2,800 communicative macroepisodes [36]. Speech transcripts add up to 1,000,000 tokens. Thus, the ORD corpus has become an unparalleled resource in allowing the study of everyday speech variation and paralinguistic phenomena in Russian.

Though the corpus has been compiled with the primary aim of studying verbal communication, it turned out that the recorded data contain large amount of non-verbal audio information, including vocal paralinguistic phenomena. Because of that, just from the very beginning of the corpus creation, we found it rational to introduce special symbols to designate the most frequent paralinguistic sounds and features which occur in everyday audio recordings and to note them in speech transcripts along with words, pauses and segmentation marks. The principles of multilevel annotation in the ORD corpus were described in [2]. The corpus is being annotated by means of two professional annotation tools – ELAN [14] and Praat [27].

Since our resource does not contain video data, it does not allow studying gestures, face expressions and other kinesic elements; therefore, speaking about paralinguistic phenomena below in this article we will mean only the audible vocal elements. Moreover, it should be taken into account that in this paper we also consider as "paralinguistic" a whole range of audible non-verbal elements which in many cases could not be considered as strictly paralinguistic, but rather physiological (e.g., cough, inhalation noise, sniffing, etc.). However, because "all these phenomena are embedded in the word chain and are often modeled the same way as words in automatic speech processing; they can denote (health) state, emotion/mood, speaker's idiosyncrasies, and the like" [33] we consider it appropriate to discuss them here.

Paralinguistic elements and features are specified in corpus annotation in two ways: either directly on the level of speech transcripts (on the same line with words, pauses and prosodic boundaries) or on the secondary annotation levels used for describing voice quality and isolated audio events.

Segment paralinguistic phenomena, independent of the verbal elements of conversation [1]—interjections, fillers, other "vocal noises" and vocal physiology sounds —are usually noted directly on the level of speech transcript (Phrase-level), and the duration of each element may be measured.

The list of the major annotation symbols for segmental paralinguistic elements used in ORD corpus is presented in Table 1. Most of these symbols have an asterisk as a prefix. Some of these symbols were used from the very beginning of the corpus annotation, the others were introduced later if a referred phenomenon turned out to be regular enough. The presented list is open for further extension. For those elements which do not fall into any category from this list we use the symbol *W. This table does not include common Russian interjections (such as *uhu, aga, nea, hm*), which are traditionally spelled like words.

Table 1. Symbols for paralinguistic phenomena in ORD speech transcripts

Symbol	Meaning
1. Paralinguistic elements which may occur independently from speech	
*B	inhalation noise (when audible)
*X	exhalation noise (when audible)
*O	sigh
*C	laughter
*L	crying/weeping
*K	cough
*3	yawn
*Z	sneezing
*Ц	tongue clicking
*S	sniffing
[a], [o], etc.	sound-like vocalization with open mouth
[m]	sound-like vocalization with closed mouth
*Г	smacking
*R	throat cleaning
*G	various glottal sounds
*W	other unclassified non-verbal sounds
*E	singing (with words, without words), humming
2. Hesitation marks	
(…)	voiceless hesitation
(a), (e), etc.	short voiced hesitations
(a-a), (e-a), etc.	long voiced hesitations
3. Speech dependent marks	
(:)	stretches of words/sounds

For example, Fig. 1 shows the annotation of the following fragment:

Participant S62: *Kakaya vstrecha!* [*What a meeting!*] *C(laugh)
Interlocutor M1-S62: *Nu da!* [*Yes, indeed!*]

It is seen from Table 1, that there is just one symbol of speech-depending phenomena which is marked on the level of speech transcripts—colon-symbol in parentheses, meaning stretches of words or individual sounds.

What concerns paralinguistic phenomena from the first group which may occur independently from speech, many of them may take place simultaneously with speech as well, overlapping it and therefore changing its characteristics: e.g., *laugh, cry, yawning*, etc. In such cases we specify these fragments of speech on the special level of *Voice* features, where the other voice qualities are marked in a free (descriptive) way: *in a tender voice, affectionately, laughter*, etc. According to Trager's classification they are *vocal characterizers*. In other approaches, they refer to the *tones of voice* [1]. The borders of the correspondent annotation indicate the location of the phenomena in concern (see Fig. 2).

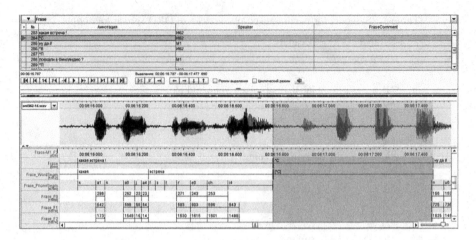

Fig. 1. Annotation of laughter between utterances.

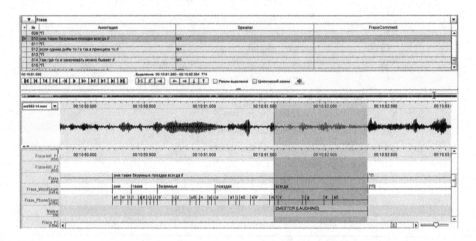

Fig. 2. Annotation of speech-laughs on Voice level.

Besides, there is a special annotation level in the ORD annotation files, which is used for indication of non-speech audio events and transcribers' comments. Here, one may also find the indications for some paralinguistic phenomena, but in rather "descriptive mode" (e.g., *"children's laughter in the background"*, *"(he) chews and swallows"*, *"sounds like she tastes the tea"*, etc.).

Speech dependent paralinguistic phenomena as well as the descriptions of paralinguistic elements given on additional annotation levels provide interesting research data, however as their annotations has not been normalized until present, it is impossible to automatically process them. Because of that, they are not discussed in this report.

3 The Frequency of Paralinguistic Phenomena in Everyday Interaction

The frequency of paralinguistic phenomena has been calculated on the base of the annotated subcorpus consisting of 100 communicative macroepisodes [5], and containing speech of 100 respondents being representatives of 20 social groups. Besides, the subcorpus contains speech of 156 interlocutors of different gender, ages, professions, and status.

Here is the list of social groups whose speech communication is presented in the analyzed subcorpus: (a) 2 gender groups (men and women), (b) 3 age groups (youth, middle-aged and seniors), (c) 10 professional groups (workers, engineers, soldiers, people engaged in natural science, people engaged in humanities, people working in education, service sector employees, IT professionals, office workers, people of creative professions), (d) 5 status groups (students and pupils, employees and specialists, executives, businessmen and private entrepreneurs, unemployed and retired) [5].

The total amount of tokens in the exploratory subcorpus equals to 187,600. It contains 27,069 phrases, 125,438 words, and 1,960 paralinguistic phenomena marked on the level of speech transcripts.

Here, it is relevant to compare these results with those obtained in [35], reporting that "paralinguistic speech acts" constitute about 3.55% of speech acts in everyday spoken interaction. However, in [35] only those paralinguistic phenomena which may be treated as "speech acts" were analyzed (e.g., laughter, tongue clicking, sighing, etc.), but not the physiological phenomena like inhalation/exhalation noises, sneezing, cough, etc.

Table 2 presents the most frequent paralinguistic phenomena observed in the subcorpus, reports the total number of occurrences for each paralinguistic phenomena and gives two percentages—the first one is calculated with respect to the number of paralinguistic phenomena (PP), the other—with respect to the number of words.

Table 2. The most frequent paralinguistic phenomena obtained on the ORD-subcorpus of 187,600 tokens

Phenomena		Absolute number	Percentage (PP)	Percentage (words)
*C	laughter	779	39.74	0.6232
*B	inhalation noise	638	32.55	0.5104
*K	cough	112	5.71	0.0896
[a], [m], etc.	vocalizations	19	4.95	0.0152
*Ц	tongue clicking	69	3.42	0.0536
*W	other non-verbal sounds	56	2.86	0.0448
*S	sniffing	37	1.89	0.0296
*R	throat cleaning	54	2.76	0.0432
*O	sigh	23	1.17	0.0184
*З	yawn	23	1.17	0.0184
*Г	smacking	20	1.02	0.0160

Thus, one may see that the most frequent audible paralinguistic phenomena turned out to be the following: laughter, inhalation noise, cough, vocalizations of different kinds (*a*-like, *e*-like, *m*-like, etc.), and tongue clicking.

What strikes the eye is the undeniable leadership of laughter in comparison with other paralinguistic events. The meaning of laughter in spoken conversation is recognized by many scientists [7, 12, 42].

Two other phenomena which are rather physiological than 'paralinguistic'—audible inhalation noise and cough—have the second and the third ranks correspondently. Tongue clicking and the other unclassified non-verbal sounds (*W) are also regular. As for phenomena marked by *W, the most frequent among them are various expressions of emotions (surprise, annoyance, interest, disappointment, etc.) or imitation of something (e.g., a working engine).

Everyday singing and humming deserve special attention. As it was shown in [38], almost one third (29%) of participants has shown the episodes of singing behaviour during the day of recording. It turned out that there are more "everyday singers" among men (33%) than among women (25%). An interesting though uncommon type of everyday singing behaviour is *singing instead of speaking*, i. e. singing in communication and interaction [ibid].

The exploratory subcorpus does not contain any crying/weeping fragments, and it should be mentioned that in the ORD recordings crying is a rather rare phenomenon.

4 Distribution of Paralinguistic Elements in Speech Communication of Different Gender and Age Groups

It was noticed long ago that paralinguistic phenomena are neither personal nor generally human, but they are culturally determined and differ from social group to social group [1, 3, 9]. In this section, we would like to compare the occurrence of paralinguistic elements between different gender and age groups.

Table 3 reports on distribution of paralinguistic elements in speech of men and women calculated on the subcorpus of 125,438 words described in the previous section. The male speech share equals to 47,135 words, whereas the female speech share amounts to 78,303 words. The percentages are calculated with respect to the number of words for each gender.

The presented numbers show that there is not much difference in our sample between the usage of many paralinguistic phenomena by men and women. It's quite predictable, that the closest numbers between groups are obtained for the inhalation noise, reflecting a common physiology factor. However, the majority of phenomena occurs slightly often in the male speech than in the female one (e.g., tongue clicking, smacking, sigh, yawn, cough, singing, humming and other unclassified non-verbal sounds). A few exceptions here, which slightly dominate in women's speech are laughter and various glottal sounds. For occurrences of everyday singing in gender and age groups in the ORD corpus see [38].

Table 3. Comparative frequencies of paralinguistic phenomena in male and female speech

Phenomena		Percentage (men)	Percentage (women)
*C	laughter	0.5898	0.6002
*B	inhalation noise	0.5071	0.5096
*K	cough	0.1040	0.0805
*Ц	tongue clicking	0.0679	0.0473
*W	other non-verbal sounds	0.0636	0.0332
*S	sniffing	0.0594	0.0115
*O	sigh	0.0297	–
*Г	smacking	0.0255	0.0102
*3	yawn	0.0233	0.0153
*X	exhalation noise	0.0191	–
*E	singing or humming	0.0127	0.0051
*G	various glottal sounds	0.0042	0.0115

Table 4 presents comparative frequencies of paralinguistic phenomena for different age groups. The following three age groups are distinguished:

Age Group I (AG I): 18–30 years old,
Age Group II (AG II): 31–54 years old,
Age Group III (AG III): 55+ years old.

Table 4. The most frequent paralinguistic phenomena obtained on the ORD-subcorpus of 187,600 tokens

Phenomena		Percentage (AG I, 18–30)	Percentage (AG II, 31–54)	Percentage (AG III, 55+)
*C	laughter	0.9087	0.4180	0.3876
*B	inhalation noise	0.5051	0.4550	0.6475
*K	cough	0.1036	0.0506	0.1065
*Ц	tongue clicking	0.0626	0.0661	0.0170
*W	other non-verbal sounds	0.0367	0.0331	0.0298
*S	sniffing	0.0324	0.0233	0.0426
*3	yawn	0.0194	0.0156	0.0255
*Г	smacking	0.0151	0.0175	0.0127
*E	singing, humming	0.0130	0.0039	–
*G	various glottal sounds	0.0086	0.0058	0.0170
*O	sigh	0.0086	0.0156	0.0426
*X	exhalation noise	0.0065	0.0117	–
*Z	sneezing	0.0022	0.0019	–

The numbers of words for each subcorpus are as follows: AG I—46,330 words, AG II—51,431 words, and AG III—23,475 words. Similar to the previous Table, the percentages here are calculated with respect to the number of words.

These data shows that there is an evident tendency to decreasing of all top-rank paralinguistic phenomena with age—laughter, tongue clicking and the variety of other unclassified non-verbal sounds. As for laughter, it is used in the youth group more than twice as likely than in the older age groups. Quite the reverse, sighing and frequently occurring "physiological" elements—audible inhalations and exhalations, cough, sniffing, and yawn—turned out to be more common for seniors.

Pragmatic annotation of the corpus allows to obtain similar data for different interaction settings, for diverse social roles of speakers, etc. We can assume that there will be more laughter and other "expressive" paralinguistic phenomena in private informal conversations than in business communication, but this hypothesis needs verification.

5 Non-verbal Interjections and Hesitations

In this section, we will present some data on usage of non-verbal interjections and hesitations. All data are given in percentages calculated for the referred social groups or subcorpus in the whole (column *Totally*).

Table 5 reports on occurrences of the most frequent non-verbal interjections, which fall into three groups. Two interjections of the first group are used in conversation to express agreement, understanding or feedback. They have the only difference—*ugu* is pronounced with a closed mouth, whereas *aga* is pronounced with an open mouth. Their functional synonym is the particle *da* (*yes*).

Table 5. The most frequent non-verbal interjections (%)

Interjections		Totally	MEN	WOMEN	AG I, (18–30)	AG II, (31–54)	AG III, (55+)
Agreement, understanding, feedback							
ugu	(uh-huh)	**0.437**	0.346	0.493	0.478	0.450	0.325
aga	(aha)	**0.100**	0.109	0.095	0.110	0.098	0.098
Disagreement							
nea	(nope)	0.012	0.008	0.014	0.012	0.007	0.000
Various emotions (depending on prosody)							
hm/gm	(humph)	0.032	0.017	0.041	0.042	0.029	0.022
ah	(ah)	0.018	0.008	0.024	0.016	0.013	0.008
oh	(oh)	0.014	0.006	0.020	0.019	0.012	0.014
eh	(eh)	0.010	0.011	0.009	0.007	0.009	0.017
aj	(aj)	0.010	0.013	0.009	0.007	0.007	0.017
oj	(oj)	**0.139**	0.082	0.174	0.109	0.157	0.143
ha	(ha)	0.012	0.014	0.010	0.025	0.004	0.006
Total		**0,783**	**0,614**	**0,889**	**0,824**	**0,785**	**0,651**

Disagreement may be expressed by non-verbal interjection *nea*—an informal variant of *net* (*no*) and its reduced form *ne*.

The third group of non-verbal interjections is used to convey emotions. The remarkable property of these paralinguistic elements is that most of them can imply a number of quite diverse feelings depending on prosody.

According to Table 5, paralinguistic interjections of agreement, understanding and feedback are the most frequent. As for interjections conveying emotions, the most popular among them turned out to be an exclamation *oj*. It is seen from the table that women use non-verbal interjections more frequently than men in order to maintain a conversation and to express emotions. This conclusion confirms our previous observations that men use less feedback than women and prefer to use the expletives (as well as their substitutes) to express emotions [37].

The evident downward trend is observed in the usage of non-verbal interjections with age: seniors use less interjections than middle-aged people, and the maximum share of interjections is observed in speech of youth.

Finally, Table 6 presents the list of the most frequent non-verbal hesitations. The variety of voiced hesitations is grouped here according to the similarity of the main sound: '*e*-like', '*m*-like', etc. One can see that the usual fillers in hesitations are vowels and sonorants. Rarely occur fillers consisting of two (or even more) sounds.

Table 6. The most frequent non-verbal hesitations (%)

Hesitations		Totally	Men	Women	AGE I, (18–30)	AGE II, (31–54)	AGE III, (55+)
(…)	hesitation pauses	0.735	0.908	0.628	0.743	0.680	0.844
(e), (e-e)	*e*-like	0.541	0.650	0.474	0.352	0.525	0.979
(m), (m-m)	*m*-like	0.120	0.134	0.112	0.104	0.102	0.194
(a), (a-a)	*a*-like	0.053	0.089	0.031	0.061	0.057	0.031
(n), (n-n)	*n*-like	0.026	0.032	0.022	0.032	0.025	0.022
(v)	*v*-like	0.008	0.013	0.005	0.003	0.015	0.006
(e-m), (a-e)	two-element	0.012	0.003	0.018	0.009	0.005	0.036
Total		1.497	1.828	1.291	1.303	1.408	2.112

Contrary to the results obtained for interjections, it is seen from Table 6 that men generally hesitate more than women (see also [37]), and the amount of hesitations increases with age.

6 Conclusion

In this paper, we aimed to present the system of annotation used for paralinguistic phenomena in speech transcripts of the ORD corpus and to obtain preliminary statistics on distribution of these elements in everyday conversations, taking into consideration gender and age differences of interlocutors.

The frequency of paralinguistic phenomena has been calculated on the base of the annotated subcorpus consisting of 100 communicative macroepisodes, and containing speech of 256 interlocutors of different gender, ages, professions, and status. The most frequent audible paralinguistic phenomena turned out to be the following: laughter, inhalation noise, cough, vocalizations of different kinds (*a*-like, *e*-like, *m*-like, etc.), and tongue clicking. We didn't find much difference in our sample between the usage of many paralinguistic phenomena by men and women. However, there is an evident tendency to decreasing of all top-rank paralinguistic phenomena (in particular, laughter, tongue clicking and the variety of other unclassified non-verbal sounds) with age.

Laughter turned out to be the most frequent paralinguistic phenomena covering about 40% of all paralinguistic elements. In our sample, laughter is used in the youth group more than twice as likely than in the older age groups, whereas there is no much difference in frequency of laughter between gender groups.

The analysis of non-verbal interjections and hesitations has been made on the same subcorpus. It revealed that the most frequent interjections are *ugu* (*uh-huh*) and *aga* (*aha*), which are used to express agreement, understanding or feedback. Among interjections conveying emotions, the most popular is an exclamation *oj*. Women use non-verbal interjections more frequently than men, while the latter prefer swear-words and their substitutes to express emotions.

The evident downward trend is observed in the usage of non-verbal interjections with age: seniors use less interjections than middle-aged people, and the maximum share of interjections is observed in the speech of youth. As for non-verbal hesitations, in contrast, men hesitate more than women in general, and the amount of hesitations increases with age.

The ORD corpus provides rich authentic data for studying the diversity of audible paralinguistic phenomena. However, analyzing real-life spoken discourse and studying its variation turned out to be extremely complex and challenging tasks. Thus, the list of paralinguistic phenomena that was proposed initially for corpus annotation has been subjected to considerable extension in the process of speech transcribing. The current annotation scheme also could not be considered to be perfect altogether. For example, it seems that some paralinguistic phenomena (in particular, laughter) deserve more fine-grained annotation, as it is made in some other resources designed for paralinguistic studies.

Basing on the ORD recordings, an audio database of audible paralinguistic phenomena is planned to be created. The creation of such a database will allow comparing actual functioning of paralinguistic elements in conversations and could help in better understanding of their semantic and pragmatic functions.

References

1. Abercrombie, D.: Paralanguage. Br. J. Disord. Commun. **3**, 55–59 (1996)
2. Asinovsky, A., Bogdanova, N., Rusakova, M., Ryko, A., Stepanova, S., Sherstinova, T.: The ORD speech corpus of Russian everyday communication "One Speaker's Day": creation principles and annotation. In: Matoušek, V., Mautner, P. (eds.) TSD 2009. LNCS (LNAI), vol. 5729, pp. 250–257. Springer, Heidelberg (2009). https://doi.org/10.1007/978-3-642-04208-9_36
3. Austin, W.M.: Some social aspects of paralanguage. Can. J. Linguist. **11**(1), 31–39 (1965)
4. Bogdanova-Beglarian, N., et al.: Sociolinguistic extension of the ORD corpus of Russian everyday speech. In: Ronzhin, A., Potapova, R., Németh, G. (eds.) SPECOM 2016. LNCS (LNAI), vol. 9811, pp. 659–666. Springer, Cham (2016). https://doi.org/10.1007/978-3-319-43958-7_80
5. Bogdanova-Beglarian, N., Sherstinova, T., Blinova, O., Martynenko, G.: Linguistic features and sociolinguistic variability in everyday spoken Russian. In: Karpov, A., Potapova, R., Mporas, I. (eds.) SPECOM 2017. LNCS (LNAI), vol. 10458, pp. 503–511. Springer, Cham (2017). https://doi.org/10.1007/978-3-319-66429-3_50
6. Burkhardt, F., Huber, R., Batliner, A.: Application of speaker classification in human machine dialog systems. In: Müller, C. (ed.) Speaker Classification I. LNCS (LNAI), vol. 4343, pp. 174–179. Springer, Heidelberg (2007). https://doi.org/10.1007/978-3-540-74200-5_9
7. Campbell, N.: Conversational speech synthesis and the need for some laughter. IEEE Trans. Audio Speech Lang. Process. **14**, 1171–1178 (2006)
8. Campbell, N.: Speech & expression; the value of a longitudinal corpus. In: LREC 2004, pp. 183–186 (2004)
9. Crystal, D.: Prosodic and paralinguistic correlates of social categories. In: Ardener, E. (ed.) Social Anthropology, pp. 185–206. Tavistock, London (1971)
10. Crystal, D.: Prosodic Systems and Intonation in English. Univ. Press, Cambridge (1969)
11. Crystal, D., Quirk, R.: Systems of Prosodic and Paralinguistic Features in English. Mouton, The Hague (1964)
12. Du Bois, J.: Transcription design principles for spoken discourse research. Pragmatics **1**, 71–106 (1991)
13. Edwards, J., Lampert, M.D. (eds.): Talking Data. Transcription and Coding in Discourse Research, Hillsdale (1993)
14. ELAN homepage. https://tla.mpi.nl/tools/tla-tools/elan/. Accessed 17 July 2017
15. Fisher, W.M., Doddington, G.R., Goudie-Marshall, K.M.: The DARPA Speech Recognition Research Database: Specifications and Status, pp. 93–99 (1986)
16. Hepburn, A., Bolden, G.: The conversation analytic approach to transcription. In: Stivers, T., Sidnell, J. (eds.) The Handbook of Conversation Analysis. Blackwell, Oxford (2013)
17. Johar, S.: Emotion, Affect and Personality in Speech. The Bias of Language and Paralanguage. Springer, Cham (2016). https://doi.org/10.1007/978-3-319-28047-9
18. Kendon, A.: Gesture: Visible Action as Utterance. Cambridge University Press, Cambridge (2004)
19. Kipyatkova, I., Verkhodanova, V., Ronzhin, A.: Segmentation of paralinguistic phonation phenomena in spontaneous Russian speech, Perm University Herald. Russ. Foreign Philol. **2**(18), 17–23 (2012)
20. Knapp, M.L., Hall, J.A., Horgan, T.G.: Nonverbal Communication in Human Interaction, 8th edn. Wadsworth, Boston (2014)

21. McTear, M., Callejas, Z., Griol, D.: The Conversational Interface. Talking to Smart Devices. Springer, Cham (2016). https://doi.org/10.1007/978-3-319-32967-3
22. Mohammadi, G., Vinciarelli, A., Mortillaro, M.: The voice of personality: mapping nonverbal vocal behavior into trait attributions. In: Proceedings of the 2nd International Workshop on Social Signal Processing, Florence, pp. 17–20 (2010)
23. Nöth, W.: Handbook of Semiotics. Indiana University Press (1995)
24. Pittenger, R.E., Hockett, C.F., Danehy, J.J.: The First Five Minutes: A Sample of Microscopic Interview Analysis. Paul Martineau, Ithaca (1960)
25. Poyatas, F.: Paralanguage: A Linguistic and Interdisciplinary Approach to Interactive Speech and Sounds. John Benjamins, Amsterdam (1993)
26. Poyatos, F.: Nonverbal Communication Across Disciplines. John Benjamins Pub. Co., Amsterdam (2002)
27. Praat homepage. http://www.fon.hum.uva.nl/praat/. Accessed 17 July 2017
28. Redder, A.: Aufbau und Gestaltung von Transkriptionssystemen. In: Brinker, K., Antos, G., Heinemann, W., Sager, S.F. (Hgg.): Text- und Gesprächslinguistik. Linguistics of Text and Conversation. Ein internationales Handbuch zeitgenössischer Forschung. An International Handbook of Contemporary Research. 2. Halbband, vol. 2, pp. 1038–1059. de Gruyter, Berlin (2001)
29. Scherer, K.G.: Vocal communication of emotion: a review of research paradigms. Speech Commun. **40**, 227–256 (2003)
30. Scherer, K.R., Ekman, P. (eds.): Handbook of Methods in Nonverbal Behavior Research, pp. 136–198. Cambridge University Press, Cambridge (1982)
31. Schuller, B., Batliner, A.: Computational Paralinguistics: Emotion, Affect and Personality in Speech and Language Processing, 1st edn. Wiley, Hoboken (2014)
32. Schuller, B., Müller, R., Eyben, F., et al.: Being bored? Recognising natural interest by extensive audiovisual integration for real-life application. Image Vis. Comput. **27**(12), 1760–1774 (2009)
33. Schuller, B., et al.: Paralinguistics in speech and language—state-of-the-art and the challenge. Comput. Speech Lang. Spec. Issue Paralinguistics Nat. Speech Lang. **27**(1), 4–39 (2013)
34. Selting, M., et al.: Gesprächsanalytisches Transkriptionssystem (GAT). Linguistische Berichte **173**, 91–122 (1998)
35. Sherstinova, T.: Speech acts annotation of everyday conversations in the ORD corpus of spoken Russian. In: Ronzhin, A., Potapova, R., Németh, G. (eds.) SPECOM 2016. LNCS (LNAI), vol. 9811, pp. 627–635. Springer, Cham (2016). https://doi.org/10.1007/978-3-319-43958-7_76
36. Sherstinova, T.: Macro episodes of Russian everyday oral communication: towards pragmatic annotation of the ORD speech corpus. In: Ronzhin, A., Potapova, R., Fakotakis, N. (eds.) SPECOM 2015. LNCS (LNAI), vol. 9319, pp. 268–276. Springer, Cham (2015). https://doi.org/10.1007/978-3-319-23132-7_33
37. Sherstinova, T.: The most frequent words in everyday spoken Russian (in the gender dimention and depending on communication settings). In: Komp'juternaja Lingvistika i Intellektual'nye Tehnologii, vol. 15, no. 22, pp. 616–631 (2016)
38. Sherstinova, T.: Some observations on everyday singing behaviour based on long-term audio recordings. In: Eismont, P., Konstantinova, N. (eds.) LMAC 2015. CCIS, vol. 561, pp. 88–100. Springer, Cham (2015). https://doi.org/10.1007/978-3-319-27498-0_8
39. Smith, H.L.: The Communication Situation. Foreign Service Institute (mimeographed), Washington (1950)
40. Steidl, S.: Automatic Classification of Emotion Related User States in Spontaneous Children's Speech. Logos-Verl. (2009)

41. Trager, G.L.: Paralanguage: a first approximation. Stud. Linguist. **13**, 1–12 (1958)
42. Trouvain, J.: Laughter, breathing, clicking—the prosody of nonverbal vocalisations. In: Campbell, Gibbon, and Hirst (eds.) Speech Prosody, pp. 598–602 (2014)
43. Wharton, T.: Paralanguage. In: Barron, A., Gu, Y., Steen, G. (eds.) The Routledge Handbook of Pragmatics. Routledge (2017)
44. Winkler, P.: Notationen des Sprechausdrucks. Zeitschrift für Semiotik **1**(2/3), 211–224 (1979)

Music Computing

Distributed Software Hardware Solution for Complex Network Sonification

Gleb G. Rogozinsky[1](✉) ⓘ, Konstantin Lyzhinkin[2] ⓘ,
Anna Egorova[3] ⓘ, and Dmitry Podolsky[1] ⓘ

[1] The Bonch-Bruevich St. Petersburg State University of Telecommunications,
22-1 Bolshevikov Pt, St. Petersburg 193232, Russia
gleb.rogozinsky@gmail.com
[2] Scientific Research Institute Rubin, 5 Kantemirovskaya St,
St. Petersburg 194100, Russia
[3] Branch ZNIIS – LO ZNIIS, 11 Varshavskaya St.,
St. Petersburg 196128, Russia

Abstract. The paper presents the hardware software solution for sonification of complex networks and systems. The sonification expands the possibilities of an analysis of complex information through using the human hearing. Auditory displays allow reducing the operator's workload and better detection of specific features and patterns in the data. The proposed sonification complex consists of two main parts. Data source located in the LO ZNIIS generates data that describes current state of a network or complex system, accumulates and redirects it. The parametric sonification layer located in the SUT converts the information into forms suitable for creating new audio environment, and represents the data as relevant timbral classes.

Keywords: Sonification · Big data · Csound

1 Introduction

In the recent years, both commercial and private consumers have been following the trend of immersion into an information society. Creating new algorithms of data monitoring and interfaces of the user/system actions mapping with the multidimensional arrays of selected parameters becomes more urgent than ever.

The composition, nature, degree of abstraction, method of presentation of parameters to display can vary within the large limits, depending on the purpose of the investigated system or area. Sometimes it is convenient to associate large data sets to be processed with any mathematical or engineering model (complex network, or mathematical graph model). It affords to use the existing well-tested instruments for data description and processing.

The annual growth of a number of devices connected to the Internet results into a vast growth of scientific interest and involving of scientists into the research of aforementioned models and instruments.

Multidimensional data sets are convenient for describing various states of complex networks and systems, since tables, lists and others abstract data structures can be

© Springer Nature Switzerland AG 2019
P. Eismont and O. Mitrenina (Eds.): LMAC 2017, CCIS 943, pp. 149–160, 2019.
https://doi.org/10.1007/978-3-030-05594-3_12

successfully processed by computers and special analytical solutions. By its very nature, such data is poorly structured. Due to the large volumes it can and does occupy, it usually referred as the Big Data.

It is often difficult for the operator of some complex system to perform an adequately full and quick analysis of raw big data through using only a set of visual toolkits. Traditional methods of modeling are not always suitable for obtaining necessary knowledge contained in the arrays of big data.

Any attempts for visualization of big data, such as representing of various complex networks and the included data as graphs, are useful in some way, but reveal the main drawback of that class of methods - the use of the visual sensory system only. The human eye is able to distinguish about ten million of colors, but it cannot keep in focus many parameters at the same time.

The architecture of a visual presentation of a complex system is not always able to correctly choose the optimal field of view - or requires special additional development (revision, additional fixing, tuning). Software models can excessively modify initial array when rendering it.

The specificity of the monitoring processes of complex systems creates an issue of development of fundamentally new interfaces for displaying big data. Regarding the auditory interface along with the visual one seems to be self-evident but is also provable by practice and science.

Deeping into the exploration and application of the auditory interfaces, we suggest to distinguish its logical components first. Rather useful approach was described in [1], applied to the telemedicine systems. We modified the proposed model according to our tasks.

2   The Modified Multidomain Model

2.1   Main Definitions

The application of non-speech auditory interfaces in the complex human-machine systems assumes solving several actual tasks, related to the problems of stability increasing and effectiveness of such systems.

For the purposes of generalization of the development process of a new interface at its initial state and better understanding of variety of solutions we should find the adequate complex of models to effectively represent the various and complex processes which take part over the whole process.

The modified multidomain model of infocommunication interaction provides general methodology, which includes the methods of a formal description of informational processes, which take place into the systems, and the ways of quantitative analysis of the parameters and characteristics of utilized signaling systems. At the same time, the model provides the possibility for accounting weakly formalized components of the interfaces, related to physiological and emotional aspects of perception.

The domain model proposed in [1] assumes dissection of the interaction field into three interacting layers (or domains), i.e. Physical Domain (PD), Informational Domain (ID) and Cognitive Domain (CD). The control of technical objects and systems assumes formation of solutions for control interactions, which alter the state of the system towards increasing of target function according to the information representation of the object.

The PD is typically concerned with the energy processes and the interaction between material world objects. The situational analysis and the intellectual activity producing evaluations and solutions are the products of mental and psychic activity happen within the CD. The ID is the area for the circulation of data used in the CD, representing the objects, phenomena and processes of the PD.

At the domain borders, the corresponding interfaces perform the informational interaction between different elements of the system. The finite number of states, represented by its own thesaurus, can characterize each object/subject of the system.

Thus, the object A of a PD with the corresponding thesaurus ξ^A, mapped onto the multiplicity of informational representations of the thesaurus ξ^B

$$\langle A \rangle^{\xi^A} \overset{Signal}{\Rightarrow} \left\langle \langle A \rangle^{\xi^A} \right\rangle^{\xi^B}. \tag{1}$$

The information is received when a new image of the source is formed within the varifold thesaurus of the target system.

$$\langle A \rangle^{\xi^A} \longrightarrow Q^{12} \langle B \rangle^{\xi^B} \longrightarrow Q^{23} \left\langle \left\langle \langle A \rangle^{\xi^A} \right\rangle^{\xi^B} \right\rangle^{\xi^C}, \tag{2}$$

Where Q^{12}, Q^{23} – mapping operators between different domains, i.e. PD, ID or CD ξ^A, ξ^B, ξ^C – thesauri of corresponding domains.

Thus mapping between the corresponding domains is actually an operation of the informational impact between entities of the domains, expressed in the discovery of maximum conformity between elements of thesauri.

Typically, sonification system of any kind is not included in the system from the beginning of system's life cycle and normally plays the role of an extension to existing system. In a language of the domain model, the thesaurus of sonification layer is a subset of information domain thesaurus. In most complete case, these two thesauri are equal, but the practical experience shows that the sonification thesaurus is sufficiently lesser.

Thus inside the *sonification subdomain* (SSD) of an ID, the information goes through three successive transformation operations, i.e. input data filtering Q^F, sonification mapping Q^M, and sound synthesis Q^S. So, the Q^F is an *intradomain* mapping operator comparing to Q^1 and Q^2, which are *interdomain* ones. It can be written as

$$\left\langle \langle A \rangle^{\xi^A} \right\rangle^{\xi^\chi} \longrightarrow Q^F \left\langle \langle A \rangle^{\xi^A} \right\rangle^{\xi^{\hat{\chi}}}, \tag{3}$$

where $\xi^{\hat{\chi}} \subseteq \xi^\chi$, i.e. thesaurus of SSD is a subset of an ID thesaurus.

Next to that operation follows the operation of sonification mapping Q^M, i.e. mapping of filtered thesaurus of ID onto a set of parameters of sound synthesizer S (with its own thesaurus ξ^S), which is a driver of an auditory display system.

The entities of SSD input thesauri ξ^X can vary within the arbitrary ranges. Thus, we have to create an adaptation between the source sonification thesaurus ξ^X and target sound synthesis thesaurus ξ^S, i.e.

$$\left\langle \langle A \rangle^{\xi^A} \right\rangle^{\xi^X} \longrightarrow Q^M \langle S \rangle^{\xi^S}. \tag{4}$$

Comparing to (3), the thesauri relations cannot be easily formalized, since all possible cases of mappings are possible, i.e. a single value of ξ^X to a single value of ξ^S, a single value of ξ^X to N values of ξ^S, and N values of ξ^X to a single value of ξ^S.

During sound synthesis controlled by mapped values, the corresponding sound signal is created. It inherits the desired features of ID representation of PD objects. Thus, the entities are represented in the thesaurus of sound systems. In that form, the audio signal can be transmitted through some communication channel, saved as an informational entity on some media, and finally reproduced through any kind of speaker, which is actually the output part of an auditory display. We cover that series of processes under Q^2 transform, as in (2). It leads to the receiver of signal or the user of sonification interface with his or her own thesaurus ξ^U.

To conclude the above, in the terms of domain model the overall sonification process can be written like following

$$\langle A \rangle^{\xi^A} \longrightarrow Q^{12} \left\langle \langle A \rangle^{\xi^A} \right\rangle^{\xi^X} \longrightarrow Q^F \left\langle \langle A \rangle^{\xi^A} \right\rangle^{\xi^X} \longrightarrow Q^M$$

$$\longrightarrow Q^M \langle S \rangle^{\xi^S} \longrightarrow Q^{23} \left\langle \langle S \rangle^{\xi^S} \right\rangle^{\xi^U} \tag{5}$$

The formula (5) describes in general the process of informational interaction between physical objects aggregate and the entities of CD through the transfer of their informational representations. Figure 1 shows the simplified graphical interpretation of (5) for the case of auditory interface.

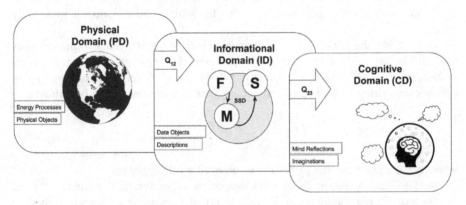

Fig. 1. Simplified graphic interpretation of a domain model

The informational representations of the PD objects (i.e. elements of technical systems) can be both visual objects (static or moving) and acoustical objects (stationary or changing). The latter are one of the research objects. The list of such objects can be expanded through the usage of olfactory (smell) and/or tactile (muscle) spaces. Such research leads us towards so-called multimodal interfaces study and corresponding design tasks [2].

Thus, at the process of development of sonification systems the following problems to be stated:

1. The problem of a set definition for the characteristics of the object, which includes the analysis of values ranges, temporal characteristics, the data rates. Generalizing, we can state that the main generators or sources of the informational streams, demanding on their interpretation in the interfaces, are *objects*, *events* and *processes*, each of which possesses the specific set of the parameters and characteristics.
2. The problem of a definition of the parameters and characteristics of a human auditory system, related to the perception of acoustical signals. This problem seems to be more or less well solved, assuming considerable research results in the different fields of acoustic studies and hearing physiology. Meanwhile, several problems related to the psychological aspects of hearing still cannot be defined as completely solved. It can be proved by considering the whole history of musical art development and such multidisciplinary subjects as a sound design.
3. The problem of an adequate and accurate mapping of the multiplicity of the entities of a PD thesaurus onto the multiplicity of ID thesaurus for the subsequent mapping onto the CD. We should mark here that just formal correlating of elements of the two thesauri, since such approach does not account psycho emotional aspects of the sound perception, and thus it requires specific multidisciplinary approaches and development of some non-trivial criteria of possible solutions estimation cannot effectively solve the latter problem.

3 Implementation of Sonification Complex

3.1 Overall View

For a practical part of the project, we developed a sonification solution for large-scale networks and systems. Figure 2 presents the structure of the developed solution, which includes the joint of two big telecom facilities of the St. Petersburg area – *The Bonch-Bruevich St. Petersburg State University of Telecommunications* (SUT) and *Leningrad Branch of Central Science Research Institute of Telecommunications* (LO ZNIIS).

The complex consists of three structural layers with different functional purposes, i.e. source generation layer, sonification layer, and auxiliary subsystems (remote libraries, backup- and remote monitoring servers).

The LO ZNIIS part of the complex is responsible for providing the data. The facility manages several post-NGN industrial solutions, thus able to provide multiple samples of big data. The complex is capable to generate the data through two fundamentally

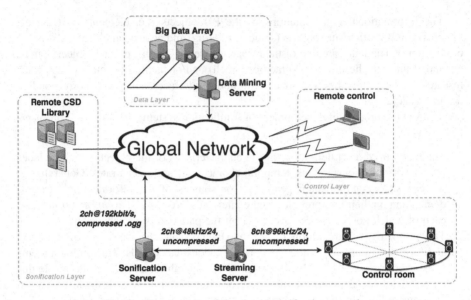

Fig. 2. The structure of developed sonification complex

different approaches: data simulation with specifying the desired characteristics of data or using a real data source with possibility to affect and modify it or simply transmit as is. Both approaches are described below in more details.

3.2   Data Simulation

The source of managed data is a cross-platform application containing a dynamic graph (based on Erdős–Rényi model [3]).

The precise parameters of the model are initially defined and specified on the application start, or can also be modified later in the process of simulation [4]. The list of most essential parameters includes following:

- Initial number of nodes;
- Probability of connection for each pair of nodes;
- Update frequency;
- Probability of (dis)appearance of a randomly selected node;
- Probability of (dis)appearance of a randomly selected connection;
- (dis)appearance of the node;
- Selection of two nodes to find the shortest path between them;

The fuzzy parameters of the model are also suitable for describing dynamical properties of the graph. They can require algorithms for their detection. Here is the list of most essential parameters:

- Relative size of the network;
- Presence/absence/appearance/disappearance of the connection property (the graph can be segmented into parts without any connections between each of them);

- Presence/absence/appearance/disappearance of clusters;
- Presence/absence/appearance/ disappearance of cyclicity;
- Unit density in total or in specified region.

3.3   Real Source

The source of real data redirection from existing network and systems with an optional data processing is an application capable to receive data through the Ethernet port and transfer it further to the processing and sonification system directly or with preprocessing. The user have an access to following blocks of information, i.e. log files of digital automatic telephone switching equipment, log files of the current working system, the output of traffic monitoring applications for the current local network, a given data array represented as a file on a media.

Further, the data analysis server selects the desired parameters for sound mapping. The software has a visual interface, and support simple logging. Data is transferred towards sonification system via OSC protocol (Open Sound Control) [5]. This protocol is developed for network interaction between multimedia devices in a real time. It supports timestamps, blobs and user-defined format of data fields, which makes it very useful for application of such kind.

3.4   Sonification

The sonification server on the receiving side uses *Csound* language for an auditory representation of the obtained data. The Csound is an open-source language, developed specially for computer music composition, digital signal processing and algorithmic composition. It runs on most of known operational systems, including main mobile platforms, as well as tiny ware, i.e. Raspberry Pi or BeagleBone [6]. There are many different instruments for various synthesis methods and processing build in Csound and accessible through the web [7].

The operator's place is located in the SUT Medialabs. The sonification synthesizer is capable to use up to eight discrete channels in an uncompressed 96 kHz 24 bit PCM format. The sound display can be reduced to quadrophonic or stereo format. For the purposes of convenience of the data monitoring, additional simplified monitoring on the source side in LO ZNIIS is also possible. All sonification servers have an access to the remote Csound library. This will allow selecting most suitable instruments by artificial intellect subsystem in future versions.

The broadcasting servers allow casting the synthesized audio like a stream of Internet radio; it helps to remotely monitor the sonification process and achieve some feedback. The auditory interface provides user the ability to manage the performance over time i.e. quality of timbres and other parameters.

Among the further steps in the development of the experimental interface, it is necessary to note the following future targets:

- Integration with one of the data visualization systems like *Gephi* and others;
- Expansion of engaged staff or interaction with other institutions;

– Increasing the database testing and keeping track of the storage base;
– Creating the web interface to control the system.

In further implementations, the auditory display should be more flexible within the range of settings for displaying and reproducing data - this will make it possible to attract people who are less resistant to cognitive loads as system operators.

Among main problems of the present study are various aspects of the psychology of perception, depending on the age, education, employment, emotional and medical state of the recipient, weather, time of the day, etc.

3.5   Sound Synthesis

We used several software synthesizers for sonification written in Csound language. The several approaches had been carried out, or in other words, several different schemes of Csound synthesizers had been chosen for the sonification system. First is the so-called all-in-one approach, where an array of mapped entities had been a source for a single synthesizer with multiple parameters to be controlled. Such approach assumes that the algorithm of synthesis, or a set of different algorithms within a composite model, has a rather big number of input parameters. The good examples of such approach are frequency modulation synthesis, additive synthesis and granular synthesis.

The opposite approach is to divide the array of entities into several set for each of numerous simple models. In the first case, the result sounds more like a complex timbral soundscape, composite by its nature, but with evolving elements. Second case sounds more like some piece of music, with different groups of instruments etc. Below we give a brief description of two synthesizers used in the process of sonification development.

The Wintermute. As an example of the first approach, we developed the Wintermute synthesizer. It was first presented at the 3rd International Csound Conference, 2015 [8]. The synthesizer is a hybrid additive-subtractive harmonic drone generator, consisting of N voices, which are uniformly distributed across the entire spectrum. Each voice consists of a white noise generator, which is controlled by a volume envelope and subsequently filtered by a bandpass filter with controllable resonance. The bandwidth of each filter can be modulated so that the sound of each voice can vary between a harsh filtered noise and a sine-like signal. LFOs and envelope generators can modulate the central frequencies of each filter. Each voice is distributed separately in the stereo field. The voices are triggered by the Gauss function. The core part structure of the synth is given on Fig. 3.

The global FX block of the synthesizer consists of a feedback delay and a stereo reverb unit.

By default, the voice filters are tuned to the corresponding harmonics of the fundamental frequency. It produces a comb-like spectrum. An additional multiplier, turning a harmonic state into an inharmonic one, can alter the frequency spread.

One of the most remarkable features of the Wintermute synthesizer is its ability to morph between quite large varieties of timbres, i.e. from a dark ambient soundscapes generator into multi stream granular synthesizer. We describe here several exemplary timbres to demonstrate the size of a possible timbre space.

1. Timbres similar to bird tweets and chirps. The number of voices is reduced to just a few. The envelope generators control pitch modulation and filter resonances are set to high values in order to achieve almost tonal results. The re-triggering rate is low.
2. Timbres similar to the boiling or bubbling liquid sounds. The number of voices is set to maximum, the re-triggering rate is set quite high and the spectrum coverage of the texture is narrowed.
3. Timbres similar to dripping liquids in a tunnel or bunker. The reverb send should be set to a high value. 'Drip' sounds are produced by using a fast modulation of a narrow filter.
4. Typical dark ambient sounds. The addition of some reverb and a little delay, then a raised attack and decay, produce quite interesting ambient soundscapes.

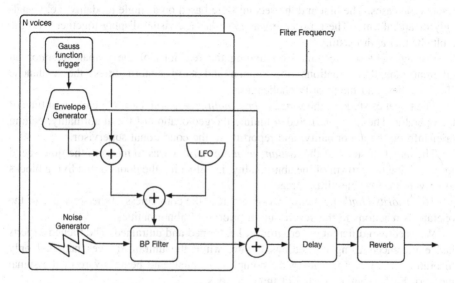

Fig. 3. The structure of the Wintermute drone generator

The Asana. The most recent approach in our study relates to the Asana synthesizer – the ambient sound generator with melodic part. It is actually a set of several synthesizers. At the SVYAZ-2017 exhibition in Moscow, we demonstrated a sonification complex for the object monitoring based on this synthesizer. We build several instruments, contrast to each other by the synthesis method, and by the time-pitch parameters. Here are the main sound components or layers of the Asana synthesizer:

1. Melody. We used the physical modeling synthesis to achieve a sitar-like sound for the leading melody. The timbre is bright and resonating. The corresponding Csound instrument is randomly triggered with some rhythmical and pitch control by a Markov chain.
2. Drone. This is an ambient layer of a complex sound. It has slowly changing low pitch controlled by another Markov chain. There are several music scales used for several situations that can occur during the monitoring of an object. Obviously,

soothing and relaxing scale corresponds to normal or stable state of the system, while dark and atonal scale symbolizes some abnormal process or malfunction.

3. Radio interference sounds. That category of sounds helps an operator to understand several types of malfunctions.

4. Earcons. The earcon space of a solution contains a set of several rhythmic sequences with rather simple, almost sine-like tones. It can represent some service information and also can be used for automatized audio based control.

4   Evaluation

To evaluate the efficiency of our experimental complex, we studied several data representation cases. The first and the second were based on a single modality, i.e. visual-only or audial-only. The third case was bimodal, i.e. visual display together with the multichannel audio setting.

During the tests we aimed on finding the reactions of the human operator on different modelled situations: the sudden and short abnormalities, the avalanche abnormalities, and the priority challenges.

The target of study of the *sudden abnormalities* was to measure the reaction time of the operator. The reaction included finding the geolocation of the abnormality, getting brief info on the abnormality, and reporting to the conditional supervisor.

The target of study of the *avalanche abnormalities* was to measure the time spend for localizing the growth of the abnormality, i.e. blocking the doors of the living blocks to prevent the zombie virus spread.

The *priority challenge* target was to estimate the correctness of the sequence of the operator's reactions to the several multi-prioritized abnormalities.

We used two different expert groups, i.e. trained and untrained. The trained experts had experienced using all settings before, while the untrained ones had had only theoretical training, i.e. reading the complex 'manual' and being aware of the signal thesauri. Each group consisted of three persons.

The improve the immersion level of the operator into the situation, and increasing the difficulty, we let other people (so-called distractors) chat with each other near the working place of an expert under test, talking funny jokes, getting in touch with an operator. At the same time, experts should chat with the friend using internet messenger, eat, and sometimes receive phone calls from the supervisor. The main goal of such measures was to increase the level of the operator's informational overload for both types of sensors.

The Fig. 4 gives results of several test series. The sudden abnormalities reaction test are given in the Sect. 1. There were three averaged parameters – detection level (DT), i.e. the normalized quantity of detected abnormal events; task completion rank (TCR), i.e. highest rank had been given to the fastest operator; geolocation detection accuracy (GDA).

The numbers 1 and 2 represent the monomodal cases, i.e. 1 – visual-only case (the most traditional one), 2 – audio-only case. Number 3 corresponds to the bimodal case.

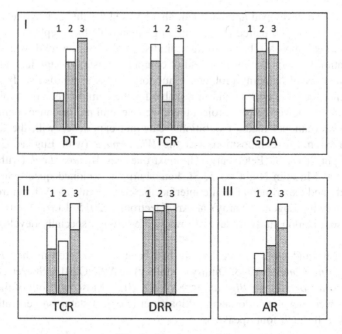

Fig. 4. The test results

White columns represent the trained experts' average results, while grayed columns are for untrained experts.

Section 2 gives average results for avalanche abnormalities detection study. Here we give task completion rank (TCR), i.e. time to localize and stop the growth of the abnormality, and the detection reaction rank (DRR).

Section 3 gives average results for priority challenge study. We give one parameter called accuracy rank (AR), i.e. the highest rank was given to the most accurately detected sequence of events.

The brief overview of the given results shows that in most cases the bimodal approach proved its efficiency. Some tasks, i.e. TCRs, were too complex to solve them using only hearing. However, more tests need to be taken with some other study of additional parameters, including visual display size, auditory displays quality and others.

5 Conclusion

The developed approach can be remarkably applied not only to the field of a system monitoring and object control as the real entities of a physical domain, but also in such promising fields as an augmented/virtual reality. The separate interesting field of the research application is the entertainment sector, which includes computer gaming, interactive art, and numerous art directions related to sound design applications and soundscapes. The developed approach can also be used for the assistive technologies, especially for visually impaired people and large mammals like elephants and whales.

The described approach has a strong multidisciplinary background, which is rather typical situation for such studies in a field of computer music. Though having focus on a theoretical study of mapping problem in auditory displays, we also study an artistic part of it, since such systems should be suitable for the comfort perception of the user.

Within the framework of our project there were several performances demonstrated at different international media exhibitions. Our first experience with the distributed network-driven music composition was the *Wintermuse* (with Eugene Cherny) at Museum Night 2013, St. Petersburg. The next one was *Memory Leak* (with Michael Chesnokov) at Museum Night 2015, St. Petersburg. It exploited quadrophonic sonification study and experimental tactile interface based on Nintendo Wii controller. The *Sonic Cities* (with Eugene Cherny) at Ars Electronica 2015, Linz, Austria, demonstrated the sonification study of several towns' life through specially developed drone synthesizer.

Less artistic and more practical study had been implemented in the *Multimodal Data Monitoring Complex* (with Dmitry Podolsky) at APINO2017, St. Petersburg and the *Sonification Complex for BigData* @ SVYAZ-2017, Moscow. Both of the last two installations were developed to map multiparametric object status on generative music system played through four speakers.

References

1. Sotnikov, A.D.: Informational communication systems and their models for health care. Informatsionno-upravliaushchie sistemy. Inf. Control Syst. **3**, 20–27 (2008). (in Russian)
2. Basov, O.O., Saitov, I.A.: Methods of transmission of polymodal information. Inf. Technol. Mech. Opt. **15**, 293–299 (2015). https://doi.org/10.17586/2226-1494-2015-15-2-293-299. (in Russian)
3. Erdos, P., Rényi, A.: On the evolution of random graphs. Bull. Inst. Internat. Statist **38**(4), 343–347 (1961)
4. Rogozinsky, G.G., Lyzhinkin, K.V., Egorova, A.N., Osipenko, I.N.: Software solution for sonification of dynamic graphs. Trudy ZNIIS. St.Petersburg Branch (Annuals of ZNIIS) **2**(2), 26–32 (2016). (in Russian)
5. Open Sound Control Homepage. http://opensoundcontrol.org
6. Batchelor, P., Wignall, T.: BeaglePi. Introductory guide to Csound on the BeagleBone and the Raspberry Pi, as well other Linux-powered tiny ware. Csound J. **18** (2013)
7. Amsterdam Catalog of Csound Computer Instruments. http://www.codemist.co.uk/AmsterdamCatalog
8. Rogozinsky G.G., Cherny E., Osipenko I.: Making mainstream synthesizers with Csound. In: 3rd International Csound Conference, pp. 132–140. SUT, St.Petersburg (2016). https://doi.org/10.5281/zenodo.50364

Automated Soundtrack Generation for Fiction Books Backed by Lövheim's Cube Emotional Model

Alexander Kalinin[1]([✉]) [iD] and Anastasia Kolmogorova[2] [iD]

[1] Verbalab, Krasnoyarsk, Russia
xyz@verbalab.ru
[2] Siberian Federal University, Krasnoyarsk, Russia
nastiakol@mail.ru

Abstract. One of the main tasks of any work of art is transferring emotion conceived by the author to its recipient. When using several modalities a synergistic effect occurs, making the achievement of the target emotional state more likely. In reading, mostly, visual perception is involved, nevertheless, we can supplement it with an audio modality with the soundtrack's help via specially selected music that corresponds to the emotional state of a text fragment.

As a base model for representing emotional state we have selected physiologically motivated Lövheim's cube model which embraces 8 emotional states instead of 2 (positive and negative) usually used in sentiment analysis.

This article describes the concept of selecting special music for the "mood" of a text extract by mapping text emotional labels to tags in LastFM API, fetching music data to play and experimental validation of this approach.

Keywords: Sentiment analysis · Lövheim's cube · Soundtrack
Multi-modal art · Emotions

1 Soundtrack for Fiction Books as Element of Multimodal Art

The main purpose of any piece of art is to transmit certain ideas and emotions strongly felt by the artist to other people. The more modalities are engaged into the process of transferring artistic message, the more powerful is the aimed emotional impact. That's why multi-modal art is being rapidly developed now with the growth of technology.

The examples of such multi-modal art communication are visual performances during musical concerts, interactive installations enabling kinesthetic experience, musical support for paintings exhibitions. All these media enabling visual, audial and kinesthetic perception channels are rising a synergistic effect on the spectator and plunge him in a certain atmosphere, in a certain emotional state.

Listening to an appropriate music while reading fiction books can facilitate emotional better perception of ideas and feelings that were expressed by the writer, and creates a sort of consensuality between author and readers. In this case, reading (visual modality) is supplemented by listening to music (audial modality) and music plays the

© Springer Nature Switzerland AG 2019
P. Eismont and O. Mitrenina (Eds.): LMAC 2017, CCIS 943, pp. 161–168, 2019.
https://doi.org/10.1007/978-3-030-05594-3_13

same role as soundtrack for films where sound creates additional effect to visual scenes. Thus, the main question arises: how to select music to supplement visual models and images, which emerge in readers' mind while reading a story?

The process of creating soundtrack for a text from a very abstract level seems to be a list of the steps below:

1. Split the text into a number of extracts.
2. Define the mood (emotion) of each extract.
3. Find the music, which corresponds to a particular emotion.
4. Map music to text extracts by emotion.

Despite limited number of steps to do and transparency of their logic, we have to solve several problems to achieve this task of selecting needed music for a given text:

1. What set of emotions to choose, i.e. what emotional model is mostly suitable for our task?
2. How to recognize a particular emotion for a given piece of text?
3. What music should we choose for a given emotion?
4. How to align the time of playing music tracks with the speed of reading?

2   Emotional Model

A corner-stone problem for the task of mapping texts to music by a certain emotion is to choose an emotional inventory – a set of possible emotional states that user can experience – thus, an emotional model. In such a case we have to engage psychology and neurology for available theoretical frames being developed in those fields. During the search for a model that can be viable for computer application building, we were guided by the criterion of the model's capacity to provide numerical or logical input scheme and explicit deterministic approach for emotions differentiation. There are 3 main models to mention as suitable for our needs:

1. Binary model
2. PAD (*Pleasure, Arousal, Dominance*) model
3. Lövheim Cube

Binary model is a very simplistic approach that assumes that emotion can be either positive or negative. This very model is developed mostly within sentiment analysis [1], an applied field of computational linguistics, and is used to estimate emotional 'color' of a text – whether the text represents positive or negative writer's attitude towards some subject under discussion. Such approach is used for tasks of evaluating different kinds of reviews like movie reviews, internet shop merchandise reviews, restaurant reviews, and also mining users' opinions on news articles, marketing research etc. [2].

As these applied tasks are dealing with the large amount of data and are computationally expensive this simple model is very handy as it doesn't bring additional complexity and can provide meaningful insights. The mentioned above model also provides continuous interpretation when emotional state can be measured between range of −1 (very negative emotion) and +1 (very positive emotion); 0 value can be interpreted as neutral emotion [3].

By the reason of the model's simplicity, the algorithms that are based on it are unable to differentiate between more nuanced kinds of positive and negative emotions, as they (emotions) don't certainly exist in one dimension. For example, anger and fear are both considered as negative emotions, but they are for sure very dissimilar, and experiencing anger is definitely different from experiencing fear. Moreover, fiction books provide much larger palette of emotions than the narrow binary system could embrace. In other words, the binary emotion model seems to be unproductive for our purposes.

PAD model [4] represents an emotion state as a point in three-dimensional space which position can be measured numerically.

The first axis is *Pleasure-Displeasure Scale* that measures how pleasant or unpleasant human feels about something. For instance, both anger and fear are unpleasant emotions and both are scored on the displeasure side. However, joy is a pleasant emotion.

The *Arousal-Nonarousal Scale* measures how energized or soporific one feels. It is not the intensity of the emotion − for grief and depression there can be low arousal intense feelings. While both anger and rage are unpleasant emotions, rage has a higher intensity or a higher arousal value. On the contrary, boredom, which is also an unpleasant state, has a low arousal value.

The *Dominance-Submissiveness Scale* represents whether one feels controlling and dominant versus controlled or submissive. For instance, while both fear and anger are unpleasant emotions, anger is a dominant emotion, whereas fear is a submissive one.

A more abbreviated version of the model uses just 4 values for each dimension, providing only 64 values for possible emotions [5]. For example, anger is a quite unpleasant, quite aroused, and moderately dominant emotion, while boredom is slightly unpleasant, quite unaroused, and mostly non-dominant.

The drawbacks of both models are conditioned by the fact they are phenomeno-logical, i.e. they put an introspection to be the main method for defining to what degree the emotion is pleasant or unpleasant, negative or positive etc. The experiencer discovers and defines the quantitative parameters of emotions, so the estimation based on such approach can be quite subjective.

The last suggested model is Lövheim's Cube. It takes objective parameters to be the arguments of emotional functions [6]. These parameters are mixtures or proportions of three monoamine neurotransmitters: serotonin, dopamine and noradrenaline. The balance of these monoamines forms a three-dimensional space represented by the following visual model (Fig. 1):

Anger according to the model is produced by the combination of low serotonin, high dopamine and high noradrenaline.

The reasons for us to choose this model instead of other two ones are following:

1. Unlike previous two models this one is not subjective and introspective and represents emotional state to be funded by neurosomatic process [7].
2. It provide 8 basic emotions as function of monoamine balance and suggests continuous numerical scale estimation for intermediate emotions, so any emotional state can be presented as a vector.

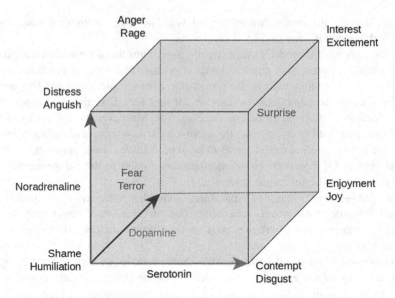

Fig. 1. Visual representation of Lövheim's Cube emotional model

3 Relevant Data Acquisition

After choosing the emotional inventory to apply for mapping texts to music we should define the mechanism of labeling certain text extract with emotions from Lövheim's cube set. Such objective can be achieved by using automated tools (like applying current sentiment analysis techniques) or manually (labeling text extras by human readers).

Unfortunately, we couldn't use automated tools based on machine learning approach. For training a model to predict a certain emotion for a given text sample we need data which had been previously labeled by human readers. The dataset must contain a sentence or a paragraph with mapped emotion label from Lövheim's cube inventory. But in spite of the fact that there lots of data with mapped binary emotions [8] and data containing PDA model metadata [9] we didn't succeed to find any text data-set with Lövheim's emotions set neither for English nor for Russian languages.

Taking into account the lack of needed data and bearing in mind the fact that our aim was only to prove the concept of soundtrack generation for a given "emotion-text" mapping, we decided not to use existing data-driven sentiment extraction pipeline and to follow some steps listed below.

1. Select Russian novel as a source of text data.
2. Split the text into small extracts showing emotional "persistence" and manifesting mainly one emotional "color".
3. Manually label the collection of extracts using evaluation from. This job should be done by at least five assessors to provide reliability in estimation and data coverage.

4. Finally, aggregate all "text-emotion" estimations by setting the most commonly selected emotion label, i.e. for each unique text extract choose label that was mostly selected by five human estimators.

As a text data source we selected Russian novel entitled "Pismovnik" ("Epistolary novel"), which consists of many letters written by a man and a woman in love while they were apart. The text from this novel mimics real personal epistolary style and represents a wide palette of emotions.

First, we had split the text into short extracts, which were considered to be emotional invariants, i.e. text where emotion sentiment is stable and doesn't fluctuate. While splitting the text of novel "Pismovnik" we discovered that the optimal length for such invariants was about 300 characters.

After splitting the text into emotional extracts we needed to label it with large number of human assessors. For quick fetching the result set, large data coverage and randomization of tasks we decided to use crowd-sourcing platform "Toloka" developed by Yandex team. The main reason we selected it was the fact that this platform provided big community of native Russian speakers who could correctly perceive the underlying emotion and label a text extract correctly.

We asked human assessors to read a text extract and to select one emotion from eight possible ones that mostly suits the sentiment of the text. Tasks with text extracts were distributed randomly, and each extract had to be assessed at least by 5 different assessors. After pushing 769 text's extracts we fetched 3893 labeled results provided by 142 native Russian-speaking assessors. Than we processed the novel text once again and labeled each extract with the label that was selected by the most times from 5 different assessments.

4 Mapping Music to Text Extras

To get meta-information relevant to music we decided to use LastFM service. The main reason to choose such resource was the availability of a big set of data concerning various kinds of music: genres, number of times played (scrobbled) and search tags assigned to different tracks by users community. This tags' folksonomy facilitated our search for different music tracks for a set of emotion labels.

For generating a list of music tracks we folded previously labeled text extras into a sequence of emotion items where no item had the same emotion as its neighbor (see Fig. 2).

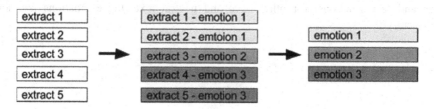

Fig. 2. Scheme for convolution of paragraphs into emotional labels sequence

For each item in this sequence we made a search query to LastFM API to get 100 tracks with search tag matching emotion label. After each tag query fetched music tracks, the list was randomized, so all the songs for each emotion item were shuffled (see Fig. 3). 100 tracks were selected to provide potentially excessive time playing of single emotion track list as we could not definitely know how long it might take to read a text extract.

Fig. 3. Pipeline for fetching track list for emotion label

5 Evaluation of Concept

It is to notice that in current project we didn't plan to solve the problem of aligning reading speed with switching track lists as reading speed is a personal constantly changing parameter, which is hard to track. Of course, such task is very crucial and definitely will arouse in case of commercial and production release of this model, but for now, we discuss a prototype with a "proof of concept" aim. The achievement of this goal presupposes the evaluation of how well a music track with certain emotion – "mood" – can supplement reading a text extract with the same mood. To answer the question we have proceeded with the estimation process.

Each of 10 volunteers was given at least 30 text extracts. Each text extract was shown on the screen. During one extract demonstration no other extracts labeled with different emotion were shown, and music from track list corresponding to the emotion was played in headphones. After reading each extract a volunteer was asked to rank the selected music track from 1 to 10, where 10 meant "music perfectly supplements the text", and 1 meant "this music is completely inappropriate for this text". After volunteer assessed a "text-music" mapping he was shown a text extract with another emotion and played music with a matching tag. Overall, 328 text extracts were evaluated. Results are presented in Table 1.

As we can see in Table 1 this concept works well for mapping distress, passion, rage and fear emotions, for other ones and neutral texts the estimations are not satisfactory.

Table 1. Results for evaluation "text-music" mappings

Emotion	Mean	Standart deviation
Anger/rage	7.3	1.43
Passion/excitement	6.9	1.21
Contempt/disgust	3.1	0.31
Enjoyment/joy	2.3	0.42
Shame/humiliation	2.1	0.35
Distress/anguish	7.9	0.51
Surprise/startle	2.8	0.39
Fear/terror	6.7	0.26
Neutral	5.2	1.17

6 Conclusion and Further Work

As our experiment has shown an approach for generating soundtracks for fiction books by mapping text to music via emotion model that uses Lövheim's Cube model can do well for a number of emotions, but not for all, and that shows that current version of our approach can't be taken as somewhat applicable. However, good results for 4 emotions encourage us to look for workarounds and further work that can involve following directions:

- Automated text labeling using sentiment analysis techniques and machine learning.
- Using extended and modified music search queries (for example look for such tags as "anger, wrath, aggression, war, battle" etc. for "rage" text label;
- Adding filters for fetched music (for example strip out tracks with lyrics as voices and song narratives can interrupt reader);
- Solving problems for automated tracking speed of reading and switching tracks intelligently.

References

1. Su, F., Markert, K.: From words to senses: a case study in subjectivity recognition (PDF). In: Proceedings of Coling 2008, Manchester, UK (2008)
2. Hu, M., Liu, B.: Mining and summarizing customer reviews. In: Proceedings of KDD 2004 (2004)
3. Kim, S.M., Hovy, E.H.: Identifying and analyzing judgment opinions (PDF). In: Proceedings of the Human Language Technology/North American Association of Computational Linguistics conference (HLT-NAACL 2006), New York, NY (2006)
4. Mehrabian, A.: Basic dimensions for a general psychological theory, pp. 39–53 (1980)
5. Lance, B., et al.: Relation between gaze behavior and attribution of emotion. In: Prendinger, H. (ed.) Intelligent Virtual Agents: 8th International Conference IVA, pp. 1–9 (2008)
6. Lövheim, H.: A new three-dimensional model for emotions and monoamine neurotransmitters. Med. Hypotheses **78**, 341–348 (2012)

7. Talanov, M., Toschev, A.: Computational emotional thinking and virtual neurotransmitters. Int. J. Synth. Emotions **5**(1), 1–8
8. Affective Text: data annotated for emotions and polarity. Dataset. http://web.eecs.umich.edu/~mihalcea/downloads.html#affective
9. EmoBank. 10 k sentences annotated with Valence, Arousal and Dominance values. Dataset. https://github.com/JULIELab/EmoBank

Characteristics of Music Playback and Visio-Motor Interaction at Sight-Reading by Pianists Depending on the Specifics of a Musical Piece

Leonid Tereshchenko$^{(\boxtimes)}$ (ID), Lyubov' Boyko (ID), Dar'ya Ivanchenko, Galina Zadneprovskaya (ID), and Alexander Latanov (ID)

M.V. Lomonosov Moscow State University, Moscow, Russia
`lter@mail.ru`

Abstract. We have analysed the basic characteristics of music playback at sight-reading of three two-line classic music selections of varying textures and complexity: a two-voice polyphonic musical piece, a theme and a variation of homophonic-harmonic musical piece. These characteristics serve as objective indicators of the musicians' skill of sight-reading, and the complexity of musical selection. Applying an original technique of eye movement recording without fixating the head, we studied the eye-hand span i.e. the time from reading the text to music playback. Our findings reveal, that the eye-hand span depends on the texture of the performed musical piece and inversely correlates with the number of errors as well as directly correlates with the rate of stability in the performance. This parameter may serve as an objective measure of the sight-reading ability. It is connected with the complexity of a musical piece and, presumably, characterizes the working memory capacity of musicians.

Keywords: Sight-reading · Eyetracking · Eye movements · Eye-hand span

1 Introduction

Playing a musical instrument is a complicated human activity, including physiological and cognitive processes taken in their multilevel complexity and simultaneity. At the physiological level this activity involves aural, visual, tactile and proprioceptive sensory systems. When playing the instrument, pianists execute complex coordinated patterns of hands and feet movements, visio-motor patterns of eye movements at sight-reading, head and body movements. Reading a musical text embraces processes of visual attention such as selecting and recognizing both single signs (notes and other signs in the musical language) and complex patterns (accords, rhythmic models), sensory and working memory of visual and aural modality, music-oriented kinesthetic memory which preserves motor patterns. With the manual performance of the recognized signs of musical notation, the working visual memory is transformed into kinetic patterns (automated motor skills, or "kinetic melodies", according to Luria [1]).

All these processes are executed through a sophisticated coordination of the visio-motor eye and hand activities. Thus, the analysis of eye movements at sight-reading of

© Springer Nature Switzerland AG 2019
P. Eismont and O. Mitrenina (Eds.): LMAC 2017, CCIS 943, pp. 169–182, 2019.
https://doi.org/10.1007/978-3-030-05594-3_14

a musical piece (which directly or indirectly reflects the above mentioned processes) opens up a new opportunity for quantitative physiological study of this complex skill.

Sight-reading suggests performing an unfamiliar musical text for the pianist. This allows establishing a certain amount and structure of new visual information presented to the pianist. And it allows to exclude the challenging individual factor of a musical piece being previously learned from the process of playing a musical instrument. Moreover, the process percepting the visual information in the form of reading a note text allows utilizing a large amount of accumulated knowledge from the adjacent area of reading verbal texts, which facilitates the development of methodological approaches to studying such a complex type of human activity.

1.1 Sight-Reading as a Musical Skill

Sight-reading is performing an unknown piece at such a tempo and by that character as it was conceived by the composer, without a preliminary fragmentary playback. This performance shall be uninterrupted, comprehensive and considering all the author's instructions. If the skill of sight-reading is well-developed, visual and aural senses, motor skills closely interact with attention, memory, intuition and creative imagination of the musician [2, 3].

We have to admit, that in course of their studies the pianists do not always master the language of piano music with the required efficiency at primary and secondary educational music schools (colleges). It results from spontaneous accumulation of experience and is largely beyond the framework of a well-conceived system. Consequently, there are often gaps in the performing skills. Therefore, the task of primary education is limited to automatizing the system of "visual senses-aural senses-motor skills" [2, 3].

The text of piano music has both horizontal and vertical dimensions. Observations and experimental data show that the horizontal comprehension of the text is easier accounting for the practice of verbal reading. But a pianist faces with a more complicated task as he must look at two and even more lines at once (three-line and even four-line records of piano music was used by F. Liszt, S.V. Rakhmaninov, K. Debussy and other composers, and also in company scores).

For successful sight-reading it is vital to learn how to structure the musical language, i.e. to divide it into syntactic units with a definite meaning [2, 3]. The understanding of how a musical thought is developed helps foresee what will happen at the next stage and significantly facilitates sight-reading. The second component of the complicated sight-reading skill is the motor execution of what been read by the performer in the musical notation [2, 3]. Three elements here are critical to achieve success:

1. Well-developed finger motor skill and basic motor patterns.
2. Ability to apply a rational finger notation in the process of reading (arrangement and alternation of fingers when playing a musical instrument)
3. Confident tactile orientation on the keyboard implies the ability to play without looking at hands (keyboard), which, in turn, requires a clear cognitive mapping of the keyboard.

Our research aims to reveal the physiological and cognitive processes involved in sight-reading. Our findings may be implemented in musical education for the development of quantitative assessment criteria of the musicians' professional skills.

1.2 Sight-Reading as a Psychomotor Processes

Piano notes are a complex set of signs, which combine a lot of factors affecting the character of eye movements while reading. First of all, the oculomotor activity depends on the complexity of the musical piece which, according to Souter [4], is stipulated by the following factors: (1) ocular complexity of a musical piece; (2) difficulty in transferring the ocular information into motor activity, which is determined by the experience of the musician; (3) difficulty in executing the motor instructions which comprise a definite finger position on the keyboard and a fine control over all the hand and arm muscles.

For a long time scientists have been studying eye movements in various aspects of human activity. Thus, a lot of effort has been invested into studying reading the verbal text in different languages, and this area has been thoroughly studied [5]. However, comparatively little research was conducted on reading the music text leaving numerous gaps in understanding this process. Yet, it was discovered that when reading a verbal text out loud [6] and at sight-reading of a musical piece with simultaneous performance [7–10] the position of visual fixation of the eyes in the notes precedes the performed passage (Fig. 1). On the basis of this phenomenon, *eye-hand span* (*EHS*) was introduced to estimate the span from the moment of reading the text up to its performance. From the very moment of fixation of the eye on the sign up to the moment of its performance, a number of physiological and cognitive processes proceed. First, the visual system perceives and deciphers visual information. Further on, the establishment and execution of the motor complex of movements take place. These constituent parts of the process as a whole most naturally require some time. Finally, a time span between the point of the gaze fixation on the musical notation and the performed note occurs [4]. The EHS parameter may be measured either (1) by the number of signs located between the note which is read and the performed note or (2) by the time from the end of the fixation to the moment the note is performed.

Sloboda [8] applied the methodology of the "fading screen" for EHS studies. In the experiments a musician was shown the monophonic notes on his screen. After a time span the duration of which was known only to the researcher, the screen was turned off, and the musician continued to play. Finally, the number of correctly played notes was estimated. The simplest measured parameter is the number of errors (notes that were played incorrectly) made during the performance. The errors were shown to correlate well with the reading skills of the musician: the most experienced musician's EHS was 6–8 notes and he made 3 errors, the least experienced musician's EHS was 3–8 notes and he made 73 errors [8].

To estimate the EHS the methodology of the "shifting frame" when a certain number of notes which preceded and followed the performed note were shown on the screen was also used. When this particular note was played, the frame moved forward [10]. This methodology revealed a correlation between eye movement's parameters and a number of notes following the performed note: among the experienced musicians, the duration of fixations decreased as the frame was enlarged, while EHS and the amplitude

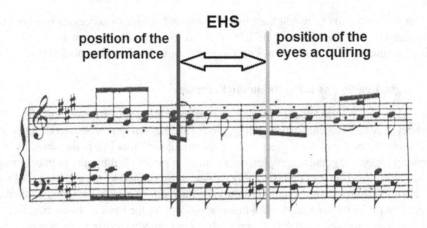

Fig. 1. The scheme of EHS (double-ended arrow) which is represented by a time span between the moment of the current gaze fixation at the musical notation (view point) and the moment performing the preceding notes which have already been read (performance point) (with modifications in accordance with [4])

of saccades increased. The results of the experiment also demonstrated that even the experienced musicians read 1–2 notes ahead most of the time, although the maximum preceding number of notes possible could reach 7 [10].

For the two-line notes, it was shown that the EHS varies greatly in the process of reading, but does not exceed 8 notes [7], and musicians read one chord forward in the event of text written in chords of three notes [11].

The EHS was first specified to have two components – one component is associated with the processing of visual information obtained through the foveal part, and the other – with the processing of information obtained through the parafoveal part of the retina [12]. Due to this fact, the professional pianists sometimes combine several notes into one sign (more frequently in passages) and that is why more information can be preserved in the buffer zone of the working memory [13].

From the technical point of view, the head retention while reading a musical text was a major problem in the experiments. Some researchers used a heavy motorcycle helmet with a video recorder to register the eye movements [11, 14], others immobilized the head with the help of a chin fixator [9, 15]. In later studies, lightweight and video quality-optimized video eye-trackers were used [16, 17]. In addition to head movements when playing a musical instrument, the pianist also makes movements with his head and torso which introduces additional difficulties when registering the eye movements. Another widespread problem is that a musician executes saccades at his hands, while sight-reading and at this particular moment the signal gets lost. Less experienced musicians execute more frequent saccades at hands than the experienced ones [4].

The recent literature on performance characteristics and eye movements at sight-reading is still rather limited. To the best of our knowledge no experiments where the eye movements could be registered without limitation to pianists' natural mobility were conducted. In all the studies referenced above, the eye movement's registration was performed with the head fixation, which inevitably affects the performance of the performed music text. In our work, we set out to investigate the characteristics of the performance with synchronous registration of eye movements at sight-reading of collections of pieces of different textures in natural conditions for pianists without fixating the head.

2 Methods

The study involved 16 students (9 men and 7 women at the age of 19–23) of Tchaikovsky Moscow State Conservatory specializing in piano. The musicians were offered one sheet of notes (2 pages) for sight-reading of three selected musical pieces of various textures and complexity: (1) Little prelude of J.S. Bach D-minor, two-voice polyphonic musical piece, (2) theme and (3) the first variation out of 13 variations of L. Beethoven for piano on the theme of aria "Es war einmal ein alter Mann" from opera "Das rothe Käppchen", which is a homophonic-harmonic musical piece. Figure 2 shows two-line selections of each musical piece. These two-line pieces are called piano lines which include two lines for upper and lower registers (for right and left hands correspondingly) combined with accolade (curly bracket on the left) for performance by both hands.

Fig. 2. Examples of piano lines from musical pieces used in the experiments. The number of each fragment corresponds to the musical pieces (see above)

Musical piece *1* consisted of two pages of five piano lines each, 28 mm wide, with a minimum distance of 6 mm between the notes, and contained 488 signs (notes, alteration signs, pauses) in 47 measures (Fig. 2.1). Musical piece *2* contained mostly quavers (eighth notes) on two pages of five piano lines, 23 mm wide, with a minimum distance of 4 mm between the notes, and contained 373 signs in 38 measures (Fig. 2.2). In musical piece *3* semiquavers prevail (sixteenth-notes) on 2 pages of seven piano lines, 20 mm wide, with a minimal distance of 3 mm between the notes, and contained 465 signs in 38 measures (Fig. 2.3). In addition to the small font of the notes, this piece contains a lot of signs of alteration, which carry additional information related to playback of the notation text.

The musicians performed the task on the company's YAMAHA piano. The distance from the keyboard to the music stand was 28 cm, the distance from the eyes to the notes slightly varied during the performance and averaged about approximately 50 cm.

The registration of the eye movements in the process of reading the notation text was executed with the use of the portable eye tracker Arrington (Scene Camera Option, Arrington Research, Inc., USA) with frequency of 30 Hz without any restrictions on the mobility of the pianist. Such conditions for eye movement's registration in the experiment did not disturb the usual pose of pianists during performance of musical pieces.

In the full mobility conditions, we encounter the problem of the head shift, and to calculate the real position of the eye, it is necessary to combine two coordinate systems: the position of the eye in relation to the notes and the position of the notes in relation to the head. To solve this problem, an original software was developed to transform the coordinate position of the eye in relation to the notes, taking into account the head movements (Fig. 3).

Fig. 3. Track of eye movements before transformation of the coordinate position of the eye (at the top) and after transformation (at the bottom)

Playback of the perused musical text was recorded by professional voice recorder Olympus LS-5 and processed with use of programme Acoustica Basic Edition 6.0.

3   Results

3.1   Characteristics of the Music Playback at Sight-Reading

Investigating the sight-reading process includes analyzing the result of the process in question, in particular, the flow of sound of the performed music text. In addition to artistic and emotional characteristics, which are experienced biased, the musical sounding may be characterized by such objective indicators as the playback tempo, taken by the pianist, the stability of tempo maintenance at reading the whole fragment of work, and the number of errors made at reading the music text. The number of errors was defined by an expert on the basis of the expert evaluation by ear.

In music, the *tempo* is a unit of time and is traditionally measured by a metronome [18] as a number of beats per minute (bpm), time between two beats equals the quarter note. Since the music pieces provided for reading have – different time signatures, calculation of the tempo for each measure in a music piece was made using the formula:

$$V_i = (m * 60) / X_i \tag{1}$$

where V_i – tempo (bpm), m – the number of quarters in one measure of a music piece, X_i – playback length of one corresponding measure (s).

The tempo indicator for each musician was defined as an average of the tempo value over all measures during performance of a particular music piece.

Using non-parametric factor analysis of variance (according to the Kruskal-Wallis criterion), a statistically significant effect on the playback tempo rate indicator of the "specifics of a music piece" factor was revealed ($H_2 = 27,31$, $p < 0,001$). While the influence of the "individual" factor, which determines individual differences, turned out to be statistically unreliable ($H_{15} = 13,19$, $p < 0,59$). Based on the results of the variance analysis, we carried out a paired-comparison experiment and revealed statistically significant differences among the playback tempo of three music pieces (Fig. 4).

The variability of the playback tempo between the measures in the music piece characterizes *the stability of the selected tempo maintenance*: a smaller variation of the playback tempo corresponds to a higher stability of the music playback, and vice versa. The stability indicator for each performance was determined as reciprocal of the standard deviation of the performance duration of measures in music pieces. In other words, the closer is the performance of the music piece to the ideal with the equal duration of each measure, the higher is the stability of tempo maintenance. By means of nonparametric factor analysis, it was shown that the influence of the "individual" factor proved to be highly reliable ($H_{15} = 32,32$, $p < 0,006$). But we did not reveal any statistically significant effect on the tempo stability of the "specifics of a musical piece" factor ($H_2 = 3,25$, $p < 0,197$),

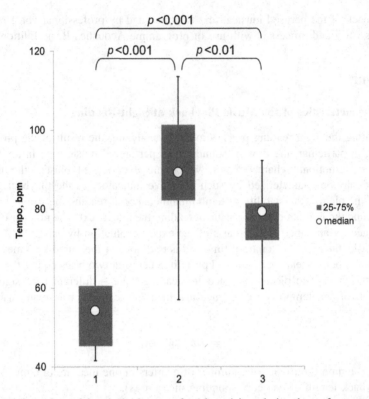

Fig. 4. Median values of the playback tempo for 16 musicians during the performance of three music pieces. The significance of statistical differences (*p*) was estimated in accordance with the Mann-Whitney criterion. References to the music pieces are given in the text above

The number of ***errors*** in a musical performance was normalized to 100 characters of the music piece, since all pieces included a different number of note signs (Fig. 5).

By method of non-parametric factor analysis, we revealed a statistically significant impact on the number of errors of the factor of a "music piece specifics" ($H_2 = 12,65$, $p < 0,002$), while the influence of the "individual" factor turned out to be quasi-reliable ($H_{15} = 23,18$, $p < 0,09$).

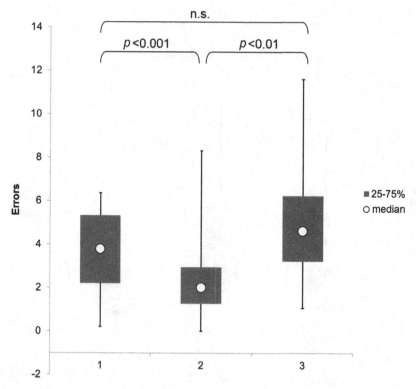

Fig. 5. Median values of the standardized error of 16 musicians during the performance of three music pieces. References are the same as for Fig. 4, n.s. – non-significant

3.2   Eye-Hand Span

The data on the eye positioning in the process of reading the notes and on performing those ones that have already been read allow us to assess the *EHS* index. EHS was determined once for each of the consecutive piano lines in a music piece at the moment when the gaze shifted to the next piano line. The final EHS index for each musician in the performance of each music piece was determined as an average for all piano lines of this music piece. Figure 6 shows EHS values (in musical symbols) averaged over all subjects for three musical texts, and Fig. 7 – distribution of EHS values.

According to the parametric two-factor analysis of variance (two-way ANOVA), a significant effect on the EHS value of the factor of the a "music piece specifics" ($F1_{2,285}$ = 17,48, p <0,001) and the "individual" factor ($F2_{15,285}$ = 15,57, p <0,001) were detected.

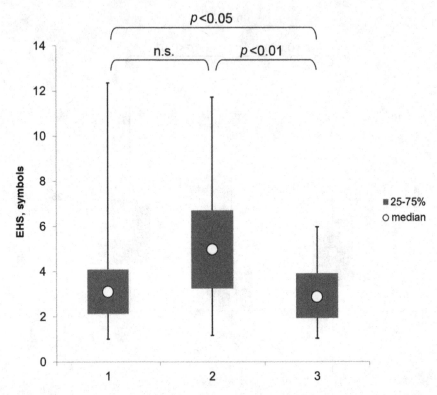

Fig. 6. Median values of EHS of 16 musicians during the performance of three music pieces. References are the same as for Figs. 4 and 5

We outlined a reliable inverse correlation ($r = -0,442$, $p < 0,01$) between the EHS value and the number of errors at sight-reading (skipped or incorrectly played note) – the objective indicators that characterize the quality of performance at sight-reading. It can be assumed that the bigger piece a pianist can hold in his working memory, the easier and more correctly he reads a piece from a sheet on the spur of the moment. A positive correlation between EHS and tempo stability was also revealed ($r = 0,37$, $p < 0,034$).

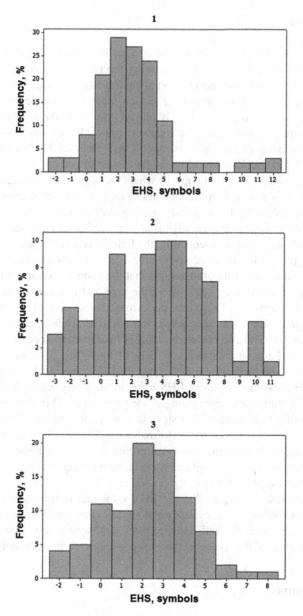

Fig. 7. Frequency distribution of EHS values of 16 musicians during the performance of three music pieces (marked by the reference numbers above the charts)

4   Discussion

The specificity factor of a musical piece influences all the analyzed characteristics of its playback except for the stability of maintaining the tempo. The complex analysis of playback characteristics of the musical text at sight-reading provides an opportunity to range the selected music pieces according to their subjective complexity. We assumed that the more complicated music piece is played, the larger the number of errors is. With other parameters being equal, at a slower tempo [4] and with less performance stability, the most complex was the music piece №3 ("Beethoven-variation"), while the music piece №2 ("Beethoven-theme") was the easiest to perform.

The stability of the selected tempo in which the significant influence of the "individual" factor was detected in combination with the number of errors committed, presumably may reflect the level of sight-reading skill of musicians.

Our results demonstrate, that the EHS is at its maximum at sight-reading of an easy musical text, and vice versa. Consequently, the EHS is a dynamic parameter that varies throughout the playback. As noted above, the EHS strongly correlates with performance errors, so it is most natural to assume that the pianist reads notes in more detail (makes more fixations) in the places where the note text becomes more complicated, and the EHS value decreases. During the performance of an easy-to-read musical piece, the pianist can make more saccades which run ahead of reading, and in this case the EHS value increases. Thus, in our study, the EHS parameter varied significantly both for each pianist and among pianists from −3 to 14 signs (Fig. 7), which is in line with other experiments with professional musicians: the EHS varied in the range of −2 up to 12 signs [10]. But the most frequent EHS value in our study was 2–3 signs, which is somewhat higher than when reading single-line notes obtained in another study – 1–2 signs [10]. Therefore, the EHS of 2–3 signs is more preferable when reading two-line notes. If the EHS value is lower, the performance quality worsens due to slowed down process of transferring the visual information into a motor response, and keeping a significant number of alternating sets of signs in the working memory is more difficult for a pianist in this type of activity.

The obtained results suggest that the EHS value can reflect the complexity of a music piece. In order to verify this assumption, an experiment which would allow to study the relation between the EHS and the errors made with a larger temporal span (for example, at the level of the measure in a music piece or even single notes) is needed.

5   Conclusions

The peculiarities of a musical piece influence all the examined characteristics of its playback except for the tempo stability.

The complex analysis of the music playback at sight-reading provides an opportunity to range the selected pieces according to their objective performance complexity. The examined qualitative characteristics may be used as the objective means for accessing the sight-reading skills among musicians to complement the experienced-based expert evaluation.

The EHS figures obtained in our research correlate well with the literary data, even taking into account a greater complexity for reading of two-line notes used in our work as compared to the single-line notes in literary data. The EHS figure may be used as an indicator of the "momentary" complexity of the note piece being read at a particular moment.

Acknowledgements. This work was supported by the Russian Foundation of Basic Research (project № 16-06-01082). The authors are thankful to consultant in musicology, associate professor of foreign music Department of the Moscow State Conservatory, Ph.D. in Art History, Filippov A.A., for the help in organization of the research.

References

1. Luriya, A.R.: Vysshie korkovye funktsii cheloveka i ikh narusheniya pri lokal'nykh porazheniyakh mozga (Higher cortical functions of man and their disturbances in local brain lesions). Publ. Moscow University, Moscow (1962). (in Russian)
2. Karacharova, T.I.: Obuchenie igre s lista na osnove aktivizatsii tselostnogo protsessa vospriyatiya i ozvuchivaniya notnogo teksta: Avtoref. diss. … kand. ped. nauk (Learning of sight-playing on the basis of intensification of overall process of perception and sounding notes. Ph.D. (Pedagogical) Thesis). Elets (2006). (in Russian)
3. Popova, K.A.: Formirovanie i razvitie navyka chteniya notnogo teksta s lista v klasse fortepiano. Nauchno-metodicheskii elektronnyi zhurnal «Kontsept» (Formation and development of the skill of sight-reading in a piano class. Scientific and methodical electronic journal "Concept"), no. 6, pp. 76–80 (2015). (in Russian)
4. Souter, T.: Eye movement and memory in the sight reading of keyboard music. Ph.D. University of Sydney (2001)
5. Rayner, K., Pollatsek, J., Alexander, B.: Eye movements during reading. In: Snowling, M.J., Hulme, Ch. (eds.) The Science of Reading: A Handbook, pp. 79–97. Publ. Blackwell Publishing (2005)
6. Levin, H., Kaplan, E.A.: Grammatical structure and reading. In: Levin, H., Williams, J.P. (eds.) Basic studies on reading. Publ. Basic Books, New York (1970)
7. Weaver, H.E.: Studies of ocular behavior in music reading. I. A survey of visual processes in reading differently constructed musical selections. In: Dashiell, J.F. (ed.) Psychology Monographs, vol. 55, no. 1, pp. 1–30 (1943)
8. Sloboda, J.A.: The eye-hand span: an approach to the study of sight-reading. Psychol. Music 2(2), 4–10 (1974)
9. Goolsby, T.W.: Eye movement in music reading: effects of reading ability, notational complexity, and encounters. Music. Percept. 12(1), 77–96 (1994)
10. Truitt, F.E., Clifton, C., Pollatsek, A., Rayner, K.: The perceptual span and the eye–hand span in sight reading music. Vis. Cogn. 4(2), 143–161 (1997)
11. Young, L.J.: A study of the eye-movements and eye-hand temporal relationships of successful and unsuccessful piano sight-readers while piano sight-reading. Ph.D. Indiana University (1971)
12. Kinsler, V., Carpenter, R.H.S.: Saccadic eye movement while reading music. Vis. Res. 35(10), 1447–1458 (1995)
13. Furneaux, S., Land, M.F.: The effects of skill on the eye-hand span during musical sight reading. Proc. R. Soc. Lond. B 266(1436), 2435–2440 (1999)

14. Halverson, D.: A biometric analysis of eye movement patterns of sight singers. Ohio State University, Ph.D (1974)
15. Smith, D.J.: An investigation of the effects of varying temporal settings on eye movements while sight reading trumpet music and while reading language aloud. Ph.D. Pennsylvania State University (1988)
16. Chang, S.: A study of eye movement during sight reading of selected piano compositions. Ph.D. Teachers College, Columbia University (1993)
17. Polanka, M.: Research note: factors affecting eye movements during the reading of short melodies. Psychol. Music **23**(2), 177–183 (1995)
18. Krasinskaya, L.E., Utkin, V.F.: Elementarnaya teoriya muzyki. 4-e izd., dopolnennoe. (Elementary music theory. 4-th ed. suppl.). Music, Moscow (1991). (in Russian)

Formalization of the Informality

The Role of Truth-Values in Indirect Meanings

Basil Lourié[1](⊠) and Olga Mitrenina[2]

[1] The National Research University Higher School of Economics (HSE),
38, Studencheskaya Str., Perm 614070, Russia
hieromonk@gmail.com
[2] Department of Mathematical Linguistics, St. Petersburg State University,
11, Universitetskaya emb., St. Petersburg 199034, Russia
mitrenina@gmail.com

Abstract. The problem of truth-values of indirect meanings is discussed within the semantic theory of indirect meaning proposed by the present authors in a dialogue with Hintikka's and Sandu's theory. The authors preserve the key notion of the latter, the meaning line, but putting it into different semantics (non-Fregean situational) and logic (paraconsistent). Like the contradictions, the indirect meanings tend to an explosion (there are always such possible worlds where they are true); to make them meaningful, there is a need of singling out the only relevant transworld connexion among the infinite number of the possible ones. The meaning line serves to this purpose. An analysis of the simplest semantic constructions with indirect meaning (tropes, humour, hints, riddles, etc.) is proposed.

Keywords: Indirect meaning · Poetical tropes · Metaphors · Humour
Riddles · Nonsense · Meaning lines · Transworld relation · Paraconsistent logic
Situational semantics

1 Introduction[1]

Among the last topics by Jaakko Hintikka was the logical theory of indirect meaning, which he approached in collaboration with Gabriel Sandu [28]. The Hintikka—Sandu theory is, in our opinion, the most inspiring for those who believe, like us, that the metaphors have, at least, some internal logic, and this logic is still within the logic of natural language. This was the first point stated by Hintikka and Sandu. At the time when they were writing, the most popular theories were—and remain now—either excluding the metaphors (and other kinds of indirect meaning) from the level of language (pushing them to deeper structures of the cognitive sphere: Lakoff *et al.* [20, 21, 31]) or limiting them to pragmatics depriving them of semantic value (partially, as Grice [24] and Searl [51], or completely, as Davidson [10]).

---

[1] The present study was supported by the Russian Science Foundation; project Nr 16-18-10202. The authors would like to express their gratitude for those who have helped them in their study, especially to Elena Chepel, Eleonora Khudoshina, Elena Ludilova, and Nadezhda Panchenko.

© Springer Nature Switzerland AG 2019
P. Eismont and O. Mitrenina (Eds.): LMAC 2017, CCIS 943, pp. 185–206, 2019.
https://doi.org/10.1007/978-3-030-05594-3_15

Hintikka and Sandu were aiming at returning metaphors (and other kinds of indirect meaning) to semantics of natural language. With the same token, they were expecting to overcome, in this way, a crisis in the formal semantic of natural language as it was established by Richard Montague and David Lewis on the Fregean ground. The very interest to the indirect meaning was provoked, in their case, with the hope to give a new impetus to the Montague—Lewis's semantics.

In our previous paper [35], we have tried to demonstrate that Hintikka and Sandu reached significant achievements in both directions. However, their resulting theory of indirect meanings, although providing the "anatomy" of the poetical trope, does not explain its "physiology," that is, *why* the logical scheme they described works in such an impressing way; and their resorting to Montague—Lewis's semantic turned out to be serving rather to refutation than confirmation of this semantic as that of the natural language. As it happens sometimes, a fruitful research can bring unexpected fruits— sometimes instead of the expected ones.

Now, we have to elaborate on Hintikka's ideas without a possibility of a personal discussion with him. Nevertheless, we can hope that he would be curious to see a reincarnation of his ideas in a different logic and semantic.

1.1 The Meaning Lines and the Paraconsistent Logic

The main idea of the Hintikka—Sandu theory of indirect meaning is the meaning lines. Like the previously known "world lines" by David Kaplan, the "meaning lines" establish a kind of transworld identity, however, their logical objects are not the individuals (as it is the case of Kaplan's world lines) but their properties (predicates). The meaning lines connect the characteristic sets of individuals in each world corre- sponding to the relevant predicate but avoid identification of the individuals themselves.

The metaphors and metonymies work, according to Hintikka and Sandu, using these meaning lines. In this way, they argued, there does not appear any specific "metaphorical" meaning having a different nature from that of the literal meaning. Instead, the indirect meanings produced through the meaning lines are subordinated to the common semantic rules of the natural language. Hintikka and Sandu answered definitively "yes" to the question whether the metaphorical (viz. metonymical) meaning can be true or false. As an explanation, they added: "…the only unusual thing about a metaphoric sentence is that the meaning lines of one of its constituent expressions are drawn in a way different from its literal cousin. But in all other respects, the same semantic rules must apply to it" [28, p. 170].

To Hintikka and Sandu, these common semantic rules are those of the Fregean semantics. Our opinion is that it is not the case.[2] Indeed, if we perform an "autopsy" of a metaphor (viz. other kind of indirect meaning), the meaning lines will be exactly what we will see—namely, the identity of some predicates shared by some quite different things, e.g. a cherry and a rolled kitty called Cherry (cf. a popular Russian cat name Вишенка, literally "Little Cherry"[3]). We would not see, however, why this name is much more fitting with its bearer than some other possible nicks based on some more fundamental features of the cats—for instance, Cow (given that both cats and cows are animals and mammals). There could be a logical point of view from which it would be preferable to call cats after animals than plants, and Cow would be a better name than Cherry—why not? Why Cow as a name of a kitty would be less poetical? At least, both names are equally allowed by the meaning lines.

The problem is that Hintikka—Sandu theory is an autopsy report of the poetical trope. This is a necessary part of research, but it does not say a word on poetical trope's "physiology," that is, why it was so expressive when it was alive.

This question has been answered by Donald Davidson in his seminal 1978 paper, although in an "anti-semantic" manner: "Metaphor makes us see on thing as another by making some literal statement that inspires and prompts the insight" [10, p. 263].

This insight is the main feature and the very *raison d'être* of communication using the indirect meanings. In our previous article [35], we have treated the Davidsonian "insight" as a direct experience of a contradiction in our mind. The kitty and the cherry, in our example above, form a subcontrary opposition, the two sharply distinct poles with no vagueness in between… but they are shown, in the lightening of the metaphor, as identical—whereas we still perfectly realise that they are not. What is seen as a meaning line in the autopsy was a true world line when the poetical trope was alive.

This is the core idea of our own theory of poetical tropes based on a paraconsistent logic (more specifically, on the logic based on subcontrary oppositions). The indirect meanings are meaningful to us when we are able to grasp an identity of things that are sharply different. The striking and insightful (in the Davidsonian sense) is this feeling

---

[2] In our previous article [35], we have shown this, among others, with a demonstration borrowed in the so-called theorem of Putnam [45]. Putnam's result in his demonstration by contradiction of the untenability of the Fregean semantics (Putnam's example: the sentence "a cat on a mat" is true if and only if there is a cherry on a tree) ceases to be absurd if we replace, in his demonstration, the Montague intentions with the meaning lines: there could be a metaphorical sense in what this result is meaningful, e.g., if Cherry is a name of a cat. This fact proves that the meaning lines are not possible in the Fregean semantics where the denotation of a sentence is its truth-value. Therefore, the meaning lines belong to situational semantics, where the denotation of a sentence is the situation it refers to. We have demonstrated further that, in the case of indirect meanings, this semantics is similar to the situational semantics by Roman Suszko (cf. [54]) but even weaker. Moreover, the so-called "metaphorical logic" proposed by Vladimir Vasjukov [57] for formalising the ontology by Alexis Meinong is applicable to the poetical tropes of the natural language. If Hintikka and Sandu are right in insisting that the sentences containing indirect meanings and those that do not have the same formal semantics (we agree with them on this point), then, the semantics of natural language as a whole is non-Fregean and situational. See Appendix for a more formal summary.

[3] We can consider this nick as a metaphor regardless of its possible usage as a personal name of a pet, because, in the case of the cat called Cherry, the metaphor is certainly not dead, in contrast with so-called dead metaphors such as "hot dog".

of identity of non-identical things themselves and not of identity of their identical predicates. The latter kind of identity might be expressed without poetical tropes, in descriptions and comparisons; it becomes visible in an autopsy of a poetical trope as a meaning line. The former kind of identity, that of non-identical things is paraconsistent and is able to work in provoking Davidsonian insights… But it is able not to work in this way.

The communication through indirect meaning is not always successful. As we have seen before, the name Cow is not quite suitable for an elegant kitty, whereas—let us dare to state this overtly—there could be other kinds of cats to whom even the name Cow would be applicable successfully. However, these would be quite different cats, not those to whom would be suitable the name Cherry.

With this problem, we step on the field of the problem marked but so far not treated, as it deserves, by both Hintikka and Sandu and us. This is the problem of truth-values in the sentences with indirect meaning.

2   *Ex Sensu Non Literali Quodlibet?*

If indirect meanings have truth-values, they could be true or false. Hintikka and Sandu acknowledged this but with a reservation: "…the question of truth and falsity normally does not arise," and this is "a consequence of their nature" [28, p. 171]. Indeed, it is easy to say that, for any sentence, there would be a possible (or impossible[4]) world where it is true, and a possible (or impossible) world where it is false. The very question "true or false" thus becomes a subject of an "explosion": *ex sensu non literali quodlibet*, as someone would say. — This conclusion is, however, counterintuitive and false.

We have seen above that, for a cat, the "true" metaphor is either "cherry" or "cow" but not both simultaneously. Let us consider a case that is more complicated, the poem we have referred to in our previous article [35] (Boris Pasternak, *Improvisation*, 1915):

Я клавишей стаю кормил с руки	I fed out of my hand a flock of keys
Под хлопанье крыльев, плеск и клекот.	To clapping of wings and shrill cries in flight.
Я вытянул руки, я встал на носки,	Sleeves up, arms out, on tiptoe I rose;
Рукав завернулся, ночь терлась о локоть…	At my elbow I felt the nudging of night…
	(Translation by Eugene M. Kayden)

One can ask whether it is true that the poet played the piano (and, indeed, there are such worlds, actual or not, where he did), but this question is senseless: the poem is certainly not about that. It is about the very nature of the act of playing: whether it is mirrored in the actual world where the player is oriented downside and has keys *under* his fingers, whereas in some *true* world (whatever it means) he is oriented upwards, and the player has not keys but birds *above* his fingers. In other words, the poem is about the transworld connexion. The readers who like the poem consider this connexion as a

---

[4] "Impossible world" is a kind of possible worlds where are broken the logical laws that are presumed to be in force in this world.

valuable finding of the poet, which is, for them, certainly real and true. For some other readers—those who dislike such symbolic (or so-called "suggestive") lyrics—the poem sounds false. In both cases, however, the appreciation of the poem depends on the evaluation of its truth-value.

In this example, we were comparing two different situations (belonging to different possible worlds), whereas in the previous example we were dealing with individuals (cat, cherry, cow). Below we will consider the individuals as the elementary cases of "situations" in the sense of situational semantics, that is, states of affairs.

In the expressions containing indirect meanings, it is the transworld connexion that makes some truth-values to be true or false in a non-trivial way.

It can be evaluated as true or false differently by different people, but this is a common destiny of any human sentence, even the most literal one: some people would disagree with it. The criteria of truthfulness or falsity are out of our scope now.

Let us retain that a metaphor (or any other kind of indirect meaning) could be either true and, therefore, appreciated as successful, or false and, therefore, considered unsuccessful if not overlooked at all.

If we ignore the paraconsistent logic underlying the use of indirect meaning, we would have to acknowledge the explosion: *ex sensu non literali quodlibet (sc., sequitur)*, that is, from the non-literal indirect meaning follow both true and false. Moreover, if the non-direct meanings are always trivially both true and false, whereas these meanings, according to Hintikka and Sandu (and we agree with them in this matter), are of the same nature as other meanings in natural language, then, any meaning in natural language is both true and false[5].

Hintikka and Sandu stopped one step before this conclusion that would ruin their allegedly Fregean semantics. However, if one hopes not to fall into the abyss of triviality, one has to take into account the relevance. It is the notion of relevance that prevents us from falling into the abyss of triviality and the explosion.

The question whether the poet played piano is irrelevant; the relevant question is about the transworld connexion only—say, whether the keys are the birds, and so on. For those who recognised, in a Davidsonian insight, these birds in the keys, the metaphor is successful and true; for the others, not.

In the same way, it is also irrelevant whether Putnam's cat is on the mat, and whether Putnam's cherry is on the tree. The relevant is only the question whether this cat is, according to its *true* nature opened to a poetically minded connoisseur, rather a cherry or a cow.

In other words, relevant is only the transworld identity between different situations established with using an indirect meaning (e.g., a poet playing the piano and some person feeding birds). This relevance is grasped in both cases, whether the proposition

---

[5] Here we avoid a discussion of semantics of natural language in general and a detailed distinction between direct and indirect meanings. In our previous paper [35], we have briefly discussed incompatibility of Hintikka—Sandu's approach with the Fregean semantics of natural language (in the wake of Richard Montague and David Lewis), despite their own intention to overcome a "crisis" in this discipline.

containing an indirect meaning is considered as true (e.g., when a metaphor is appreciated as a good one) or false (e.g., when a metaphor is understood but considered as unhelpful—that is, false).

3   When the Truth-Value Matters: Tropes *vs* Jokes

The indirect meanings imply a transworld connexion, as we would formulate it in the possible world semantics. There are, however, other means to describe the phenomenon, more familiar to either philologists or psychologists.

For the philologists, we would recall the old term *double entente* and many others referring to the possibilities to understand the same expression in mutually incompatible ways. It is not limited to poetry, or, better, one can say that it is present everywhere in the human life, where is, at least, some minimal poetry. It is easier to enumerate where it is absent: where all other meanings except the literal are impossible. No, this is not the case of natural sciences, despite Rudolf Carnap's dream of a purely extensional language for them.[6]

The exclusively literal thinking is a feature of early childhood or some psychical disorders, especially those accompanied with a high level of depression. This is why, among the rules for the staff in the mental hospitals, there is a strict prohibition of humour and jokes with the patients.[7] Indeed, the humour requires a capacity to think in two different levels simultaneously—that is, in two different possible worlds. Freud has defined this mechanism as a kind of dialogue between *ego* and *super-ego*.[8] The modern theories, even psychoanalytical ones, could be different in details concerning the so-called tripartite structure (*ego*, *super-ego*, *id*), but, anyway, they require, for the ability to understand humour, a more or less mature and healthy structure of personality.[9]

The psychological mechanism here has the same logical structure as it is required for understanding poetry. It is almost impossible not to succumb to temptation to quote here the famous Freud's formula: "The pleasure in a joke arising from a 'short-circuit' like this seems to be the greater the more alien the two circles of ideas that are brought together by the same word…"[10] One can repeat about the poetical tropes the same: it is also enlightening as a "short-circuit" between two logical objects quite distant from

---

[6] Cf. his hypothetical "Thesis of Extensionality" [8, pp. 245–247].

[7] Unless humour and jokes become a constituent part of the therapist's technics, serving, most often, to reduce patient's paranoid sadistic impulses and aggression. In such cases, humour and jokes are used for restoring patient's personality (transforming the transference-countertransference relationship between him and the therapist). If this succeeds, the patient starts to realise the humoristic nature of therapist's words. For a discussion of this complicated matter, s. [4].

[8] In his 1927 article "Humour" ("Der Humor") [16]. For placing the Freudian psychoanalytic approach to the humour into the context of the 20th-century interdisciplinary humour studies, s. [38].

[9] For a larger than Freudian psychoanalytic approach to the humour, s. [41]. This approach, inspired, in a large part, by Ignacio Matte Blanco, could be the most interesting for a logician.

[10] From his 1905 book "Jokes and their relation to the unconscious" ("Der Witz und seine Beziehung zum Unbewußten") [17, p. 120].

each other. Here Freud's wording on joke is quite close to Davidson's "insight" as the way of our understanding of the metaphor.

As it was demonstrated in details by Tzvetan Todorov in his 1977 book "Théories du symbole" (but first noticed long before him), Freud (in his classification of kinds of humour in "Jokes and Their Relation to the Unconscious") described, in fact, nothing but poetical tropes.[11] The causes of misunderstanding of poetical tropes are, too, analogous to the causes of misunderstanding humour.[12]

What is different between the poetical trope and the joke, is not the semantic structure but what we are interested in here—the truth-values. This fact was first noticed in 1967 by Paul Grice who was dealing with the difference between the irony and the metaphor. Irony implies a contradiction between its plain (literal) meaning and the intended meaning: the former is true whereas the latter is false (or *vice versa*), e.g., "X is a fine friend," whereas the audience knows about X something sharply different [24, p. 34].[13] We can add, to this Grice's analysis, an explanation of the fact why this ironical manner could be more effective than a direct attack on X: because of the Davidsonian "insight," or the Freudian "short circuit" that is produced by a paraconsistent transworld identification of the real X with an imaginary X who is a good friend. The audience able to perceive this irony understands that, for this ironic sentence, the pretending truth-value "true" points to the real truth-value "false."

Another Grice's example where metaphor and irony are combined could be useful for grasping both identity of their semantic structure and difference in their dealing with truth-values. The hearer has to perform an interpretation in two stages: "I say *You are the cream in my coffee*, intending to hearer to reach first the metaphor interpretant 'You are my pride and joy' and then the irony interpretant 'You are my bane'" [24, p. 34]. Victor Raskin, elaborating on these Grice's ideas on irony, provided an analysis of humour as a kind of "non-*bona-fide* communication" [46].[14]

Applying Raskin's terminology, we have to classify the poetical tropes within the *bona-fide* communication. If the transworld identities they establish are not perceived as "true," this means that the metaphor (or another poetical trope) fails.

Unlike the poetical tropes, the humour deliberately changes the labels "true" and "false" on its propositions. Those who do not catch this game do not understand a given piece of humour (but it occurs that the person to be blamed is not the hearer but the utterer of a joke).

The poetical trope uses expressions with indirect meanings that are non-trivially true. The humour uses such expressions that are non-trivially false. The two Grice's examples above show two ways how the indirect meaning could be non-trivially false: in both cases, there is a meaning pretending to be non-trivially true that turns out to be false.

---

[11] The corresponding chapter is entitled "Freud's Rhetoric and Symbolics" [56, pp. 247–254].

[12] Cf. a detailed and rich monograph [6].

[13] This Grice's seminal paper has been written in 1967 and first published in 1975; cf. also its 1987 continuation [23, pp. 53–54].

[14] Ralph Müller [40] provides a concise introduction to the problem, albeit without any specific logical theories and attention to the truth-values either. Salvatore Attardo [3] implies a cognitive (Lakoff-styled) theory of metaphor, which undermines its interest to our purpose.

In the case of a "pure" irony ("X is a fine friend"), the non-trivial truth-value "true" denied by the irony is the literal (direct) meaning of the sentence "X is a good friend"; no indirect meaning is involved here at the first glance. The indirect meaning appears on the next step, that of irony, when one should realise that the sentence means the opposite to its literal meaning, thus changing its truth-value from "true" to "false."

In the case of an ironic sentence using a poetical trope ("You are the cream in my coffee"), the first non-trivial truth-value "true" is that of the metaphor. At the stage when one realises the irony one have to notice that the intended meaning of the sentence is the opposite, thus changing its truth-value from "true" to "false."

Anyway, the humour requires the indirect meaning with the truth-value non-trivially "false." This becomes possible only with denying the truth-value non-trivially "true." The truth-value "true" denied by the humour might be acquired in any non-trivial way, either with using an indirect meaning or without.

We will meet later (Sect. 7) a specific kind of humour based on blocking the expected non-triviality of indirect meaning. This could serve as a proof by contradiction of the non-triviality of the indirect meanings in all genres where they occur.

4   Lyrics or a Joke? It Depends…

The identity of the internal semantic structure between the poetical tropes and the pieces of humour leads to the theoretical conclusion, that there is no way to discern between the "true" and humorous metaphor (poetical trope) judging from its internal structure only. For instance, whether a given text is a "serious" poem or a parody we can define uniquely from its cultural context. Thus, a famous Russian romance (a kind of sentimental sung poetry extremely popular in the 19th- and early 20th-century Russia) was written as a parody poem in 1847, but in 1848 was provided with the music that transformed it into a completely serious song.[15] It is often performed until now.

Of course, such story is not unique. Perhaps, now the most known in the world is the case of John Kander's (music) and Fred Ebb's (lyrics) song *Tomorrow Belongs To Me* written for their 1966 Broadway musical *Cabaret* (and more known as a movie). The authors, two American Jews, composed this allegedly early 1930s Nazi youth hymn ironically and, of course, in English, but it became one of the anthems of the modern extreme rights, including the Neo-Nazis, who are arguing, here and there on the web, whether it was first composed in German or Italian.

---

[15] Ivan Panaev's poem *Будто из Гейне* (*As if from Heine*), a parody on the Russian poetical translations from and imitations of Heinrich Heine. With the music by N. D. Dmitriev (1848)—which Panaev himself called "beautiful" in 1855,—it became a famous romance *Густолиственных кленов аллея…* (*The alley of thick-foliage maples…*), and this despite its obviously humoristic wording, alliterations, and paronomasias. Paradoxically, as a parody, the poem was unusually successful: it "killed" (as contemporary critics said) the epigonous lyrics it was aimed at. See, for the text and a commentary, [26, pp. 650, 1040]. We are grateful to Eleonora I. Khudoshina for having pointed us out this story.

Finally, we could refer to a beloved metaphor for the female beauty, "she-camel." Indeed, it sound less attractive outside the lyrical poetry of the Arabs, but, in the classical Arab culture, even the words *ğamal* "camel" and *ğamāl* "beauty; beautiful woman" are the closest relatives (cf., e.g., [29, p. 237; 36]). Nevertheless, in the classical Indian *Pañcatantra*, a collection of moralistic stories where all characters are animals, camel's name is Vikaṭa "ugly," and he perishes out of his stupidity.[16] Therefore, if somebody is metaphorically called "camel," it is not necessarily out of her/his beauty, because the meaning varies according to the cultural contexts—even though the semantic skeleton of the metaphor is always the same.

5 The Poetical Trope Inside Out: The Riddle

Before this point, we were dealing with the usages of indirect meanings, where at stake was the transworld identity *per se*. In these cases (let us formulate this in situational semantics terms), both situations *a* and *b* belonging to different possible (or impossible) worlds were considered to be known by audience beforehand. The situation *b* was, in these cases, known either in literally sense (as it was in the case of irony or in the cases where both *a* and *b* are individuals, that is, elementary situations) or, at least, in the sense that they are described with trivially true propositions (as it was in the case of Pasternak's poem describing an imaginary situation of feeding some birds etc.: there is certainly some possible or impossible world where it is true).

The human culture would hardly miss an opportunity to create another kind of texts, where the situation *b* is to be found out, whereas the transworld identity is considered as more or less known. Such texts could be in general called riddles,[17] whereas the real extension of the corresponding genre range is much wider than one could expect looking from the modern European culture.

We say about the *a priori* knowledge of the transworld identity "more or less," given that the number of theoretically possible meaning lines is always infinite, and there is always a problem to find out the right path. In fact, this is the only difficulty when we, knowing the situation *a*, are trying to resolve the riddle for finding the situation *b*.

Another peculiar feature of the riddle in comparison with the poetical tropes and the humour is that, in their case, it is the situation *b* that belongs to the world presumed to be actual, whereas the situation *a* belongs to a world built with the help of imagination.[18]

Aristotle (*Poetics* XXII, 1458 a 22-30) was the first to notice that the riddles use metaphors: among the expressions that include the words used in an indirect or unusual meaning (πᾶν τὸ παρὰ τὸ κύριον), the one which uses metaphors, is a riddle (ἂν μὲν οὖν ἐκ μεταφορῶν, αἴνιγμα). "The main idea of the riddle is the following: to say as about

---

[16] Story I, 12 [44, pp. 105–111].

[17] For an orientation in the ocean of literature on the riddle by folklorists and anthropologists, s., e.g., [1]. The most of this literature could be of only tangential interest for a logician. Among the recent most comprehensive studies, s. especially those of Savely Senderovich [52, 53].

[18] In the most archaic structures of riddle, there are not two but three situations involved, thus establishing the transworld connexion between three possible worlds; cf. more on them below, Sect. 8.

something real what is impossible to put together with each other; it is not to be produced using a combination of other words, whereas it could be done with metaphors"[19] (translation is ours). Nevertheless, in our epoch, the logical study of riddles became much less lucky than that of metaphors and humour.[20]

In our opinion, of special theoretical importance remains the 1984 paper by Tatiana Ya. Elizarenkova and Vladimir N. Toporov "On the Vedic Riddle of *Brahmodya* Type."[21] It takes into account semantics of the riddle in the religious practices, which escaped even the attention of such a universal researcher as Savely Senderovich.[22]

Elizarenkova and Toporov said about the nature of the riddle something very similar to what Davidson said about the metaphor and Freud about the joke:

> "[T]he question of the riddle and its answer are tautologies but constructed in such a manner that the two tautological parts are directed differently (at least, on the superficial level): placing these two structures at the maximal possible distance not only 'hides' the aspect of identity but becomes an analogue, in some way, of transmitting of the meaning of the world outside or, more precisely, retaining of the extremely great distance between the meaning (the answer of the riddle) and the question about it; in other terms, preserving of such maximal tension between the tautological members, when their tautology is hidden as much as possible. From this principle, it follows that, in fact, one has to consider the resolution of a riddle not its answer alone (the riddle is least of all having to do with guessing and improvisation but [first of all,] with knowledge and the art of its engendering), but the answer as a 'curled up' sign of the whole procedure of explication of the hidden identity of the two parts of the riddle."[23]

---

[19] [55, pp. 203.26–204.2]: αἰνίγματός τε γὰρ ἰδέα αὕτη ἐστί, τὸ λέγοντα ὑπάρχοντα ἀδύναται συνάψαι· κατὰ μὲν οὖν τὴν τῶν ἄλλων ὀνομάτων σύνθεσιν οὐχ οἷόν τε τοῦτο ποιῆσαι, κατὰ δὲ τὴν μεταφορῶν ἐνδέχεται.

[20] Beside Senderovich's monorgaphs [52, 53], the most interesting, from a logical point of view, is the chain of three articles [5, 27, 37] by Ian Hamnet, who elaborated the topic on the role of inconsistency and ambiguities in various kinds of human interaction, not only the riddles. He specified, moreover, that the kind of ambiguity involved here is not vagueness but indetermination: it results not from lack of specification, as vagueness, but because the text or ritual "fails to indicate which of two (or more) references is intended, though each possible reference may be fairly specific in itself" [27, p. 383]. In this way, Hamnet distinguished, even though without strict logical terminology, between the subcontrary and contrary oppositions, stating that only the first is involved in the archaic rituals, riddles etc.

[21] We will quote the first publication [15]; cf. French and German translations [13, 14].

[22] Who does not mention [15] in his [52, 53].

[23] "…вопрос загадки и ее ответ суть тавтологии, но построенные таким образом, что обе тавтологические части разнонаправлены (по крайней мере на поверхностном уровне): разведение этих двух структур на максимально возможное расстояние не только «скрывает» аспект тождества, но и представляет собой своего рода аналог выведения смысла мира *вовне* или, точнее, удержание предельно большого расстояния между смыслом (ответом загадки) и вопросом о нем, в других терминах — сохранение такого максимального напряжения между тавтологическими членами, когда сама тавтологичность предельно скрыта" [15, pp. 16–17]. "Из этого принципа вытекает, что, по сути дела, решением загадки должен считаться не просто *ответ* (загадка вообще менее всего связана с угадыванием и импровизацией, но со знанием и искусством его порождения), а ответ как свернутый знак *всей процедуры экспликации скрытого тождества* обеих частей загадки" [15, p. 38, n. 7]. The passage starts in the main texts and continues in an endnote, but we do not interrupt the textual flow in our translation.

Like Freud, Elizarenkova and Toporov said about a "tension" and "the maximal distance" between the opposing transworld situations, but they went so far as to grasp the "hidden identity" that becomes, when the riddle is resolved, explicit and striking. We have to notice that this "hidden identity" is paraconsistent—and this is why it is "hidden" from any ordinary reasoning. All this is common in the riddles, poetical tropes, and humour.

The role of the riddle as, first of all, the art of engendering knowledge of the situation b, but also the knowledge of the right logical path from a to b. This means that the riddle is also dealing with the nature of the transworld identity in a given case. This path is never known *a priori*. In the modern Western culture, the riddle implies reasoning in some kind of inductive logic (the logic where the available data are never sufficiently complete for ensuring the strict classical reasoning and that, therefore, operates with likelihoods). In other societies, this path together with the answer of the riddle are subjects of esoteric knowledge, which is not supposed to be grasped through guessing—it must be revealed by the bearer of this knowledge.[24] The meaning lines between the transworld situations could be drawn, as always where the indirect meaning is involved, in an infinite number of ways, but the modern riddle contains some hints how to single out the "right" logical path, whereas the archaic riddle is "concealed" for the outsider and requires, for being resolved, an access to hidden knowledge.

It is only natural that the knowledge of the situation b and that of the path from a to b are inseparable (even in the modern riddles where guessing is appropriate). It could be only approached from different sides, but, in itself, it is a whole and unique: the knowledge of the situation b and of the right logical path to it from an already known situation a. The poetical tropes and the humour approaches from the side of the path, and the riddle approaches from the side of b.

Beside the riddle, where the logical path from a to b is hidden, there is its simplified relative, the hint. In the hint, the logical path is either explicit or supposed to be easily perceivable. In this way, Jesus said to the crowd about the adulteress: "He that is without sin among you, let him first cast a stone at her" (John 8:7 KJV). Here the logical path is explicit: look at yourself and decide. The situation b referred to is "nobody of you is authorised to judge according to the Law of Moses." The theoretical necessity of lapidating is not under the question, but the situation a (Jesus's enforcement of the Moses Law) is the requirement that only sinless people are authorised to cast stones at the adulteress.

The hints are the simplest riddles supposed to be guessed even in the non-western and non-modern cultures.

6 The "Incomplete" Riddles in the "Anti-Humour"

We have noticed above that the humour appears where the indirect meanings acquire the truth-value "false" in a non-trivial way, and that, for this, they have to be constructed as a negation of a proposition having the truth-value "true" in any non-trivial

---

[24] See, for details, [27, 52, 53].

way (containing an indirect meaning or not). Is it possible, for an indirect meaning proposition, to acquire the truth-value "false" without referring to another proposition with truth-value "true"? In other words, is it possible to be false without specifying what exactly is false? The answer is positive, but, in this case, the non-specified proposition that turns out to be false is enigmatic. In other words, we have to deal with a kind of riddles.

This genre is sometimes called in English "anti-humour" and is a part of the culture of nonsense. It is constructed according the standard scheme of indirect meaning but either (1) the transworld situation b or (2) the transworld meaning line from a to b is lacking. In both cases, it turns out that *de facto* are lacking both b and the logical path from a to b, but the causes are different: in the case (1), there is no path because there could be no path to nowhere, whereas, in the case (2), there is simply no path, although the situation b seems to be inaccessible but existing.

An example of the case (1) is the nineteenth-century English joke (first appeared in 1847):

Question: Why did the chicken cross the road?
Answer: To get to the other side.

This is a riddle with lacking transworld situation at all. A transworld situation b seems to be implied in the question but its existence is denied with the answer. The reason of the chicken is simply to do what they did. It turns out to be possible to deny a non-specified and even non-existing indirect meaning. The humour here implies the truth-value "false" but ascribed to the proposition represented with a void set of meaning. We can perceive, from that, that the void set is not the same as nothing, or, in other words, that the non-existing meaning is nevertheless a meaning and, therefore, could be perceived and denied: otherwise, this "anti-humoristic" joke could not be successful. The non-specified and, therefore, somewhat hidden transworld meaning requires that the text is shaped as a riddle.

No wonder that this "anti-humour" riddle has served as the pattern for dozens or even hundreds "normal" humoristic riddles, where the transworld situation b is explained with a reference to some thinker or religion or something else: "Why did the chicken cross the road? — Nietzsche: Because if you gaze too long across the Road, the Road gazes also across you" (and so on).

An example of the "anti-humoristic" riddle of type (2) is that of the Hatter in the *Alice's Adventures in Wonderland* (ch. 7 "The Mad Tea Party"): "Why is a raven like a writing-desk?" This is a question about a transworld connexion (between a raven and a writing-desk). Eventually, as one recalls, "Alice sighed wearily" classifying this riddle among those "that have no answers." Many readers follow Alice committing the same mistake. Many others (including Lewis Carroll in his 1896 preface to a new edition of the *Alice*) try to guess an answer,[25] thus repeating the initial move by Alice together with her self-confidence ("'Do you mean that you think you can find out the answer to

---

[25] See Martin Gardner's note 5 to ch. 7 in [9, pp. 71–73]. Lewis Carroll himself wrote about his answer (*ibid.*): "This, however, is merely an afterthought; the Riddle, as originally invented, had no answer at all." Our question is whether this "at all" means to be absolute (ontological) or merely epistemological.

it?' said the March Hare. 'Exactly so,' said Alice"). However, the true bearers of the hidden knowledge are only the Hatter and the March Hare (and not even Lewis Carroll). And this knowledge consists precisely in the fact that it is not and could be not known by anybody, in the way that any guesses are senseless. The line of transworld connexion is either epistemically inaccessible or non-existing (the text does not allow to choose between these variants).

Here the transworld situation b is not non-existing but inaccessible: the situation exists (both worlds containing a raven and a written-desk exist) but the meaning line between them does not. Nevertheless, a non-existing meaning line is still a meaning line. It works and makes the riddle of the Hatter provoking (even if not for everyone: not for Alice).

In both examples of anti-humour, something is implied to be existing but does not exist. These non-existing objects (such as the goal of chicken's movement) and non-existing meaning lines (such as the answer to Hatter's riddle), without being existing, are at work. These objects do not exist even in the Meinongian sense, because they do not exist precisely in the (im)possible worlds they belong to[26]. Nevertheless, at the initial stage, their existence appears as evident: otherwise, the very phenomenon of anti-humour would be impossible.

For becoming successful, an "anti-humour" joke needs to create confidence in existence of some object and, then, discover that the proposition(s) implying its existence is (are) false—because this object do not exist. This "false" is the non-trivial truth-value that features any kind of humour.

7 "Wax and Gold": The Riddles and the Logic of Discovery

With the riddles, especially in their religious usage, we are reaching fundamental questions of the epistemological function of the indirect meaning. Unlike Carnap and the neo-positivists from the Vienna circle, the human civilisation considers the indirect meaning as much more powerful vehicle of knowledge than the literal "extensional language" (even if the ideal of such language would be reachable).

Savely Senderovich in his analysis of the riddles [52, 53] concludes that, in its archaic form, the riddle had two answers—that is not one but two situations b_1 and b_2—where the first resolution was simply funny or curious, whereas the second one was always belonging to the hidden sexual contents. Such a limitation for the "hidden" contents looks unfounded: it comes from a methodological limitation of Senderovich's study which hardly takes into account religion. The Elizarenkova's and Toporov's study [15] is sufficient for grasping, at least, a general idea of the religious value of archaic riddles.

Nevertheless, Senderovich's analysis is already sufficiently profound for providing the necessary means for establishing the mutual relations between the riddle and the exegesis or hermeneutics in different cultures. The sacred text as a whole (or even a text

---

[26] For the transworld meaning lines, we can postulate a specific (im)possible world, where the meaning lines belonging to the "anti-humour" of type (2) do not exist.

with the value approaching that of a sacred text, such as the Homeric epos in the Hellenistic culture) is considered as being similar to a riddle according to its multi-level semantics.[27] Its "right" understanding requires the same procedures as those that are necessary for resolving the riddles: there could be some hints that must be found out within the text and that are subsequently to be processed with a given set of exegetical rules, and, the most necessary, there is a need of obtaining an access to the "hidden knowledge"—ether through a direct revelation or an exegetical tradition.

Similarly to the structure of the archaic riddle where two different answers belong to the two different possible worlds, the exegesis of a sacred text would reveal several levels of meaning which are to be reached beyond the literal ones. In the Christian tradition going back to Origen (first half of the 3rd cent. CE, the founder of the so-called Alexandrian [Christian] exegetical school), the literal meaning is called "carnal," and the deeper meanings are called "psychic" (= ascetic) and "pneumatic" (= truth about God); the carnal meaning of the Scripture could be, in some places, even lost or not intended at all, whereas the two others are ever-present.[28] The Alexandrinian Christian School, however, albeit having inherited from the Second Temple period Jewish exegetical traditions many particular exegeses did not inherit any system of strict exegetical rules.

In these cases, the elementary riddle-like structure where there is only one trans-world identity between only two situations belonging to the different (im)possible worlds becomes more complicated through recursion: there are several transworld situations, which are not necessarily connected with each other. For instance, the "psychic" and the "pneumatic" meanings of the Scripture in the patristic exegesis normally do not have any perceivable mutual connexion. However, the different is the traditional Ethiopian culture of ambiguous sayings with poetical tropes called, in Amharic, *säm-ənna wärq* "wax and gold." The "wax" means here the surface meaning, often very elegantly represented, and the "gold" is the intended meaning, which is not always easy to discover (the name is alluding to the work of a silversmith who pours molten gold into a clay form filled with a wax model; the wax melts away, and the gold takes the shape of the wax). The "wax" could be considered as a usual poetical trope, whereas the "gold" is the answer to an implied riddle. The art consists here in combining the two indirect meanings together while creating the maximal tension between the two [42].[29]

> Mohammed Girma [22] relates a story about the late 19th-century churchman and poet *äläqa* ("master") Gäbrä Ḥänna, who once saw a rat jumping out of the *mäsob* (breadbasket) of a family that invited him for a dinner. In his prayer after the meal, he said the following two-verse poem: *Bälanäw ṭäṭanäw kä änğäraw kä wäṭu / Ɜgziäbḥer yäsṭäləñä kä mäsobu äyṭu* "I ate and drank with *enjera* (bread) and stew, / And I pray to God that you may not lack (*äyṭu*) for your breadbasket." So was the "wax." The "gold" was provided with the homonymy, because "rat" in Amharic is *äyṭ*, which made the prayer less pleasant to the hosts (but still within the limits of gentle irony)—asking God to grant rats for their breadbasket.

---

[27] Cf. a comparative study of several hermeneutic traditions: [58].

[28] Origen, *On the Principles*, books III and IV; cf., on this feature of the traditional Christian exegesis, Henri de Lubac's studies, starting from [11].

[29] For the use in the exegesis, s. [22].

Even now, the art of the "wax and gold" is one of keystones of the traditional education among the Amhara people. It penetrates into the modern Amharic culture in such an extent that it creates difficulties in communication with those who know the Amharic language but do not share the Amharic cultural background (being, for instance, Tigreans) [2]. The phrases with "wax and gold," especially the verses, are used for all kinds of poetry, irony, secret communication, theology, and biblical exegesis. In the exegesis, the number of indirect meanings of the same passage could be, of course, much more than two...

In the Jewish exegesis, unlike the Christian, the rules were shaped into a logically explicit system. It is presently known as it was formulated by the Talmudic and post-Talmudic sages [7],[30] but its main rules were already established to the late Second Temple period and are omnipresent in the earliest Christian texts as well, including the New Testament—sometimes with explicit hints to use a particular rule of exegesis, more often without them.

We limit ourselves to a simplest example, where a New Testament text contains an explicit hint to use, for a deeper understanding, the exegetical rule called by the rabbis *gezerah šawah* (גזרה שוה) "an equivalent regulation" (one passage may be explained by another, if there are similarities in their wording). In John 19:36, the fact that the soldiers "brake not his [Jesus's] legs" (John 19:33) is explained with a reference to Exodus 12:46 "For these things were done, that the scripture should be fulfilled, 'A bone of him shall not be broken' (KJV)" (cf. [39, pp. 147–166]). Even without the explicit reference to Exodus 12:46 ("neither shall ye break a bone thereof" KJV), the competent reader would have had to grasp the similarity between this situation with Jesus's body on the cross and the commandment about the eating of the paschal lamb, thus concluding—according to the *gezerah šawah* procedure—that the two situations are identical, and, therefore, Jesus became the very paschal lamb, that is, the reality which symbolic "prefiguration" was the sacrificial lamb prescribed by the Law of Moses.

The exegesis of sacred or "semi-sacred" texts is the topic that is, in the traditional cultures, very close to the exegesis of "the book of Nature," or the natural sciences. The anthropologist Donald N. Levine (1931–2015), famous by his first book on the Ethiopian culture of "wax and gold," dedicated a monograph precisely to the problem of ability of thinking with ambiguities—or lack thereof—in the modern western culture ([32]; cf. [33]). This problem certainly touches "resolving the riddles of nature" and leads us to the elusive verge between the artistic imagination and the scholarly intuition...

Let us finish with the words of a baroque theoretician who was especially sensitive to a deep kinship between the logic of poetical tropes and the logic of natural sciences and mathematics, the Polish Jesuit Maciej Kazimierz Sarbiewski (1595–1640), also known for his analysis of the contradiction lying in the base of the poetical trope:

---

[30] For a logical analysis, s. especially [48–50].

Solus poeta numquam mentitur, nam etsi ea dicat, quae non sunt, non dicit tamen eo animo, ut credantur, sed ut cognoscantur veluti perfecte expressa, ut ex cognitis ulterior quaedam veritas sub fabula latens colligatur [47, p. 28].[31]

Only a poet never lies, but even if he says what does not exist, he says this not with the purpose of making believe but for making this (non-existing) recognised, with having it perfectly expressed, and for collecting, from these recognised (things), some posterior truth hidden under the tale.

8 Conclusion

Following Hintikka and Sandu, we interpreted the indirect meaning as establishing some transworld relation. Unlike Hintikka and Sandu, we consider this relation to be a paraconsistent identity of sharply different things ("situations" in the sense of situational semantics, where the individuals are to be taken as elementary situations). However, this identity is established along the meaning lines in the sense of Hintikka and Sandu.

Therefore, the simplest semantic structure containing an indirect meaning is the following

$$(a \neq b) \wedge (a \equiv b) \wedge (a \unrhd b),$$

where a and b are different situations belonging to the different (im)possible worlds, $\equiv$ is identity, and $\unrhd$ is the meaning line (s. Appendix for the details).

In the simplest structure, there are only two situations belonging to the different (im)possible worlds, which are connected with a transworld relation. In other cases, such as archaic riddles, multilevel scriptural exegesis, Ethiopian "wax and gold" wordplay art etc., the number of transworld situations could be higher, and their mutual relations could be either involved into the construction of the whole or not. Anyway, there is always one situation that is considered as "given."

Limiting ourselves to the simplest semantical structures containing an indirect meaning, we need to consider two transworld situations a and b and the transworld relation between them. In our notation, a is the situation known beforehand; it could be foreknown in either literal sense or in the sense of being described with propositions that are trivially true (that there is some possible or impossible world where they are true). Therefore, the new knowledge acquired with the indirect meaning could be either that of the situation b or the transworld relation between a and b.

The trivialisation of the propositions containing non-direct meanings is avoided due to the condition of relevance. For instance, for the poem we have quoted above, it is irrelevant whether a poet was playing the piano, and it is trivially true that there are some worlds where he did. However, it is relevant that the situation of a poet playing the piano is identical to the situation of somebody feeding birds. One can discuss this identity, whether it is true or false. For those to whom it is true, the poem with its metaphors is good. For those to whom it is false, the poem is not good. In both cases,

---

[31] In the context of the present paper, the most relevant literature on Sarbiewski are [19, 30, 34, 43].

however, the implied set of propositions confirming the relevant identity is true or false in a non-trivial way.

The truth-values of the propositions describing the situations are external to the situations themselves. This is why the same indirect meanings could be taken as either serious or humoristic in different cultural contexts.

The core of the indirect meaning is a paraconsistent transworld identity based on a subcontrary opposition between (at least) one pair of situations belonging to the different (im)possible worlds. This transworld relation of identity either establishes a non-trivial connexion between two foreknown situations or points out a non-trivial transworld counterpart for one foreknown situation. In both cases, the paraconsistent identity connexion or the transworld situation pointed out by it could be non-trivially denied when recognised as being false.

Outside any context, any situation is both trivially true and trivially false, because there are such (im)possible worlds where it is either true or false. The non-triviality of the unique truth-value that is singled out is to be granted with the relevance, and the relevance is pointed with the transworld connexion established by the indirect meaning. Either this transworld connexion itself or the transworld situation b it points out is to be evaluated as non-trivially true or false.

There is a natural classification of the expressions containing indirect meanings, which is presented in Table 1 for the simplest structures (with only two transworld situations a and b). The indirect meanings are divided into two types according to their structure, depending on whether they bring new knowledge on the transworld situation b or the transworld relation between a and b. Moreover, each of these two types is further subdivided into two subtypes according to the truth-values[32]. The truth-value "false" makes the expression humoristic or belonging to a nonsense genre.

Table 1. The simplest structures containing indirect meaning

Known beforehand	Gained through insight	Type of indirect meaning
Transworld situation: True	Transworld relation	Poetical trope
Transworld situation: False	Transworld relation	Humour
Transworld relation: True	Transworld situation	Riddle
Transworld relation: False	Lacking/Inaccessibility of transworld situation	"Anti-humour" riddle

---

[32] For the sake of brevity, we apply, in Table 1, truth-values "true" and "false" to the situations and the relations, taking in mind that they are applicable to the propositions that describe situations and relations.

Appendix: Situational (Non-Fregean) Semantics for Poetical Tropes (Basics Concepts)[33]

The so-called Fregean axiom as formulated explicitly by Roman Suszko:

$$(\text{FA}) \qquad (p \leftrightarrow q) \rightarrow (p \equiv q)$$

In words: the logical equivalence of the formulae (sentences) p and q entails the identity of their denotations. Thus, the denotations of all sentences are their truth-values. The sign $\equiv$ means "(extensionally/referentially) identical to."

The Non-Fregean axiom of the situational semantics by Roman Suszko:

$$(\text{NFA}) \qquad (p \equiv q) \rightarrow (p \leftrightarrow q)$$

In words: the sentences are identical (their denotations are the same) if and only if the situations they describe are the same.

The equivalent of the Principle of Identity of Indiscernibles (PII) in Suszko's semantics (PII-S):

$$(\text{PII-S})\, (a \sqsubseteq b) \leftrightarrow \forall\varphi(\varphi(a) \Rightarrow \varphi(b)),$$

where φ is a formula, $a \sqsubseteq b$ means "a situationally entails b," $\Rightarrow$ is Suszko's non-Fregean connective "referentially leads to" defined through NFA: the connective $\equiv$ "referentially identical to" is the same Suszkean connective in both directions (one could write $\Leftrightarrow$).

Vasjukov's weakening of Suszko's semantics in his formalisation of Meinong's ontology (in his "metaphorical logic")—his weaker than PII-S equivalent of PII, the Principle of Similarity of Indiscernibles from a Preconceived Viewpoint (PSIPV):

$$(\text{PSIPV}) \qquad (a \unrhd b) \leftrightarrow \exists\varphi(\varphi(a) \Rightarrow \varphi(b)),$$

In words: in some preconceived aspect, a referentially leads to b. Here $\unrhd$ means "indiscernibles from a preconceived viewpoint." Connective $\Rightarrow$ means "referentially leads to from some preconceived viewpoint" (a weaker analogue of the Suszkean non-Fregean connective $\Rightarrow$). It means that, at least, one situation where a does occur must be involved, in some sense (from a preconceived viewpoint), into the situations where b does occur.

PSIPV could be considered as well as a generalisation of Peter Geach's concept of relative identity.[34] The difference is that PSIPV deals with the situations and not necessarily with individuals. Within PSIPV, one can interpret an individual as a kind of situation, an elementary one, whereas Geach's relative identity concept does not embraces the situations. Dealing with the indirect meaning, we need to take into account, in general case, the transworld identity between the situations as well as

---

[33] For a detailed explanation, s. [35].

[34] See, for a detailed bibliography, [12].

between the individuals (e.g., in Pasternak's poem dealt with above). Therefore, the relative identity framework would be not sufficient for us.

PSIPV is nothing but the formula for the meaning lines of Hintikka and Sandu. The phrase "from a preconceived viewpoint" is quite suitable not for the poetical trope itself but for its anatomical description in its autopsy report, when one describes the ground on which a metaphor or metonymy was created (respectively, relation of similarity or contiguity, according to Roman Jakobson's 1956 definition used by Hintikka and Sandu).

To formalise the poetical trope *in vivo*, one has to consider a conjunction of PSIPV and the paraconsistent conjunction $(a \neq b) \wedge (a \equiv b)$. Thus, the logical formula of the indirect meaning (IM) could be written as the following triple conjunction:

$$(\text{IM}) \qquad (a \neq b) \wedge (a \equiv b) \wedge (a \trianglerighteq b)$$

Without the third element, $a \trianglerighteq b$, any communication using indirect meaning is doomed to failure, because the conjunction $(a \neq b) \wedge (a \equiv b)$ alone would look silly: it does not result in discovering a new meaning. This third component is the meaning line first described by Hintikka and Sandu. Without comprehensibility of the connexion $a \trianglerighteq b$, no indirect meaning could be perceived. This is a necessary condition, whereas not a sufficient one.

There is always an infinite number of ways to draw meaning lines between the situations a and b belonging to different (im)possible worlds, but only one of them, in a given context, could be perceived as pointing to some non-trivial paraconsistent identity, $a \equiv b$.

References

1. Abrahams, R.D., Dundes, A.: Riddles. In: Dorson, R.M. (ed.) Folklore and Folklife: An Introduction, pp. 129–143. University of Chicago Press, Chicago (1982)
2. Aronsson, K.: Language practices and the visibility of language. Reflections on the great divide in the light of ethiopian oral traditions. In: Säljö, R. (ed.) The Written World: Studies in Literate Thought and Action. Springer Series in Language and Communication, vol. 23, pp. 73–83. Springer, Berlin (1988)
3. Attardo, S.: Humorous metaphors. In: Brône, G., Feyaerts, K., Veale, T. (eds.) Cognitive Linguistics and Humor Research. In: Applications of Cognitive Linguistic, 26, pp. 91–110. Mouton de Gruyter, Berlin (2015)
4. Baker, R.: The Delicate balance between the use and abuse of humor in the psychoanalytic setting. In: Barron, J.W. (ed.) Humor and Psyche: Psychoanalytic Perspectives, pp. 109–130. The Analytic Press Inc., Hillsdale (1999)
5. Barley, N.F.: Structural aspects of the anglo-saxon riddle. Semiotica **10**, 143–175 (1974)
6. Bell, N.: We are not amused: failed humor in interaction. In: Humor Research, 10. Mouton de Gruyter, Berlin (2015)
7. Boyarin, D.: Sparks of the logos: essays in rabbinic hermeneutics. The Brill Reference Library of Judaism, 11. Brill, Leiden (2003)
8. Carnap, R.: The Logical Syntax of Language, tr. A. Smeaton (Countess von Zeppelin). International Library of Psychology, pp. 245–247. Routledge, London (2001)

9. Carroll, L.: The Annotated Alice. The Definitive Edition. Introduction and notes by M. Gardner. W. W. Norton & Co., New York (2000)

10. Davidson, D.: What Metaphors Mean. In: Idem, Inquiries into Truth and Interpretation, pp. 245–264. Clarendon Press, Oxford (1984) [repr. 1991]

11. de Lubac, H.: Histoire et Esprit. L'intelligence de l'Écriture d'après Origène, Théologie, 16; Paris: Aubier (1950); 2nd edn. Cerf, Paris (2002)

12. Deutsch, H.: Relative identity. In: Zalta, E.N. (ed.) The Stanford Encyclopedia of Philosophy (Fall 2017 Edition), forthcoming https://plato.stanford.edu/archives/fall2017/entries/identity-relative/

13. Elizarenkova, T.Ya., Toporov, V.N.: L'énigme védique du type brahmodya. In: Permiakov, G. (ed.) Tel grain tel pain: Poétique de la sagesse populaire, pp. 207–251. Progrès, Moscow (1988)

14. Elizarenkova, T.Ya., Toporov, V.N.: Zum vedischen Rätsel des Typs brahmodya. In: Eismann, W., Grzybek, P. (eds.) Semiotische Studien zum Rätsel: Simple forms reconsidered II. Bochumer Beiträge zur Semiotik, 7, pp. 39–73. Studienverlag Brockmeyer, Bochum (1987)

15. Elizarenkova, T.Ya., Toporov, V.N.: On vedic puzzle brahmodya. In: Permyakov, G. (ed.) Paremiologicheskie issledovania. Issledovania po folklore i mifologii Vostoka. Moscow: Nauka, 14–46 (1984); reprinted in: Nikolaeva T.M. (ed.) Iz rabot Moskovskogo semioticheskogo kruga. Yazyk, semiotika, kultura, pp. 303–338. Yazyki mirovoy kultury, Moscow (1997). (in Russian)

16. Freud, S.: Humour. In: [18], vol. 21, pp. 159–166

17. Freud, S.: Jokes and their relation to the unconscious. In: [18], vol. 8

18. Freud, S.: The Standard Edition of the Complete Psychological Works of Sigmund Freud. Translated from German. Ed. by Strachey, J. Freud, A., 24 vols. The Hogarth Press and the Institute of Psycho-Analysis, London (1956–1974)

19. Fullenwider, H.F.: Concors discordia: Sarbiewski's De acuto et arguto (1627) and Jean de Serres' Commentary on Plato's Timaeus (1587). Bibliothèque d'Humanisme et de Renaissance **46**, 619–624 (1984)

20. Gärdenfors, P., Löhndorf, S.: What is a domain? Dimensional structures versus meronomic relations. Cogn. Linguist. **24**, 437–456 (2013)

21. Gärdenfors, P.: The Geometry of Meaning: Semantics Based on Conceptual Spaces. MIT, Cambridge (2014)

22. Girma, M.: Whose meaning? the wax and gold tradition as a philosophical foundation for an ethiopian hermeneutic. Sophia **50**, 175–187 (2011)

23. Grice, P.: Further notes on logic and conversation. In: [25], pp. 41–57

24. Grice, P.: Logic and Conversation. In: [25], pp. 22–40

25. Grice, P.: Studies in the Way of Words. Harvard University Press, Cambridge (1989)

26. Gusev, V.E.: Songs and Romances by Russian Poets: Introduction. Sovetskiy pisatel', Moscow. (in Russian) (1965)

27. Hamnett, I.: Ambiguity, Classification and Change, vol. 2, pp. 379–392. The Function of Riddles, Man, N.S (1967)

28. Hintikka, J., Sandu, G.: Metaphor and other kinds of nonliteral meaning. In: Hintikka, J. (ed.) Aspects of Metaphor. Synthese Library 238, pp. 151–188. Kluwer Academic Publishers, Dordrecht (1994). Repr. in: J. Hintikka, Selected Papers, vol. 4: Paradigms for Language Theory and Other Essays, pp. 274–310. Kluwer Academic Publishers, Dordrecht (1998)

29. Jabbur, J.S., Jabbur, S.J.: Bedouins and the Desert, transl. L. Conrad. State University of New York Press, Albany (1995)

30. Lachmann, R.: 'Problematic Similarity': Sarbiewski's Treatise De acuto et arguto in the Context of Concettistic Theories of the 17th Century. Russ. Lit. **27**, 239–252 (1990)
31. Lakoff, G.: The contemporary theory of metaphor. In: Ortony, A. (ed.) Metaphor and Thought, 2d edn, pp. 202–251. Cambridge University Press, Cambridge (1993)
32. Levine, D.N.: The Flight from Ambiguity: Essays in Social and Cultural Theory. The University of Chicago Press, Chicago (1985)
33. Levine, D.N.: Wax and Gold: Tradition and Innovation in Ethiopian Culture. The University of Chicago Press, Chicago (1965)
34. Li Vigni, A.: Poeta quasi creator. Estetica e poesia in Mathias Casimir Sarbiewski. Aesthetica Preprint, Supplementa, 13; Palermo: Centro Internazionale Studi di Estetica (2005)
35. Lourié, B., Mitrenina, O.: Semantics of poetical tropes: non-fregeanity and paraconsistent logic. In: Arkadiev, P., et al. (eds.) Donum semanticum: Opera liguistica et logica in honorem Barbarae Partee a discipulis amicisque Rossicis oblata, pp. 177–191. LRC Publishers, Moscow (2015)
36. Mahmud, H.A.-S.: Classical Arab Poetic convention by the Umayyad period: a psychological study of imagination. Asian Afr. Stud. **21**, 35–69 (2012)
37. Maranda, E.K.: Structure des énigmes. L'Homme **9**(3), 5–48 (1969)
38. Matte, G.: A psychoanalytical perspective of humor. Humor **14**, 223–241 (2001)
39. Menken, M.J.J.: Old Testament Quotations in the Fourth Gospel: Studies in Textual Form, Contributions to Biblical Exegesis and Christology, 15. Kok Pharos Publishing House, Kampen (1996)
40. Müller, R.: Metaphorical perspective on humour. In: Brône, G., Feyaerts, K., Veale, T. (eds.) Cognitive Linguistics and Humor Research. Applications of Cognitive Linguistic, 26, pp. 111–128. Mouton de Gruyter, Berlin (2015)
41. Newirth, J.: Jokes and their relation to the unconscious: humor as a fundamental emotional experience. Psychoanal. Dialogues **16**, 557–571 (2006)
42. Nosnitsin, D.: Sämənna wärq. In: Uhlig, S. (ed.) Encyclopaedia Aethiopica, vol. 4, pp. 507–509. Harrassowitz, Wiesbaden (2010)
43. Otwinowska, B.: "Concors discordia" Sarbiewskiego w teorii konceptyzmu. Pamiętnik Literacki **59**(3), 81–110 (1968)
44. Panchatantra and Hitopadesha Stories. Translation and Introduction by A. S. P. Ayyar. 2nd rev. and enlarged ed. Madras: V. Ramasvamy Sastrulu & Sons (1960)
45. Putnam, H.: Reason, Truth, and History. Cambridge University Press, Cambridge (1981)
46. Raskin, V.: The sense of humor and the truth. In: Ruch, W. (ed.) The Sense of Humor: Explorations of a Personality Characteristic. Humor Research, 3, pp. 95–108. Mouton de Gruyter, Berlin (1998)
47. Sarbiewski, M.C.: O poezji doskonałej czyli Wergiliusz i Homer (De perfecta poesi, sive Vergilius et Homerus). Opracował S. Skimina. Biblioteka Pisarzów Polskich; Wrocław: Wyd. PAN (1954)
48. Schumann, A.: Logical cornerstones of judaic argumentation theory. Argumentation **27**, 305–326 (2013)
49. Schumann, A.: Qal wa-homer and theory of massive-parallel proofs. Hist. Philos. Log. **32**, 71–83 (2011)
50. Schumann, A.: Talmudic Logic; Studies in Talmudic Logic, 6. College Publications, London (2012)
51. Searl, J.R.: Metaphor, in idem, Expression and Meaning. Studies in the Theory of Speech Acts. Cambridge UP, Cambridge (1979). [repr. (2005)]
52. Senderovich, S.: The Riddle of the Riddle: A Study of the Folk Riddle's Figurative Nature. Kegan Paul Ltd., London (2005)

53. Senderovich, S.: Morphology of a puzzle. Studia Philologica. Yazyki slavyansloy kultury, Moscow (2008) (in Russian)
54. Suszko, R.: The abolition of the Fregean axiom. In: Parikh, R. (ed.) Logic Colloquium: Symposium on Logic Held at Boston, 1972-73. Lecture Notes in Mathematics, vol. 453, pp. 169–239. Springer, Berlin (1975)
55. Tarán, L., Gutas, D.: Aristotle, Poetics. Editio maior of the Greek Text with Historical Introductions and Philological Commentaries. Mnemosyne, Supplements, 338. Brill, Leiden (2012)
56. Todorov, T.: Theories of the Symbol. Tr. by C. Porter. Ithaca, NY: Cornell University Press, (1984)
57. Vasjukov, V.L.: A Non-Fregean Guide to Husserl's and Meinong's Jungles. I-II (in Russian), Logicheskie issledovaniya No 11, 99–118 (2004); No 12, pp. 146–161 (2005)
58. Visotzky, B.L.: Midrash, Christian Exegesis, and Hellenistic Hermeneutic. In: Bakhos, C. (ed.) Current Trends in the Study of Midrash, Supplements to the Journal for the Study of Judaism, 106, pp. 111–131. Brill, Leiden (2006)

Linguistic Approaches to Robotics: From Text Analysis to the Synthesis of Behavior

Artemy Kotov[1,2(✉)] , Nikita Arinkin[1,2] , Ludmila Zaidelman[1,2] ,
and Anna Zinina[1]

[1] National Research Center "Kurchatov Institute",
pl. Kurchatova, 1, Moscow, Russia
kotov_aa@nrcki.ru
[2] Russian State University for the Humanities,
Miusskaya pl., 6, Moscow, Russia

Abstract. We examine the problem of "understanding robots" and design an F–2 emotional robot to "understand" speech and to support human-like behavior. The suggested system is an applied implementation of the theoretical concept of robotic information flow, suggested by M. Minsky ("proto-specialists") and A. Sloman (CogAff). This system works with real world input – natural texts, speech sound – and produces natural behavioral output – speech, gestures and facial expressions. Unlike other chatbots, the system relies on semantic representation and operates with a set of d-scripts (equivalents to proto-specialists), extracted from advertising and mass media texts as a classification of basic emotional patterns. The process of "understanding" is modelled as the selection of a relevant d-script for the incoming utterance.

Keywords: Syntactic parsers · Semantic processing · Robot companions
Emotional agents

1 Introduction

M. Minsky has suggested that the basic architecture underlying information processing of living beings and future robots should be based on "proto-specialists": simple reactive units, detecting negative or positive situations on one side and executing behavioral reactions on the other [1]. According to Minsky, "proto-specialists" are responsible for basic drives and emotions (hunger, thirst, aggression, flight etc.). They constantly compete for the body's resources: the winning proto-specialist controls the behavior (e.g. direction of movement), while the others remain on standby. Further, A. Sloman has extended the architecture with a triple layer model with sophisticated conflict handling [2, 3]. While basic drives and emotions remain on the first (basic) level, their activation may be suppressed by deliberative reasoning (second level) and meta-management – reflective processing (third level). This describes the interaction between rational and emotional processes: while rational processing may control emotions to a certain degree, reflexes grab control when an organism needs to recoil from a snake or a falling object. This architecture was implemented in the CogAff project for the design of emotional agents [4], and underlies the architecture of many

© Springer Nature Switzerland AG 2019
P. Eismont and O. Mitrenina (Eds.): LMAC 2017, CCIS 943, pp. 207–214, 2019.
https://doi.org/10.1007/978-3-030-05594-3_16

agents in artificial societies. Such agents have very limited sets of input events and output actions – although designed as models for living beings (humans) or as software prototypes of future robot companions, which will live in the real world and should handle natural language texts (and other semiotic systems) as their input, showing believable emotional behavior as their output. In this work we demonstrate the application of this theoretical architecture to a robot companion, which receives natural language speech as its input and generates speech, gestures and facial expressions for its output.

In our studies we solve two main problems:

(a) develop a system for natural text understanding, which also draws conclusions from the received statements and suggests possible reactions for an utterance;
(b) develop a system to execute behavioral reactions on a robot companion.

The general architecture of the system is represented in Fig. 1.

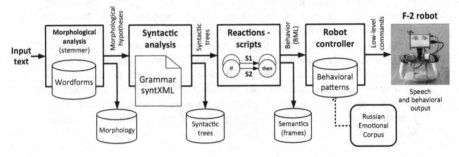

Fig. 1. Processing workflow for the emotional robot F-2.

The system accepts written texts in Russian as the input or decodes input audio instructions with Yandex Speech API. Further, the text is processed by morphological and syntactic components. Syntactic trees are transferred to the reaction component, which extracts from each tree a shallow semantic representation and compares it to the scripts – models of emotional and rational reactions. The winning script(s) form output behavioral reactions with utterances in BML (Behavior Markup Language) – which are combined and processed by the robot controller, and further executed by the F-2 robot. During the execution of BMLs, the robot controller retrieves the behavioral patterns from a database, designed following the research on real behavior in emotional dialogues in the Russian Emotional Corpus (REC).

2   Text Analysis and Sentiment Extraction

Present technologies of sentiment analysis usually rely on the "bag-of-words" method, in which a text is represented as a set of wordforms [5–7]. "Emotion" is calculated as an average score of emotional words present in the text. Although this approach is suitable for text classification and even for some dialogue systems, it omits an important aspect: emotion is triggered by an event and in text comprehension emotion is triggered by an event representation in text semantics. Semantic roles are crucial in this representation: the message X *conquered* Y has different emotional contents for X and for Y. Further, *You are an idiot!* should sound like an insult to the addressee, not like a neutral statement of the evaluation 'N is bad/stupid'. Several approaches in automatic text analysis and sentiment extraction rely on partial syntax parsing and extraction of T-expressions (three-element tuples <*subject, relation, object*>) [8] or four-element sets (subject, relation, actant, negation) [9]. Modern compound projects, like ABBYY Compreno parser [10] or Sentilo project [11], suggest constructing a syntax tree of the whole sentence and adding the semantic information to the nodes of the tree. In these cases semantic facts or emotional assertions can be found as substructures of the extended syntactic trees. Within our project we design a system which should recognize a set of "emotional" semantic patterns in the incoming text. Therefore the text parser should analyze the morphological/syntactic structure of the text and construct its semantic representation – suitable for the recognition of emotional meanings.

2.1 Semantic Parser for Natural Text Analysis

At the first stage of analysis, the parser divides incoming text into wordforms and retrieves possible morphological hypotheses from a dictionary that contains approximately 737,000 wordforms for 48,000 lexemes. Wordforms from the analyzed text are represented as lexemes and are assigned grammatical and semantic attributes. Semantic attributes are retrieved from a semantic dictionary; it assigns to each lexeme a set from a list of 660 semantic markers – main semantic categories, like 'human' or 'object', and emotional markers like 'intensive' or 'inadequate'. 28,000 words are annotated by semantic markers: from 1 to 18 markers per word (on average 2). Homonymic and polysemic meanings are distinguished: a marker can be assigned to a specific meaning of a word.

At the second syntactic stage the parser builds a syntactic tree for each sentence. At each step it adds the next wordform to a stack and tries to reduce the stack head with the available rules. The syntactic component relies on the rules described in syntXML format [12]. A rule is represented as a possible reduction, in which the right-hand side is reduced to the left-hand head h (1). Head h can also be a member of the right-hand side (2):

$$h \rightarrow <a, b, \ldots n>$$
(1)

$$h \rightarrow <a, b, h \ldots n> \text{ or } <a, b, h^{\text{head}}, \ldots n>$$
(2)

This rule structure allows us to combine rules from immediate constituent grammars as well as from dependency grammars. In our case we use "immediate constituent" rules for conjunction groups (*John and Pete* are reduced to a "virtual head" – [John_and_Pete]) and dependency rules for most other cases (*red house* is reduced to [house]).

A syntactic rule indicates a semantic role for an actant in the future semantic representation. For example, if *John walks* is reduced by subject + verb rule, *John* is excluded from the stack and is assigned an *agent* (or **ag**) semantic role. Other actants of a verb fill in other semantic valences – *patient, instrument, cause* etc.

The syntax component outputs syntactic trees: numerous trees for a sentence can be constructed, taking into account morphological or syntactic homonymy. No trees are generated if the sequence of words is considered to be "ungrammatical" and cannot be reduced by the syntactic rules to a single head.

2.2   Model of Emotional Reactions

Labels of semantic roles, assigned by syntactic rules, are used to construct a semantic representation: the semantic markers of each word are transferred to the corresponding semantic valence. For a single clause, a semantic representation (semantic predication) is a table of semantic valencies, filled with semantic markers for each valency. Each additional clause in a sentence adds another semantic predication. As shown in [12] the utterance *A real man is always interested in the life of the beloved girl* gives the following semantic predication.

Each semantic predication is compared with the inventory of scripts, the typical emotional reactions of the robot. Proximity to one of the scripts allows the parser to resolve homonymy and choose a preferred tree from a set of alternatives, if multiple trees have been constructed at the syntactic stage.

The system of scripts is represented in [13, 14]. Scripts are extracted by content analysis of publicity materials, leaflets and advertisements, etc. The inventory contains rational scripts (or **r-scripts**, corresponding to deliberative reasoning in CogAff architecture) and dominant scripts (**d-scripts**, corresponding to reactions or alarms in CogAff architecture). D-scripts are represented by 21 positive scripts – for compliments, expression of joy, advertising – and 13 negative scripts – for conflict, lamentation, or negative influence.

The scripts model emotional reactions to an incoming utterance and produce output behavioral patterns. For each sentence, a measure of proximity to each script is calculated. The script is activated depending on its affinity with the incoming utterance and proportionally to the "mood" or "temperament", simulated by the robot (the scripts have current activation levels and "sensitivity", which allows the robot to imitate a temperament). In particular, the semantic predication in Table 1 activates negative d-scripts (PLAN: somebody plans something frightening against me – 'man makes an evil plan against woman' – and SUBJV "Subjectivity": somebody is narrow-minded, thinks only about one thing – 'all men think about are women') and positive d-scripts (ATTENTION: subject is pleased, because somebody pays him attention – 'woman is happy because of the men's attention' – and APPROVAL: somebody acts like a hero, does something right – 'real men do well to pay attention'). The tendency to prefer negative or positive scripts can be controlled by the simulated robot character. The most activated script produces a robot output – a speech utterance and an element of nonverbal behavior to be executed by the F-2 robot.

Table 1. Semantic representation (semantic predication) for the utterance *a real man is always interested in the life of the beloved girl*

p (predicate)	ag (agent)	pat (patient)
think, pay-attention, frequently	object, somebody, man, positive	abstract, time-period, existence, object, somebody, woman, of-minimal-age, positive

3 Development and Execution of Emotional Behavioral Patterns

Future robot companions should communicate fluently with people, attain and maintain emotional contact, and maintain an interface, similar to normal personal interaction. In order to execute the generated reactions we developed a control system of behavior for the personal robot F-2 (Fig. 2). We extract behavioral patterns from a multimodal corpus and combine these patterns during the execution by the robot to enrich its behavior and the expression of emotions.

Fig. 2. F-2 emotional robot.

Fig. 3. Conversion of an emotional gesture from REC corpus to Blender 3D character for further use of the gesture by F-2 robot to express a certain communication function, in this case joy.

3.1 Research and Design of Communication Patterns

Activated scripts generate elements of communicative behavior, represented by packages in BML – Behavior Markup Language [15, 16]. These packages contain speech utterances and expressive patterns (gestures, facial expressions). BML packages refer to gesture movements stored in a database – during the execution these movements are retrieved from the base, linearized, and executed by the F-2 robot.

Elements of communicative behavior are developed with the help of emotional patterns from the multimodal corpus REC, Russian Emotional Corpus [17]. The REC includes video records of real emotional interactions: university exams, customer service in a municipal office, interviews with people engaged in art. The corpus is marked up with the help of ELAN software – a professional tool for complex annotation of video and audio resources. We marked up speech of participants as well as the facial expressions and gestures of one of the interlocutors (student, client, respondent). A separate level of markup sets the communicative function of a mimic movement or gesture if this function can be definitely determined [18]. Thus the corpus allows us to select typical elements of behavior to express a specific function. These elements are drawn in the Blender 3D editor and saved to the database (Fig. 3). Such a library of BML reactions is developed for each script.

3.2   Behavior Execution

The developed system simulates the behavior of the robot depending on the script activation and expresses the modeled gestures using the robot's motors, screen and audio system. As the input the system receives messages with the following information:

- script identification;
- weight of script activation,
- BML, produced by this script.

This information is processed and queued in descending order of activation. The system tries to activate tags of BMLs from the top of the queue. During BMLs scanning tags check if the execution device (hand, head etc.) for this tag is free. Tags with free devices become active while others stay in the queue waiting for the corresponding device to be unlocked. Preparation of tags consists of three mechanisms:

- acquisition of the instructions from the database and their parameterization;
- generation of instructions based on the environment model;
- generation of speech.

Prepared data represents instructions based on time stamps. Each tag has its own timer, which returns instructions associated with the active time stamps. Received instructions are transferred to the corresponding device (gesture instructions to robot motors, facial expressions to screen, utterances to audio system). After the processing of all time stamps for each tag according to the timer triggers, the tag completes, which lets the system find further tags to execute. If all tags of a BML are complete then the information on the script that has generated the BML is deleted from the queue and the activation of the script is reduced. If the robot activates several scripts then the BMLs from different scripts can be combined: robot can demonstrate a gesture of denial by hand and reverie through its head (turning the head and eyes up and sideways) (Fig. 2). To produce miscellaneous combinations we have formed a hierarchy of body parts, which allows us to describe instructions for one or several expression devices (e.g. for one hand or both hands). This hierarchy is used in the process of tag activation to choose the most convenient way to show a behavior on the robot.

Moreover the elements of behavior can be synchronized in between. For each gesture, facial expression or utterance it is possible to allocate the following main points:

- beginning;
- end;
- peak – marked as "stroke".

For example, the robot can start to think by looking away and turning its head left, right or up, then speak with an appeal – directing its hand to the interlocutor. In this way the gesture "appeal" is synchronized with the utterance, which allows the robot to express emotions more accurately. In general, such combinations of elements allows us to make the communicative behavior of the robot richer, more complex and more attractive to people. Thus we develop a cycle for the information processing, which constructs and executed compound behavior on different robot actuators for the given activation of scripts – in particular, expressing conflicts in the behavior, when contradictory scripts are activated and expressed at the same time (similar to script activation in Sect. 2.2).

4   Conclusion

The suggested system is an applied implementation of the theoretical concept of robotic information flow, suggested by Minsky and Sloman. This system works with real world input – natural texts, speech sound – and produces natural behavioral output: speech, gestures and facial expressions. Unlike other chatbots, the system relies on operations with semantics and operates with a set of d-scripts (equivalents to proto-specialists) extracted from advertising and mass media texts as a method of classification of basic emotional patterns. The process of "understanding" in this system can be modelled as the selection of a relevant script for the incoming utterance. At the same time, emotional relevance is subjective – one may be happy and/or confused, while being the center of attention. Here we suggest that the selection of one "most" relevant reaction is not reasonable – several highly activated emotional reactions may be mixed in the output, forming compound behavior of an artificial agent (robot), able to express emotions with numerous output devices.

Acknowledgements. Design of the syntactic parser was supported by RFBR grant 16-29-09601 ofi_m, development of negative emotional patterns was supported by RSF grant 17-78-30029, and design of the F-2 robot was supported by the NRC "Kurchatov Institute" (05.07.2018 № 1601).

References

1. Minsky, M.L.: The Society of Mind. Touchstone Book, New-York, London (1988)
2. Sloman, A.: Beyond shallow models of emotion. Cognit. Process. **2**, 177–198 (2001)
3. Sloman, A., Chrisley, R.: Virtual machines and consciousness. J. Conscious. Stud. **10**, 133–172 (2003)

4. Sloman, A.: Varieties of affect and the CogAff architecture schema. In: Johnson, C. (ed.) Proceedings Symposium on Emotion, Cognition, and Affective Computing, AISB'01 Convention, York, vol. 10, pp. 39–48 (2001)
5. Su, F., Markert, K.: From words to senses: a case study of subjectivity recognition. In: Proceedings of the 22nd International Conference on Computational Linguistics, vol. 1, pp. 825–832. Association for Computational Linguistics, Manchester (2008)
6. Chetviorkin, I.I.: Testing the sentiment classification approach in various domains – ROMIP 2011. Comput. Linguist. Intellect. Technol. 2(11), 15–26 (2012)
7. Poroshin, V.: Proof of concept statistical sentiment classification at ROMIP 2011. Comput. Linguist. Intellect. Technol. 2(11), 60–65 (2012)
8. Katz, B.: From sentence processing to information access on the world wide web. In: AAAI Spring Symposium on Natural Language Processing for the World Wide Web (1997)
9. Mavljutov, R.R., Ostapuk, N.A.: Using basic syntactic relations for sentiment analysis. Comput. Linguist. Intellect. Technol. 2(12), 91–100 (2013)
10. Anisimovich, K.V., Druzhkin, K.J., Minlos, F.R., Petrova, M.A., Selegey, V.P., Zuev, K.A.: Syntactic and semantic parser based on ABBYY Compreno linguistic technologies. Comput. Linguist. Intellect. Technol. 2(11), 91–103 (2012)
11. Recupero, D.R., Presutti, V., Consoli, S., Gangemi, A., Nuzzolese, A.G.: Sentilo: frame-based sentiment analysis. Cognit. Comput. 7, 211–225 (2014)
12. Kotov, A., Zinina, A., Filatov, A.: Semantic parser for sentiment analysis and the emotional computer agents. In: Proceedings of the AINL-ISMW FRUCT 2015, pp. 167–170 (2015)
13. Kotov, A.A.: Mechanisms of speech influence in publicistic mass media texts. Ph.d. thesis. RSUH, Moscow (2003, in Russian)
14. Kotov, A.A.: Mechanisms of Speech Influence. Kurchatov Institute, Moscow (2017)
15. Kopp, S., et al.: Towards a common framework for multimodal generation: the behavior markup language. In: Gratch, J., Young, M., Aylett, R., Ballin, D., Olivier, P. (eds.) IVA 2006. LNCS (LNAI), vol. 4133, pp. 205–217. Springer, Heidelberg (2006). https://doi.org/10.1007/11821830_17
16. Vilhjálmsson, H., et al.: The behavior markup language: recent developments and challenges. In: Pelachaud, C., Martin, J.-C., André, E., Chollet, G., Karpouzis, K., Pelé, D. (eds.) IVA 2007. LNCS (LNAI), vol. 4722, pp. 99–111. Springer, Heidelberg (2007). https://doi.org/10.1007/978-3-540-74997-4_10
17. Kotov, A., Budyanskaya, E.: The Russian emotional corpus: communication in natural emotional situations. Comput. Linguist. Intellect. Technol. 11(18), 296–306 (2012)
18. Kotov, A.A., Zinina, A.A.: Functional analysis of nonverbal communicative behavior. Comput. Linguist. Intellect. Technol. 1(14), 299–310 (2015)

Semantics and Syntax Tagging in Russian Child Corpus

Polina Eismont$^{(\boxtimes)}$ (iD)

Saint Petersburg State University of Aerospace Instrumentation,
Bolshaya Morskaya str. 67, 190000 St. Petersburg, Russia
polina272@hotmail.com

Abstract. The paper describes a new semantic and syntax tagging that is applied to annotate Russian child corpus "KONDUIT" – the corpus of oral unprepared elicited narratives produced by Russian monolinguals at the age of 2;7–7;6. This annotation allows uncovering some links between verb semantics and syntax that influence the steps of verb acquisition. A case study of verbs of speech and their comparison to the ones of mental activity shows that children acquire verb semantic and syntax structures on the base of verb semantic classes gradually progressing from one structure to the next one. On the other hand the results prove that syntax acquisition depends not only on verb semantics but also on such parameters as reference or part of speech. Along with the acquisition of narrative skills and the rules of referencing children widen their sets of possible syntactic structures.

Keywords: Language acquisition · Semantic tagging · Syntax tagging
Corpus annotation · Spoken narrative

1 Introduction

Verb is considered to be the center of any utterance, and its syntactic and semantic features determine the syntax and semantics of the whole sentence. Such complexity of verbs and their mostly abstract meaning (actions are more implicit in the reality than objects) lead to the fact that verbs are acquired later than nouns or even some adjectives [1, 2]. The acquisition of Russian semantics and syntax has never been a subject of a prolonged study, but all linguists agree that it is a long and complex process [3, 4]. Computational linguistics and corpus methods provide some new and productive possibilities of language acquisition studies, but due to the peculiarities of child language the methods and mechanisms suggested for Natural Language Processing need to be somehow updated for the child data.

A brief review of different approaches to syntax-semantics interaction is given in Sect. 2. Sections 3 and 4 provide detailed description of the study: the collected data of Russian child language and the elaborated semantic and syntactic tagging. A case study of structural correspondences between different verb semantic classes (such as verbs of speech and verbs of mental activity) is discussed in Sect. 4. Section 5 outlines some future steps in the development and scientific application of the suggested annotation.

© Springer Nature Switzerland AG 2019
P. Eismont and O. Mitrenina (Eds.): LMAC 2017, CCIS 943, pp. 215–224, 2019.
https://doi.org/10.1007/978-3-030-05594-3_17

2 Semantics vs. Syntax: Which One Is Initial?

Any linguistic theory that study the questions of either semantics or syntax, or both of them, has to understand their role in speech processing and to find out the links between them. Any attempts to study syntax or semantics separately have failed and are no longer acceptable.

Most linguists agree that syntax and semantics are tightly linked but the balance between them and the direction of these links are arguable. Formal theories started with the priority of syntax to any other disciplines. Theta roles that represent a prominent part of the Government and Binding Theory [5] are embedded into the syntactic structures though some scholars state that they are closely related to both the functional structure of sentence and the argument structure of predicates (cf. lexical-functional grammar by Falk [6]).

Other theories state that semantics and syntax are equal; they should be studied in parallel. Van Valin in [7] maps semantic and logical structure of sentences into syntactic rules of their expression, this mapping is called the syntax-semantics interface. Construction Grammar also argues the need to analyze both semantics (meaning) and syntax (form) of any construction as only their distinct unity allows an expression to become a specific construction [8, 9]. Constructions are formally represent in a special database Framenet [10] that consists of lexical units and their semantic frames – a set of frame elements that project all possible semantic links. Such frames have become a start point for semantic role labeling in language processing [11].

The notion of semantic roles (or thematic roles) was introduced by Charles Fillmore in 1968 [12] and describes the thematic relations between predicate and its arguments (cf. syntactic theory by Tesniers who developed dependency grammar according to the relations between predicates and their arguments [13]). At the same time the idea of the semantic structure priority was suggested by Russian linguists Mel'čuk, Zholkovsky, Apresjan and others. They proposed a detailed semantic tagging to annotate each seme and every argument of any lexical item. This tagging also included morphosyntactic information and could be used for speech production as the description provided by means of the so called models of government limited the word collocations [14]. The proposed semantic tagging is now embodied in Russian National Corpus [15] and allows to solve such problems as word sense disambiguation or to improve the machine translation mechanisms [16]. The advantages of corpus methods and machine learning in studying syntax-semantics interaction on the base of lexical-semantic tagging have been revealed for English [17, 18], Italian [19], Japanese [20] and others.

But none of these studies may give the final answer to the head question: which one (syntax or semantics) is initial? The study of language acquisition may give a key to this question. When children acquire their native language they may follow either semantic or syntactic bootstrapping [21–23]. If semantics is initial children acquire new words by mapping their meaning into the semantic structures of the previously known tokens. On the other hand, if syntax is initial, children apply their notion of syntactic structures to the new acquired words and thus understand their meaning. Both hypotheses have their pros and cons, some scholars argue that both semantic and syntactic bootstrapping are equally effective [24, 25], but each of these points requires new experimental and corpus studies to be approved or disapproved.

The idea of using child corpora to study syntax-semantics interaction that may help to unfold the answers to these questions is not new [26, 27], but they have never been studied on the base of a Russian child corpus. Russian child language studies are primarily focused on the issues of phonetics and morphology acquisition, and those few Russian child corpora that are available provide only phonetic and morphological annotations [28, 29]. The present study relies on the data of a specially collected corpus that will be discussed in the following section.

3 Data

The tagging has been elaborated on the base of the corpus "KONDUIT" (KOrpus Nepodgotovlennyh Detskih Ustnyh Izvlechennyh Tekstov – Corpus of Child Unprepared Elicited Oral Narratives; [30]) that comprises 213 unprepared narratives (or quasi-narratives), elicited during a series of experiments with Russian native children aged 2;7–7;6. All children were divided into 5 age groups, each has been provided with a specially elaborated experimental design depending on their cognitive development [31].

The youngest children (aged 2;7–3;6) took part in a game with two experiment assistants who performed different actions with 4 glove puppets. These actions had to be described using the verbs of 14 different semantic classes, e.g. verbs of motion, verbs of communication, emotional verbs, verbs of object manipulation, etc. The second group (children aged 3;6–4;6) had to retell a picture book "Three kittens" (by Vasily Suteev) that consists of 15 pictures and represents a story of three small kittens who hunter a mouse, a frog and a fish, but they fail and have to return to their home wet, tired and hungry. The three oldest age groups had to retell a cartoon about a kitten who makes a disorder at home and goes for a walk instead of tiding everything up. All stories were audio- and video- recorded, they had to be elicited simultaneously with either picture book or cartoon watching without any previous preparation. The orthographic annotation of all the recordings has been performed by the experimenter who conducted the experiment with all children. All actions performed both in the picture book and in the cartoon may be described using the verbs of the same semantics that were expected in the experiment with the youngest children.

The experiment was carried out in accordance with the Declaration of Helsinki and the existing Russian and international regulations concerning ethics in research. The parents signed informed consents for their children to take part in the experiment.

The corpus includes 25689 tokens, 6521 of them verbs representing 661 verb lexemes. These verbs have been divided into 14 semantic classes. Children of all age groups used the verbs of all but one of these semantic classes as may be seen in Table 1:

Table 1. Statistics of verb tokens and lexemes, and their semantic classes in all 5 age groups (* - 46 verbs repeat for all 5 age groups)

Age group	Verb tokens	Verb lexemes	Number of semantic classes	Missed semantic class
2;7–3;6	368	109	13	Verbs of behaviour
3;7–4;6	1002	187	14	None
4;7–5;6	1603	290	14	None
5;7–6;6	1808	338	14	None
6;7–7;6	1740	330	14	None
Total	6521	660*	14	None

4　Verb Tagging and Discussion

The annotation model consists of two lists that represent all possible semantic and syntactic structures of each verb. These lists have been manually made by means of tagging semantic and syntactic structure of each verb token of the "KONDUIT" corpus. Thus, we have made a list of tagged verbs with all their semantic roles and the corresponding morphosyntactic forms.

These lists have become the ground of a rule-based algorithm of automatic verb parsing. Morphological analysis is performed by pymorphy2 [32] which identifies the verb token and restores its lexeme. At the next step the parsing algorithm attributes the semantic class of this verb and specifies all possible semantic structures of the verbs of this semantic class. The last step provides suitable syntactic structures for the chosen semantic structures. This scheme is shown in Fig. 1.

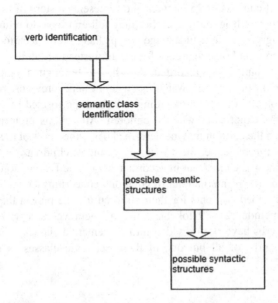

Fig. 1. Scheme of verb semantic and syntactic structure identification.

Such semantic and syntactic tagging allows studying the process of verb acquisition with a vice-versa analysis. Parser identifies the morphosyntactic structure of an utterance, matches it to the appropriate semantic structure and predicts the semantic class of a verb in case of its omission either in the utterance or in the verb list.

Let us consider the following examples. Verbs of speech represent one of the most frequent semantic class in the "KONDUIT" corpus (508 tokens for all 5 age groups). These verbs have three arguments – Agent (Ag, the one who produces the act of speech), Addressee (Addr, the other participant of the act of speech) and Theme (the topic of the act of speech). On the one hand, each of these arguments may be omitted according to some pragmatic or grammatical rules [33]. On the other hand, the roles of Addressee and Theme may be expressed differently (cf. Table 2) and in most contexts there is no explicit rules to prefer one expression to another.

Table 2. Arguments of the verbs of speech and their morphosyntactic forms (*о – preposition 'about'; с – preposition 'with'; что – conjunction 'that').

Agent	Theme	Addressee
Nominative	Accusative/Direct speech	Dative
Nominative	о* + Prepositional /о том, что + clause	с + Instr.
Nominative	что + clause	Dative

All possible semantic and some corresponding syntactic structures for the verbs of this semantic class are shown in Fig. 2.

Due to their abstract semantics and complex argument structure children acquire the verbs of speech quite late – at the age of 3;6 and later. As you may see in Fig. 3, none of three possible argument slots has been fulfilled by the youngest children in most cases, while the children of three eldest age groups explicitly name only two roles – those of Agent and Theme. The role of Addressee is much less significant and only few children of the age 5;7–7;6 have fulfilled it.

Their morphosyntactic correlations are also acquired gradually. Figure 4 represents all syntactic structures of two possible corresponding semantic structures – Ag-Theme and Theme (with omitted Agent). This plot shows that the younger the children are the more often the use of direct speech or subordinate clause is. But at the same time the use of subordinate clause depends on the presence of the role of Agent: younger children use this structure mostly with pronominal subject while elder children may both use nominal subject or just omit it. Children of any age try to avoid structures with both pronominal arguments, but prefer to express the role of Theme with direct speech in Ag-Theme structure independently of Agent form.

The same two arguments construct the semantic structure of verbs of mental activity: Agent (Ag, the one who performs mental actions) and Theme (the object of mental activity). Both roles may be expressed with the same morphosyntactic forms as those of the verbs of speech. But if we compare their realizations in the KONDUIT corpus, we shall notice that children use different syntactic structures of the same semantic structures for the verbs of different semantic classes (cf. Fig. 5).

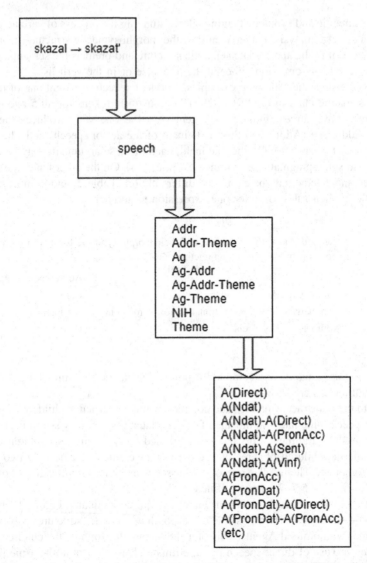

Fig. 2. All semantic and some syntactic structures of the verbs of speech (NIH – all arguments are elliptic).

These two plots show that the youngest children do not fulfill the role of Theme with the verbs of mental activity (they used a few verbs of this semantic class, but they were either lack of both roles (two tokens) or had only one explicit role – the role of Agent (1 token). Opposite to the verbs of speech the use of the verbs of mental activity shows that the elder the children are, the more they express Theme with direct speech or subordinate clause. On the other hand, subordinate clause is more frequent within

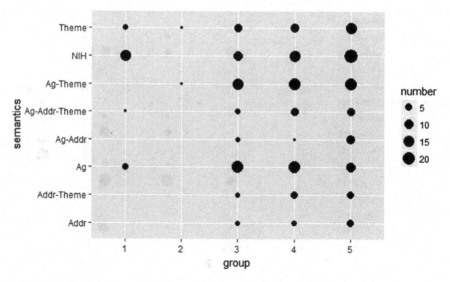

Fig. 3. Verbs of speech and their semantic structures in the KONDUIT corpus (NIH – all arguments are elliptic).

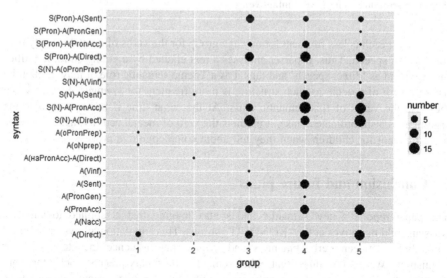

Fig. 4. Verbs of speech: syntactic structures of two corresponding semantic structures (Ag-Theme and Theme) in the KONDUIT corpus (S-syntactic subject; A – other argument; Pron – pronoun; N – noun; Sent – clause; Gen – genitive; Acc – accusative; Direct – direct speech; Prep – prepositional; Vinf – verb infinitive).

the stricture with pronominal subject in the texts by the children at the age of 4;7–5;6, while the same structure but with nominal subject is more frequents in the texts by the children at the age of 6;7–7;6.

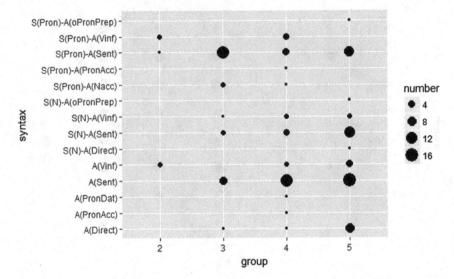

Fig. 5. Verbs of mental activity: syntactic structures of two corresponding semantic structures (Ag-Theme and Theme) in the KONDUIT corpus (S-syntactic subject; A – other argument; Pron – pronoun; N – noun; Sent – clause; Dat – dative; Acc – accusative; Direct – direct speech; Prep – prepositional; Vinf – verb infinitive).

Direct speech is less frequent for any age group for the verbs of mental activity than for those of speech. Thus, if parser analyses a text elicited by a young child, identifies the argument as 'direct speech' and tags it as a Theme semantic role, it may predict the use of a verb of speech, as such structure is more frequent for younger children when they use the verbs of this semantic class. At the same time if parser identifies the argument as a subordinate clause, it predicts the verb of mental activity, as this form is more frequent for children when they tell about some cognitive process.

5   Conclusion and future plans

The paper reports a new semantic and syntax tagging that is applied to annotate Russian child narratives at the "KONDUIT" corpus. This annotation allows uncovering some links between verb semantics and syntax that influence the steps of their acquisition. We cannot affirm that either semantics or syntax precede each other, but these results show that children acquire verb semantic and syntax structures on the base of verb semantic classes gradually progressing from one structure to the next one. The use of different morphosyntactic structures shows that syntax acquisition depends not only on verb semantics but also on such parameters as reference or part of speech. Along with the acquisition of narrative skills and the rules of referencing children widen their sets of possible syntactic structures.

The revealed tendencies (also they still need to be approved with other data, for example, with the data of child spontaneous speech) allow applying the suggested tagging to develop a semantic parser. Such parser will be able to assign the appropriate semantic structure according to the used syntactic structure and to predict the verb or at least its semantic class. Statistic information provided in the "KONDUIT" corpus will help to identify the age of a child who is the most probable author of the analyzed utterance. Such parser and Russian child corpus of unprepared narratives may be used as a start point for the future applying of corpus methods in the Russian child language studies.

Acknowledgements. The work is supported by the research grant number 16-04-50114-RFH from the Russian Foundation for Basic Research.

References

1. Tomasello, M.: First Verbs: A Case Study of Early Grammatical Development. Cambridge University Press, Cambridge (1992)
2. Gagarina, N.: The early verb development and demarcation of stages in three Russian-speaking children. In: Bittner, D., Dressler, W.U., Kilani-Schoch, M. (eds.) Development of Verb Inflection in First Language Acquisition: A Cross-Linguistic Perspective, pp. 131–169. de Cruyter, Berlin (2003)
3. Eliseeva, M.B.: The development of the individual language system of a child (in Russian). Iazyki slavianskoi kul'tury (2014)
4. Lepskaia, N.I.: Child language (development of verbal communication). (in Russian). Filologicheskii fakul'tet MGU im. M. V. Lomonosova (1997)
5. Baker, M.: Incorporation: A Theory of Grammatical Function Changing. Chicago University Press, Chicago (1988)
6. Falk, Y.N.: Lexical-Functional Grammar: An Introduction to Parallel Constraint-Based Syntax. CSLI, Stanford (2001)
7. Van Valin Jr., R.D.: Exploring the Syntax-Semantics Interface. Cambridge University Press, Cambridge (2003)
8. Goldberg, A.E.: Constructions: A Construction Grammar Approach to Argument Structure. University of Chicago Press, Chicago (1995)
9. Fried, M., Boas, H.C. (eds.): Grammatical Constructions: Back to the Roots. John Benjamins, Amsterdam & Philadelphia (2005)
10. Baker, C.F., Fillmore, C., Cronin, B.: The structure of the framenet database. Int. J. Lexicogr. **16**(3), 281–296 (2003)
11. Jurafsky, D., Martin, J.H.: Speech and Language Processing, 2nd edn. Prentice-Hall Inc., Upper Saddle River (2009)
12. Fillmore, C.: The case for case. In: Bach, E., Harms, R.T. (eds.) Universals in Linguistic Theory. Holt, Rinehart and Winston, New York (1968)
13. Tesnière, L.: Éléments de Syntaxe Structurale. Librairie C. Klincksieck, Paris (1959)
14. Mel'čuk, I.A., Zholkovsky, A.K., Apresjan, J.D., et al.: Explanatory Combinatorial Dictionary of Modern Russian: Semantico-Syntactic Studies of Russian Vocabulary. Wiener Slawistischer Almanach, Wien (1984)
15. Apresjan, J.D., Boguslavsky, I.M., Iomdin, B.L., et al.: Syntactically and semantically annotated Russian corpus: modernity and perspectives. In: Natsionalny korpus russkogo jazyka, 2003–2005, Moscow, Indrik, pp. 193–214 (2005). (in Russian)

16. Kobricov, B.P., Lyashevsky, O.N., Toldova, S.J.: Verb sense disambiguation with the help of semantic models retrieved from electronic dictionaries (2007). https://cache-mskstoredata06.cdn.yandex.net/download.yandex.ru/IMAT2007/kobricov.pdf. (in Russian)

17. Haynes, S.: Semantic Tagging Using WordNet Examples. In: SENSEVAL@ACL, pp. 79–82 (2001)

18. Kawahara, D., Peterson, D.W., Popescu, O., Palmer. M.: Inducing example-based semantic frames from a massive amount of verb uses. In: Proceedings of the 14th Conference of the European Chapter of the Association for Computational Linguistics (EACL 2014), pp. 58–67 (2014)

19. Corazzari, O., Calzolari, N., Zampolli, A.: An experiment of lexical-semantic tagging of an italian Corpus. In: LREC (2000)

20. Shibata, T., Kawahara, D., Kurohashi, S.: Neural network-based model for japanese predicate argument structure analysis. In: Proceedings of the 54th Annual Meeting of the Association for Computational Linguistics (ACL 2016), pp. 1235–1244 (2016)

21. Grimshaw, J.: Form, function, and the language acquisition device. In: Baker, C.L., McCarthy, J.J. (eds.) The Logical Problem of Language Acquisition, pp. 165–182. MIT Press. Cambridge (1981)

22. Höhle, B.: Bootstrapping mechanisms in first language acquisition. Linguistics **47**(2), 359–382 (2009)

23. Bowerman, M.: Linguistic typology and first language acquisition. In: The Oxford Handbook of Linguistic Typology. Oxford University Press (2010)

24. Abend, O., Kwiatkowski, T., Smith, N., Goldwater, S., Steedman, M.: Bootstrapping language acquisition. Cognition **164**, 116–143 (2017)

25. Gauthier, J., Levy, R., Tenenbaum, J.B.: Word learning and the acquisition of syntactic-semantic overhypotheses. CoRR, abs/1805.04988 https://arxiv.org/abs/1805.04988 (2018)

26. Chang, F., Lieven, E., Tomasello, M.: Using child utterances to evaluate syntax acquisition algorithms. In: Proceedings of the Annual Meeting of the Cognitive Science Society, vol. 28, pp. 154–159 (2006). https://escholarship.org/uc/item/3fh4h2t4

27. Colletta, J.-M., Kunene, R.N., Venouil, A., Kaufmann, V., Simon, J.-P.: Multi-track annotation of child language and gestures. In: Kipp, M., Martin, J.-C., Paggio, P., Heylen, D. (eds.) MMCorp 2008. LNCS (LNAI), vol. 5509, pp. 54–72. Springer, Heidelberg (2009). https://doi.org/10.1007/978-3-642-04793-0_4

28. MacWhinney, B.: The CHILDES Project: Tools for Analyzing Talk. Erlbaum, Mahwah (2000)

29. Lyakso, E.E., Frolova, O.V., Kurazhova, A.V., Gaikova, J.S.: Russian infants and children's sounds and speech corpuses for language acquisition studies. In: Proceedings of International Conference INTERSPEECH, pp. 1878–1881 (2010)

30. Eismont, P.M.: "KONDUIT": corpus of child oral narratives. In: Proceedings of the International Conference "Corpus Linguistics – 2017", pp. 373–377. Saint-Petersburg State University, St. Petersburg (2017). (in Russian)

31. Ambridge, B., Rowland, C.F.: Experimental methods in studying child language acquisition. Wiley Interdiscip. Rev. Cogn. Sci. **4**(2), 149–168 (2013)

32. Korobov, M.: Morphological analyzer and generator for Russian and Ukrainian languages. In: Khachay, M.Y., Konstantinova, N., Panchenko, A., Ignatov, D.I., Labunets, V.G. (eds.) AIST 2015. CCIS, vol. 542, pp. 320–332. Springer, Cham (2015). https://doi.org/10.1007/978-3-319-26123-2_31

33. Michaelis, L.A.: Constructions License Verb Frames. In: Rudanko, J., Havu, J., Höglund, M., Rickman, P. (eds.) Perspectives on Complementation, pp. 7–33. Palgrave MacMillan, London (2015)

When Language Survived, Music Resurrected and Computer Died: To the Problem of Covert Ontologies in Language

Anastasia Kolmogorova[(⊠)] [iD]

Siberian Federal University, Krasnoyarsk, Russia
nastiakol@mail.ru

Abstract. Creating formal ontologies is one of the current information science trends. However, in the context of taxonomies existing in natural languages another type of class hierarchy seems to be more important – the so-called "covert ontologies" that categorize entities in terms of crypto classes or hidden classes.

The research aims to examine localization of the three entities in the Russian language natural ontology, which seem very different from the formal point of view. These entities are: "language" (i.e. belongs to the formal class of systems), "music" (i.e. represents the formal class of perception or activity), and, finally, "computer" (i.e. embodies the formal class of equipment).

According to our preliminary observations, all three entities under discussion are conceptualized in Russian language as living systems. Our further analysis of 500 occurrences in which the three entities' names adjoin verbs designing different steps of vitality cycle showed that "music" enters the class of mythic heroes or Demiurges, "language" belongs to the covert class of Humans; at last, "computer" integrates the class of pets.

The revealed properties of natural categorization due to the effects of covert ontology also influence the eventual semantic roles of exploring entities' names.

Keywords: Covert ontologies · Formal and natural semantics
Crypto classes

1 Introduction

The present paper pursues the aim to highlight and then to discuss an assumption that a human mind is able to conceptualize the Universe not only by exemplifying all its entities in the strictly rational and formal way which we imitate building formal ontologies but also by using rudimentary classification principles which are less explicit and, at the same time, more natural. Such covert ontology manifests itself in natural languages world usage from which we can see arising so-called "crypto-classes". Even if we compare the place of such disparate phenomena as language, music and computer in formal ontologies and the covert one, we will see that the mentioned entities are differently categorized. However, what categorization is more valid for such a living system as a Human? I argue that the response to this question

© Springer Nature Switzerland AG 2019
P. Eismont and O. Mitrenina (Eds.): LMAC 2017, CCIS 943, pp. 225–233, 2019.
https://doi.org/10.1007/978-3-030-05594-3_18

does not seem clear and the hesitancy invites discussion about the status of formal ontologies as a preponderant framework for the knowledge building systems.

2 Theoretical Ground and Methodology

2.1 Concept of Ontology

The concept of ontology is deeply rooted in Antique and European philosophy. Aristotle was the first to postulate the importance of the study of being in general that he called the "first philosophy" [1]. The Latin term of *ontologia* had penetrated into the European metaphysic discourse in 1606, thanks to the German thinker Jacob Lorhard [2]. It became a key term of the Husserlian phenomenology two centuries later.

For Husserl [3], logic is the theory of science because it is concerned with a closed collection of meanings and associated meaning-instantiating acts, so that the unity which is characteristic of the science must involve both: (1) an interconnection of truths (or of propositional meanings in general), and (2) an interconnection of the things to which these truths (and the associated cognitive acts) are directed. To grasp and to structure units of a science the latter uses formal ontology, its sister discipline, that relates to object categories such as object and property, relation and relatum, manifold, part, whole, state of affairs, existence etc. In this way, modern science is due to Husserl notions of formal logic and formal ontology: as formal logic deals with properties of inferences which are formal in the sense that they apply to inferences in virtue of their form alone, so formal ontology deals with properties of objects which are formal in the sense that they can be exemplified, in principle, by objects in all material spheres or domains of reality [4].

The ontological bias found its systematic treatment in the philosophical conception of Husserl's disciple Hartmann [5], who, unlike his predecessor, focuses on the objective and immanent aspect of world categorization postulating that categories deal with what is universal and necessary, they specify configurations, structures and contents, not forms of existence. For him, categories are immanent to the world: they do not form a second world. They form the network of internal, dynamic determinants and dependencies, which articulate the furniture of the world.

2.2 Formal and Natural Ontologies

As previously mentioned, Hartmann's objectivist intention was to describe the "furniture of the world" and gave the recent emphasis on formal ontology building as the possibility of knowledge sharing and reuse across different applications of knowledge engineering. Today, formal ontologies are largely used in computer science, particularly, in the practice of knowledge-based systems building. Despite the enormous variety of definitions specifying the notion of ontology, there is a set of permanent features regularly ascribed to this phenomenon, such as the following: explicit description of the concepts and their hierarchical relationships that can exist for an agent or a community of agents and can be designed for use in supporting information retrieval, analysis and integration in scientific and other domains [6–8]. An ontology defines a common vocabulary for researchers who need to share information in a domain. It includes machine-interpretable definitions of basic concepts in the domain and relations among them [9].

The most known ontologies are the upper level formalizations: SUMO (Suggested Upper Model Ontology), SENSUS, WorldNet. They all are based on cognitive agents' conceptual maps of the world governed by strictly logical rules and axioms.

However, this formal approach is not the only one used by Humans to categorize the world. Husserl was the first to distinguish natural or so-called "naive" ontology and formal one. As the name implies, natural "furniture of the world" does not demand any specific operation to present the observer's mind "work" more explicitly. On the contrary, it reflects a spontaneous human's world perception far from being accessible to any intentional analysis of the cognitive agent himself. Since the works of von Humboldt [10], linguistics has been aspiring to find out some of its traces or vestiges across natural language data. By introducing the notion of crypto-type, B. Whorf gave life to a new linguistic trend. Accordingly to his definition, "a crypto-type is a linguistic classification like English gender, which has no overt mark actualized along with the words of the class but which operates through an invisible "central exchange" of linkage bonds in such a way as to determine certain other words which mark the class, in contrast to the phenotype, such as gender in Latin" [11 : 78].

The idea of some covert classificatory map existence resulting from specific human cognitive strategies for interpreting their environmental niche, the world around them, was met by linguists with enthusiasm and found its development in the field. For many researchers, language became a productive data to denude the hidden meshwork that is sometimes inherited from mythological conscience.

Thus, the famous Russian scientist V.A. Vinogradov, used the notion of covert class to elaborate the typology of non-grammaticalized nominative classes in African languages [12]. By his works, he proved, that despite the lack of formal morphological marks, some names in African languages let the researchers see their categorical status through the tendency to meet in the context adjectives or verbs belonging to the same covert class, for example, class of "what is liquid" or "what is sharp". Such mechanism of semantic concordance was given the name of "echosemy". Its motivation is the universal Human's wondering to see the similarity in very different and heterogeneous things: river runs, time runs, thoughts run.

In similar vein, another Russian linguist A.A. Kretov, has developed Vinogradov's suggestion proposing the term of "crypto class". He defines the latter as "a lexico-grammatical category of noun that consists in noun distribution into classes according to their semantic features in the case if (1) the class corresponds leastwise to one morphemically expressed grammatical category in any language in the world; (2) the marker of class obligatory manifests in the utterance structure under the forms of grammatical construction or word combination, word form" [13 : 9].

While aided by the key concept mentioned above, O.O. Boriskina degages and describes 6 of such crypto classes in modern English language [14]. The researcher calls them by using Latin names Res Filiforms, Res Liquidae, Res Longa Penetrantes, Res Acutae, Res Parvae, Res Rotundae. For example, class Res Liquidae embraces all the English nouns whose semantics manifests features "making allusion" to the properties of any liquid substance (water e.g.): information, knowledge, music, song, news, world, speech etc. The case illustrates the crucial principles of crypto classes building – first, it is based on the naive projection of the world formed in experience of everyday life and, secondly, it largely uses the principle of similarity inherited from a mythological world vision.

In the next section, I am going to compare in what classification case formal and natural or covert ontologies put such three different entities such as music, language and computer.

2.3   *Music, Language* and *Computer* in Ontologies and Thesauri

As it is shown below, searching for exemplifying the world formal ontologies build up a hierarchy of categories and their subcategories where each entity finds its localization.

Music, language and computer are limited within rather different categories (except for the Worldnet ontology where music and language are perceived as constituents of the same communication class): language is categorized within the classes of Property or Process, Communication or System; music – the classes of Activity, Communication and Art; computer enters those of Machine, Internet or Electronic device (see Table 1).

Table 1. Music, language and computer in meshwork of formal ontologies and thesauri

Entity/Type of ontology	SUMO	Worldnet	RuThez	Roger's Thesaurus
Language	**Property or Process**	Communication	**System**	Communication
Music	**Activity**	Communication	**Art**	Art
Computer	**Machine**	Internet	**Electronic device**	Machine

Even from the view of formal logic, the examined phenomena are far from being classified always in the same way. This example is meant to highlight the assumption that the formal categories are neither absolutely objective nor immanent to the real world configuration. They are more explicit due to the deeply rooted metaphysical tradition, but they do not represent the only way to perceive and understand the world around us. Their alternative, being less explicit, but, as it seems, having the same relevance and importance for the human mind, is covert "natural" categorization that manifests in natural language functioning.

2.4   *Music, Language* and *Computer* Through Natural Language Collocations (on the Material of the Russian Language)

The observations of linguistic data of Russian language prompted me to the preliminary conclusion that from a naïve cognitive agent's point of view, *language, music* and *computer* are conceptualized as living organisms. In this way, we can speak about upper level conceptual metaphor LANGUAGE, MUSIC and COMPUTER ARE LIVING ORGANISMS in Lakoff's and Johnson's sense of the term.

To be able to retrieve the metaphorical occurrences relevant to this study from our corpora we adopted the Metaphorical Pattern Analysis method (MPA) proposed by Stefanowitsch. The researcher defines "metaphorical pattern" as 'a multi-word expression from a given source domain (SD) into which one or more specific lexical items from a given target domain (TD) have been inserted' [15 : 66].

In this way, I was preoccupied in the search for metaphorical patterns for music, language and computer, as I discovered a large range of collocations of these words (in Russian) containing classificatory marks of living organism class. As such classificatory markers, I consider verbs denoting the main processes and properties of living systems: (1) main properties – nutrition, breathing, motion, reactivity, reproduction; (2) main processes – birth, growing up, reproduction, aging and death. As a result, the corpus of 97 Russian verbs that contain semantic components related to the above-mentioned properties or processes was built: *родиться, рождаться, есть, кушать, вкушать, питаться, завтракать, обедать, ужинать, дышать, вздохнуть, выдохнуть, дыхнуть, расти, взрослеть, возмужать, вымахать, стареть, стариться, дряхлеть, бежать, прыгать, падать, идти, двигаться, съежиться, отпрянуть, вздрогнуть, родить, заболеть, болеть, стареть, стариться, умирать, умереть, сдохнуть, подохнуть, загнуться* etc.

Using a corpus-based approach to metaphor, I retrieved more than 500 instances with collocations containing lexemes *язык* '*language*', *музыка* '*music*', *компьютер* '*computer*' and verbs as their metaphorical predicates from the list mentioned above.

As sources for my data corpus, the contexts from National Corpus of Russian Language, Russian Corpus of Leeds University, the database of Modern Russian Papers "East View.com", services of "Google Ngram Viewer" and "Google Trends" were used.

Having checked the list of 97 verbs (i.e. eventual markers of the class of living systems) by applying the MI score (a measure of how strongly two words seem to associate in a corpus, based on the independent relative frequency of two words [16]), I selected 14 verbs from my data collection that regularly occur in the same contexts with three words under discussion. All retrieved collocations were with the MI score more than 3 that is for Russian language the sufficient score for considering such collocates as statistically relevant word combination [17]. The 14 verbs list includes the following lexemes: (1) *родиться* 'to be born', (2) *жить* 'to live', (3) *расти* 'to grow up', (4) *выжить* 'to survive', (5) *пережить* 'to face, to experience', (6) *страдать* 'to suffer', (7) *болеть* 'to be ill', (8) *(по)родить* 'to give birth', (9) *стареть* 'to get old', (10) *умереть* 'to die', (11) *сдохнуть* / (12) *помереть* / (13) *кинуть кони* / (14) *околеть* – everyday speech synonyms of *to die*.

3 Results

The analysis of collocations shows that not all 14 mentioned above Russian verbs do occur with *music* (*музыка*), *language* (*язык*) and *computer* (*компьютер*). It means, not all the three entities possess the same properties of living systems (see Table 2).

Table 2. Verbs' occurrences with music, language and computer in research data corpus

Entity/Verb	Be born	Live	Grow up	Survive	Experience	Suffer	Be ill	Give birth	Get old	Die/its everyday synonyms
Language	+	+	+	+	+	+	+	+	+	+/−
Music	+	+	+	+	+	−	−	+	−	+/−
Computer	−	+	−	+	+	−	+	−	+	+/+

The Further Metaphorical Patterns Analysis also Revealed Some Particularities in Using *Music*, *Language* and *Computer* in Collocations

1. In collocations where *music* is ascribed to be born the verb is predominantly used in the Present Tense (*музыка рождается* '*music is born*'). In this way, music is conceptualized as someone who is appearing in front of our faces so that we can observe his/her birth. It is similar to the scenes of god's or goddess's birth frequent to Greek mythological narrations: the birth of Zeus, the birth of Apollonius, the birth of Athena etc.

2. Only *music (музыка)* and *computer (компьютер)* can occur with the verb *воскреснуть* 'to rise from the death' as if they were divine beings or if they had experienced some divine influence:

   (1) *Музыка воскресла. Музыка встала на дыбы и рассыпалась* (*Music has risen from death. Music has reared up and has broken*) (V. Nabokov "King, queen, knave").

   (2) *Компьютер воскрес! Ура, товарищи* (*Computer has risen from death! Hurrah comrades!* (from the technical support blog).

3. Only *computer (компьютер)* combines with some rather rude and low-colloquial synonyms of the verb *умереть* ('to die'), such as *сдохнуть, околеть, помереть, кинуть кони*. The Russians largely use all of them when speaking about pets, but, in contrast, they employ such words to talk about people only in pejorative way.

4. Only two of the entities under discussion could be perceived as being ill or becoming sick (*болеть, заболеть*):

   (3) *Русский язык заболел суффиксами* (*The Russian language became sick of suffixes*) ("Nevskoe vremja", 15.04.2017);

   (4) *Заболел компьютер. Что делать? (My computer is ill. What I can do?)* (from the technical support blog).

The figure below (see Fig. 1) displays the frequency of different vital cycles verbal markers occurring with each of the three words. We can see that the blue line of language has little pics on the three relevant events and properties: birth, surviving and death. In contrast, this lexeme is never associated with the ideas of growing up, reproduction nor resurrection. The red line of music is rather smooth – its focal points on the vital cycle vector are birth, death and resurrection. Finally, the green line of computer rose twice – on surviving and death, but also reveals the importance of properties to get old and to rise from death.

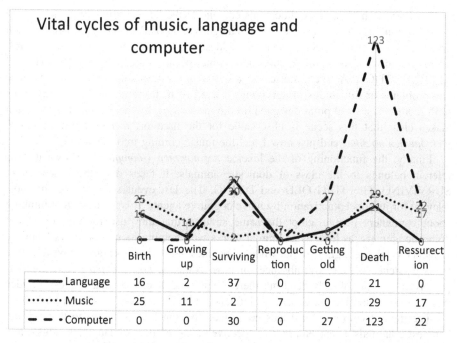

	Birth	Growing up	Surviving	Reproduction	Getting old	Death	Ressurection
—— Language	16	2	37	0	6	21	0
···· Music	25	11	2	7	0	29	17
— — · Computer	0	0	30	0	27	123	22

Fig. 1. The frequency of verbal markers of the category "the living system" for music, language and computer

4 Discussion

As can be seen from the linguistic data, the three entities under discussion are conceptualized in the naïve projection of the world within a large source domain of living organism. However, they "represent" different subspecies of such organisms. To continue with the idea of crypto classes, we argue, that music, language and computer belong to the different crypto classes of living being in frame of this natural covert ontology. The corpus of linguistic collocations shows that they have specific sets of classificatory markers.

Focusing on such processes or events in the living system vital cycle as BIRTH, SURVIVING, GETTING OLD and DEATH, language's existence, as naïve cognitive agents perceive it, seems to be very close to human life. In other terms, Russians speak about язык (*'language'*) as if it was a human being. They use verbal markers of this crypto class to predicate properties to the language. Indeed, Russian speakers conceptualize language as a member of covert category of "human being", which is less explicit than, for instance, categories of "systems" or "communication" in formal ontologies, but, instead, more natural and cognitively relevant for them.

In contrast, the Russian collocations containing the lexeme *музыка* (*'music'*) lead us to the conclusion that in naive world categorization of Russians music enters such crypto class as "divine beings, gods or goddesses". In our corpus, *музыка* (*'music'*) meets predicates that highlight three key-points of its being: BIRTH, DEATH and RESURRECTION. As such, music escapes from any sort of suffering, it does not face any problems or difficulties of surviving. Instead of it, in narrations about music, its birth represents a focal point designed, in the most cases, by the Present Tense, which makes clear that this scene is observable for the narrator: *и вот теперь музыка рождается во мне* (and just now I feel the music coming into the world).

Finally, the functioning of the lexeme *компьютер* (*'computer'*) shows that its referent belongs to the class of domestic animals: it faces only the processes of SURVIVING, GETTING OLD and DYING. The last event seems to be the most relevant for its conceptualization by naïve cognitive agents. It is to stress, that thinking about computers people adopt the same strategy that they use for thinking about domestic animals: as long as an animal works well helping its master in his labor, its existence is taken for granted, but when it becomes old or dies, its master pays attention to its existence or, already, absence. In most contexts, *компьютер* (*'computer'*) is perceived as being already dead but there are some collocations that suggest the idea that sometimes the Divine Grace can influence it and can give it a second birth.

The three crypto classes discussed above ("human beings", "divine beings" and "domestic animals") that embrace, respectively, the entities of language, music and computer on the level of covert categories displayed in Russian, influence the semantic properties of the lexemes themselves. Indeed, the ideas of non-autonomy of the computer, of autonomy of the language and of the upper or supernatural position of the music determine the mentioned lexemes' central semantic roles, according to Fillmore's theory of semantic cases, respectively, of an Experiencer, Patient and Agent or Stimulus e.g. *уход за компьютером, забота о языке, восхищение* музыкой.

5 Conclusion

Increased attention to the formal ontologies building is due to the interest of modern computer science to the universal inventory of the "furniture of the world", a sort of window on a portion of reality that specialists in very different domains could share. However, searching for a ready way to complete and to unify human knowledge specialists in computer science seem to be excessively attracted by the metaphysical idea of the immanent nature of world classes and categories. All concur, therefore, that cognitive agents such as humans implement not only formal principles to build up strongly hierarchical systems of classes to structure their environment. They have some deeply rooted cognitive strategies enabling them to conceptualize the world in terms of crypto classes. We believe that for naïve cognitive agents, such covert natural ontologies are very important. Seen through natural language collocations, crypto classes provide the most comprehensive framework for perceiving and understanding the world in our everyday life.

References

1. Aiken, D.W.: Essence and existence, transcendentalism and phenomenalism: aristotle's answers to the questions of ontology. Rev. Metaphys. **45**(1), 29–55 (1991)
2. Øhrstrøm, P., Andersen, J., Schärfe, H.: What has happened to ontology? In: Dau, F., Mugnier, M.-L., Stumme, G. (eds.) Conceptual Structures 2005, ICCS, pp. 135–147. Springer, Heidelberg (2005)
3. Husserl, E.: Formal and transcendental logic. Matinus Nijhoff, Nederlands (1969)
4. Smith, B.: Logic and formal ontology. In: Mohanty, J.N., McKenna, W. (eds.) Husserl's Phenomenology: A Textbook, Lanham, pp. 29–67. University Press of America, Lanham (1989)
5. Hartmann, N.: New Ways of Ontology. Henry Regnery Company, Chicago (1953)
6. Hovy, E., Knight, K., Junk, M.: Large Resources. Ontologies (SENSUS) and Lexicons. http://www.isi.edu/natural-language/projects/ONTOLOGIES.html. Accessed 24 May 2017
7. Gruber, Th.: What is an Ontology. http://www-ksl.stanford.edu/kst/what-is-an-ontology.html. Accessed 31 May 2017
8. Guarino, N.: Understanding, Building, and Using Ontologies. http://ksi.cpsc.ucalgary.ca/KAW/KAW96/guarino/guarino.html. Accessed 05 Jun 2017
9. Protégé. http://protege.stanford.edu/publications/ontology_development/ontology101.pdf. Accessed 01 June 2017
10. Humboldt, W.v.: On language. On the Diversity of Human Language Construction and its Influence on the Mental Development of the Human Species. Cambridge University Press, Cambridge (1999)
11. Whorf, B.L.: Language: Thought and Reality. Cambridge University Press, Cambridge (1956)
12. Vinogradov, V.A.: Nominative categories in songai. In: Vinogradov, V.A. (ed.) Foundations of African linguistics. Nominative categories, vol. 1. Aspect Press, Moscow (1997)
13. Kretov, A.A., Titov, V.T.: The role of covert categories in typological description of Romance languages. Bull. Voronej State Univ. Linguist. Cross-Cult. Commun. **1**(6), 7–12 (2010)
14. Boriskina, O.O.: Crypto Classes in English. Publishing House Istoky, Voronej (2011)
15. Stefanowitsch, A.: Words and theirs metaphors: A corpus-based approach. In: Stefanowitsch, A., Gries, Th. (eds.) Corpus-based Approaches to Metaphor and Metonymy, pp. 63–105. Mouton de Gruyter, Berlin (2006)
16. Church, K., Hanks, P.: Word association norms, mutual information, and lexicography. Comput. Linguist. **1**(16), 22–29 (1996)
17. Zakharov, V., Khokhlova, M.: Study of effectiveness of statistical measures for collocation extraction on Russian texts. Comput. Linguist. Intellect. Technol. **9**(16), 137–143 (2010)

Author Index

Printed in the United States
By Bookmasters